This book is dedi... ...nd Chris Gierke.
And to Patrick ... ...lso, to Jeni Jo
McCormick for ... ...nnot forget our
mother and gra... ...nd enthusiasm for
all our projects, ... has instilled in us
a love for fo... ...randma Marge
Sawtelle who ha... ...sely to her family ... ...e owned her own
roadside stand.

Copyright © 1997 by:
Creekside
Publishing
All Rights Reserved
No part of this book may be reproduced in any form or by any means, electronic or mechanical, including photocopying, recording, or by any information store retrieval system without permission in writing from the publisher.

ISBN 9-9658650-0-2
Library of Congress Catalog Card No.: 97-92223

Cover Illustration by Ruth Pittman, inspired by Chris Gierke

Thanks for your encouragement: Sue Kinzer, Puget Sound Editor, Farm Direct Marketing Association, Linda Watson, and to those wonderful farming families who truly represent the heart and soul of this great country.

Printed in the United States by
Pacific Printers
1359 North Pacific Highway
Woodburn, Oregon 97071

Farm Trails
of
California, Oregon, Washington
County Farm/Roadside Stands & Farmers' Markets

TABLE OF CONTENTS

How to Use This Travel Guide	1
Tips for Visiting Farm Trail Produce Stands	2
Canning Conversion Table	3
California Counties' Farm Trail Seasonal Guides, Maps & Farm Listings	5
Calaveras	7
Contra Costa	11
El Dorado	19
Fresno	29
Lake	37
Napa	41
Nevada & Placer	45
San Mateo	51
Santa Clara & Santa Cruz	57
Sonoma	67
Farmers' Markets for all California counties	79
Oregon Counties' Farm Trail Seasonal Guides, Maps & Farm Listings	99
Clackamas, Multnomah & Washington	101
Hood River	115
Linn	121
Marion, Polk & Yamhill	127
Farmers' Markets for 25 areas in Oregon	135
Washington Counties' Farm Trail Seasonal Guides, Maps & Farm Listings	141
Bainbridge Island, Skagit, Snohomish, Vashon Island, Whatcom & Whidby Island	143
King County North, King County South, Skagit, Snohomish, Pierce & Vashon Island	153
Snohomish	171
Spokane	179
Thurston	185
Yakima	193
Farmers' Markets for 53 areas in Washington	203
Order form	211
Index	212
Reference	213
Credits	214

How to Use This Travel Guide

Before planning your next vacation or outing, be sure to take along your copy of ***Roadside Stands and Farmers' Markets: A Travel Guide To Westcoast Produce.*** It is a good idea to check out your state maps to see which roadside stands and farm trails may be on your route.

1. Look at the seasonal guide at the beginning of each county to determine if the produce you want is in season. Remember that seasons vary as much as two weeks because of weather conditions.

2. Now look at the local map. The listings of the farms are divided into geographic areas and are located by numbers. It is always a good idea to call ahead to check availability. Each farm listing includes address, phone number and produce that they provide. Changes, however, do occur.

3. Then on the following pages you will find a listing of the farms and the produce they offer. Again, their location is indicated with a number corresponding to their number location on the map.

4. Tell a friend about this book and remember it would make a wonderful gift for someone special. (See order form on page 211)

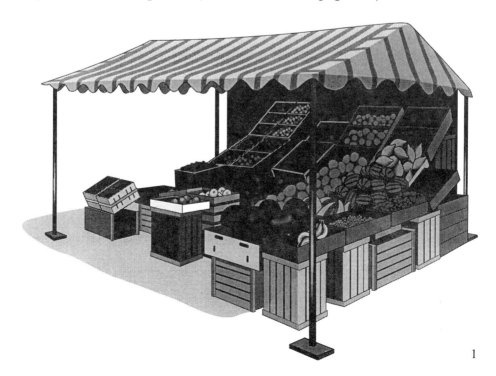

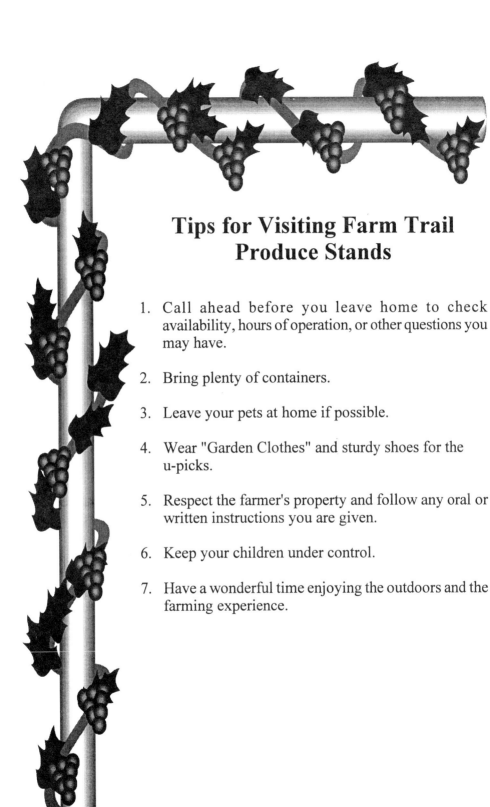

Tips for Visiting Farm Trail Produce Stands

1. Call ahead before you leave home to check availability, hours of operation, or other questions you may have.

2. Bring plenty of containers.

3. Leave your pets at home if possible.

4. Wear "Garden Clothes" and sturdy shoes for the u-picks.

5. Respect the farmer's property and follow any oral or written instructions you are given.

6. Keep your children under control.

7. Have a wonderful time enjoying the outdoors and the farming experience.

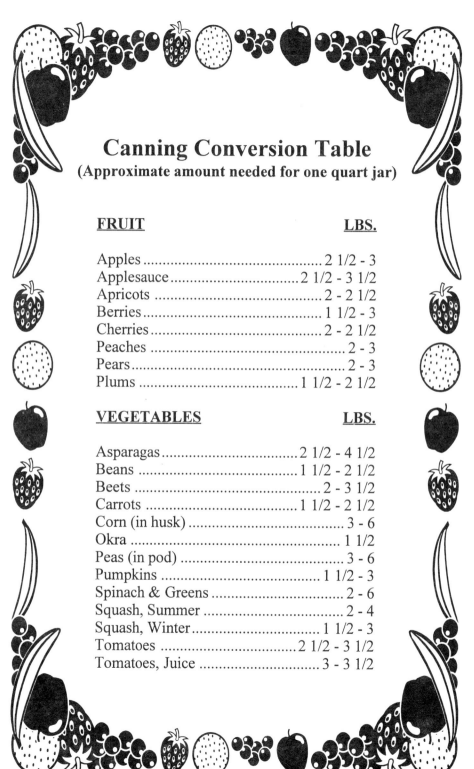

Canning Conversion Table
(Approximate amount needed for one quart jar)

FRUIT   LBS.

Apples .... 2 1/2 - 3
Applesauce .... 2 1/2 - 3 1/2
Apricots .... 2 - 2 1/2
Berries .... 1 1/2 - 3
Cherries .... 2 - 2 1/2
Peaches .... 2 - 3
Pears .... 2 - 3
Plums .... 1 1/2 - 2 1/2

VEGETABLES   LBS.

Asparagas .... 2 1/2 - 4 1/2
Beans .... 1 1/2 - 2 1/2
Beets .... 2 - 3 1/2
Carrots .... 1 1/2 - 2 1/2
Corn (in husk) .... 3 - 6
Okra 1 1/2
Peas (in pod) .... 3 - 6
Pumpkins .... 1 1/2 - 3
Spinach & Greens .... 2 - 6
Squash, Summer .... 2 - 4
Squash, Winter .... 1 1/2 - 3
Tomatoes .... 2 1/2 - 3 1/2
Tomatoes, Juice .... 3 - 3 1/2

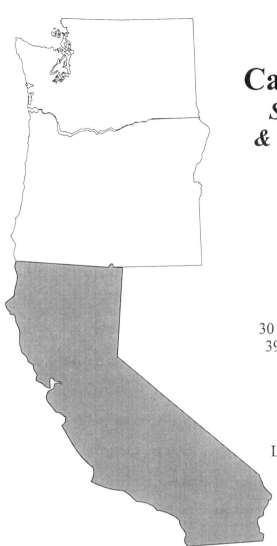

California State
Seasonal Guides & Farm Trail Maps

499 California Farms
and
301 Farmers' Markets
Featured

California Farm Facts:
76,000 farms
30 million acres of farm land
391 acres average per farm
Toll Free Travel Info:
1-800-862-2543

State Fair:
Sacramento
Late August - September

California, with its moderate temperatures and rich soil in the state's growing regions, produces some of the world's finest fruits and vegetables. Tourists flock to the vineyards of Napa Valley near San Francisco and drive along the highways of the fertile San Joaquin Valley. The state harvests crops from farms in more than eighteen of its counties. Whether it's u-pick, farm picked, organically grown or commercially harvested, you will probably find it in this agriculturally rich state.

Source: 1995 World Almanac and Book of Facts, *Funk & Waganalls*

Calaveras County

Calaveras Farm Trails

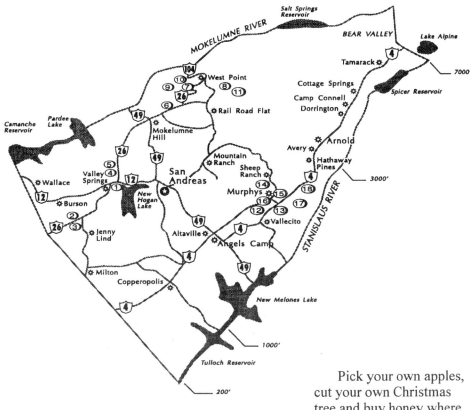

Commodity Directory

6, 12, 18	Apples
11	Bantams
5, 12	Cattle
3, 7, 9, 10, 12	Christmas Trees
6	Dairy Goats
2	Dried Flowers
8	Fish (Trout)
4	Gems & Minerals
6	Grapes
2	Herbs
6, 16	Honey
1	Native Trees
6	Peaches
6	Pears
11	Ponies
12, 13, 14, 15, 16, 17	Wine

Pick your own apples, cut your own Christmas tree and buy honey where the bees are the nearest neighbors.

Use the Farm Trails listing to discover the variety and importance of agriculture in Calaveras County.

Enjoy the beauty of the land as you thread through the backroads to reach these farms and producers. The fine products you'll purchase make the experience of buying "at the source" even more satisfying.

Explore the growing side of the Gold Country.

Credit: Calaveras County Master Gardeners

Calaveras Farm Trails Participants

1 CALAVERAS NURSERY
1622 Hwy 12, Valley Springs, 209-772-1823
NATIVE TREES: Nursery stock, specializing in quality California native trees. Open by appointment only, so please call ahead.

2 RHETTLAND HERBARY
7867 Burson Rd., Valley Springs, 209-786-2667
HERBS, DRIED FLOWERS: Plants, tours, cooking and craft classes, herbal wreaths, garlic braids, books, herbal products and gifts. Herb gardens emphasize drought and frost tolerant plants. Take Hwy 26 south from Valley Springs about seven miles to Burson Road and turn right. Open Saturday and Sunday (except rainy days and Holidays) from 11:00 AM to 4:00 PM. No children or pets, please.

3 JENNY LIND CHRISTMAS TREE FARM
10044 Roach Dr., Valley Springs, 209-786-2406
CHRISTMAS TREES
From Valley Springs, take Hwy 26 south to Jenny Lind turnoff, app. eight miles. Take Jenny Lind Rd. to Milton Rd. then turn right, and proceed to Roach Dr. Open the day after Thanksgiving until Christmas from 9:00 AM until dusk.

4 SNYDER RANCH
1290 Paloma Rd., Valley Springs, 209-772-1265
VALLEY SPRINGS POW-WOW: Gem and Mineral Show, over 200 booths offering arts and crafts, produce and jewelry. Beginning of May from 8:00 AM to dark. Free admission, day parking and entertainment. From Valley Springs, take Paloma Rd. north two miles. Ranch is on right.

5 VALLEY SRPINGS REGISTERED HEREFORD RANCH
1290 Paloma Rd., Valley Springs, 209-772-1265
HEREFORD CATTLE
From Valley Springs, take Paloma Rd. north two miles. Ranch is on right.

6 HUMBUG CREEK ORGANIC FARM
17425 Hwy 26, Glencoe, 209-293-7907
HONEY, APPLES & CIDER, PEARS, PEACHES, GRAPES, DAIRY GOATS: Rare antique varieties of just as good as what Grandma ate. Standard varieties as well. Two miles east of the Glencoe Store on Hwy 26. Please call ahead.

7 CAL-SIERRA TREE FARM
250 Stanley Rd., West Point, 209-293-7232
CHRISTMAS TREES: White Fair, Silver Tip, Douglas Fir, other varieties. Picnic area available. Free boughs. Take Stanley Rd. from Hwy 26, one mile south of West Point. Open the day after Thanksgiving through December 24th, from 9:00 AM until dark.

8 KEMOO TROUT FARM, LTD.
2710 Jurs Road, West Point, 209-293-7940
RAINBOW TROUT: Off sale and public fee fishing. Lodging with advanced reservatons. Trout sales are year round. Fishing during State Fishing Season only. High quality recreation environment. Take Hwy 26 to Winton Rd., travel 1.5 miles to Bummerville and turn right, then proceed to 2710 Jurs Road.

9 LONGS TREE FARM
PO Box L, West Point, 209-293-7087
CHRISTMAS TREES: Douglas Fir, Scotch Pine trees up to 12 feet. Christmas items such as dolls, decorations. Free coffee, chocolate, boughs, cones and mistletoe. Look for sign four miles west of West Point on Hwy 26, and take Woodhouse Mine Road for 3/4 mile. Open seven days a week following Thanksgiving weekend.

10 ALTO FARMS
839 Spink Road, West Point, 209-293-4936
CHRISTMAS TREES
From Main St. in West Point, take Spink Rd. 2/10 mile west. Open the day after Thanksgiving, 9:00 AM to 4:30 PM weekends, and Noon to 4:30 PM weekdays. Closed Monday.

11 CAPRICORN PONIES
5700 Gold Trail, Wilseyville, 209-293-4827
PONIES: Shetland and Welsh, pony equipment, Shetland stud service, Old English GAME BANTAMS. Take Hwy 26 to Wilseyville turnoff, proceed to Blue Mountain Rd. and turn right. Turn left at Gold Trail and proceed quarter mile to first wire-fenced field on right. By appointment only, so please call after dark.

12 KAUTZ VINEYARDS AT HAY STATION RANCH
Six Mile Road, Murphys, 209-728-1251
PREMIUM WINES, APPLES, CHRISTMAS TREES, REGISTERED POLLED HEREFORDS: Winery features two aging caverns, each 200 feet in length. From Main Street in Murphys, take Six Mile Rd. south one mile, Winery open for tours and tasting Thursday through Sunday, 11:00 AM to 4:30 PM.

13 CHATOM VINEYARDS
1969 Hwy 4, Douglas Flat, 209-736-6500
PREMIUM WINES: Bottled wine, wine-related items, sweatshirts. Largest grape grower in Calaveras County. Winery on site of historic vineyard. Take Hwy 4 north from Angels Camp app. six miles to Chatom sign on right. Winery open daily 11:30 AM to 4:30 PM.

14 STEVENOT WINERY
2690 San Domingo Rd., Murphys, 209-728-3436
PREMIUM WINES: Bottled wine, special Library wines, gifts, lunch items, picnic grounds. Unique "Alaska House" tasting room. From Main St. take San Domingo Rd. north at the Stevenot sign for 2.5 miles, to winery on left. Open daily 10:00 AM to 5:00 PM.

15 BLACK SHEEP VINTNERS
634 French Gulch Rd., Murphys, 209-728-2157
PREMIUM WINES: Produced from grapes of the Sierra Foothills. Bottled wine and gift items. Located at the end of Main Street in Murphy's, at the intersection of Murphys Grade Rd. Open for tours and tasting Saturday and Sunday from Noon to 5:00 PM, during the week by appointment.

16 MILLIAIRE
276 Main St., Murphys, 209-728-1658
PREMIUM WINES, LOCAL HONEY: Produced from grapes of the Sierra Foothills. Bottled wine and gift items. Winery located in a former carriage house next to Murphy's Creek. Open daily for tasting and sales form 11:00 AM to 4:30 PM.

17 INDIAN ROCK VINEYARD
1154 Pennsylvania Gulch Road, Murphys, 209-728-2266
PREMIUM WINES: Proprietor's Reserve Chardonnay, other bottled wines, gift items, picnic tables. Located on the site of once-thriving Gold Rush boomtown, in a spring-fed meadow. From Hwy 4 north at Murphys, turn right at Pennsylvania Gulch and proceed 1.5 miles to winery on right. Open Saturday, Sunday, and Holidays 11:00 AM to 5:00 PM. Other times upon request.

18 THE RED APPLE
DARBY RANCH
Five miles east of Murphys on Hwy 4, 209-728-3272
APPLES, CIDER: Fresh apples, cider, baked goods, gifts, produce. Open August to January seven days a week from 8:00 AM to 5:30 PM.

Contra Costa County

Harvest Time in Brentwood, Inc.

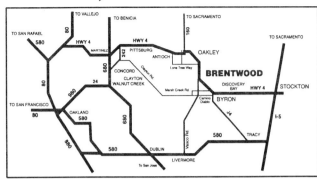

USE LADDERS SAFELY
1. Set ladder securely.
2. Do not stand on top 3 steps.
3. Do not rest ladder against any part of tree.
4. Keep your balance when reaching for fruit.
5. Report a broken ladder to the grower.
6. PLEASE no children on ladders.

TIPS:
Wear comfortable clothing and sensible shoes. Come in the morning--it's cooler. Group buying saves Time and Gas.
PLEASE BRING CONTAINERS.

Credit: *Harvest Time in Brentwood, Inc.*

Choose your grower... then look for locations on map at left

ALMONDS
August 20 thru December 31
- **4** Brentwood Ranch Eggs-P
- **6** Slatten Ranch-P
- **30** Gursky Ranch-P
- **32** Harris Apples-P
- **33** Smith Family Farms-P

APPLES/APPLE JUICE
July 15 thru September 10
- **2** Dwelley Farms-P
- **3** Lopez Ranch-P/U
- **6** Slatten Ranch-P/U
- **11** Nunn Better Farms-P
- **17** Papini Farms-P/U
- **20** The Gerrys' Fruit Bowl-P/U
- **21** The Farmer's Daughter Prdc-P
- **27** McKinney Farms-P
- **30** Gursky Ranch-P
- **32** Harris Apples-P
- **33** Smith Family Farms-P/U
- **35** Bob's Delta Produce-P

APPLE/FRUIT PIES
- **32** Harris Apples & Fruit Pies

APRICOTS
May 25 thru July 10
- **1** Pomeroy Farm-P
- **2** Dwelley Farms-P/U
- **6** Slatten Ranch-P
- **11** Nunn Better Farms-P
- **14** TK'S Best Produce-P
- **15** Bacchini's Fruit Tree-P/U
- **17** Papini Farms-P/U
- **16** Farias'-P
- **19** Peter A. Wolfe-P
- **20** The Gerrys' Fruit Bowl-P/U
- **21** The Farmer's Daughter Prdc-P
- **23** H.L.D. Nectarine Ranch-P/U
- **27** McKinney Farms-P

ASPARAGUS
- **2** Dwelley Farms-P

BOYSENBERRIES
May 10 thru July 5
- **15** Bacchini's Fruit Tree-P/U
- **34** Pease Ranch-P

— Please Note: —
Dates shown are approximate & will vary by the season. To be sure you're not disappointed, please call in advance. Only a partial list. Refer to listings for more items.

CHERRIES
May 21 thru June 25
- **1** Pomeroy Farm-P
- **2** Dwelley Farms-P
- **3** Lopez Ranch-P/U
- **5** Maggiore Cherry Ranch-P/U
- **6** Slatten Ranch-P/U
- **9** G. Nunn's Extraordinary Ch-U
- **11** Nunn Better Farms-P
- **13** Calabrese Ranch-P/U
- **14** TK'S Best Produce-P
- **15** Bacchini's Fruit Tree-P/U
- **16** Farias'-U
- **21** The Farmer's Daughter Prdc-P/U
- **23** H.L.D. Nectarine Ranch-P/U
- **24** Tidrick Ranch-U
- **26** Seko Cherry Ranch-P/U
- **27** McKinney Farms-P
- **34** Pease Ranch-P/U
- **35** Bob's Delta Produce-P

CORN
June 25 thru September 30
- **2** Dwelley Farms-P
- **6** Slatten Ranch-P
- **11** Nunn Better Farms-P/U
- **14** TK'S Best Produce-P
- **21** The Farmer's Daughter Prdc-P
- **27** McKinney Farms-P
- **33** Smith Family Farms-P
- **35** Bob's Delta Produce-P

CUCUMBERS
- **2** Dwelley Farms-P/U
- **11** Nunn Better Farms-P/U
- **14** TK'S Best Produce-P
- **21** The Farmer's Daughter Prdc-P
- **27** McKinney Farms-P
- **33** Smith Family Farms-P/U
- **35** Bob's Delta Produce-P

DRIED FRUIT
- **6** Slatten Ranch
- **19** Peter A. Wolfe
- **21** The Farmer's Daughter Prdc
- **24** Ridrick Ranch
- **27** McKinney Farms
- **30** Gursky Ranch
- **32** Harris Apples
- **33** Smith Family Farms

FIGS
- **13** Calabrese Ranch-P

EGGS (and poultry*)
- **2** Dwelley Farms
- **4** Brentwood Ranch Eggs*
- **6** Slatten Ranch
- **21** The Farmer's Daughter Prdc
- **33** Smith Family Farms

GRAPES
July 1 thru October 15
- **6** Slatten Ranch-P/U
- **11** Nunn Better Farms-P/U
- **23** H.L.D. Nectarine Ranch-P/U
- **32** Harris Apples-P/U
- **33** Smith Family Farms-P

GREEN BEANS, PEAS, BLACK EYES
June 15 thru September 15
- **2** Dwelley Farms-P
- **11** Nunn Better Farms-P/U
- **14** TK'S Best Produce-P
- **21** The Farmer's Daughter Prdc-P
- **27** McKinney Farms-P
- **33** Smith Family Farms-U
- **35** Bob's Delta Produce-P

HONEY
- **19** Peter A. Wolfe

MELONS
- **2** Dwelley Farms-P
- **11** Nunn Better Farms-P
- **14** TK'S Best Produce-P
- **21** The Farmer's Daughter Prdc-P
- **27** McKinney Farms-P
- **33** Smith Family Farms-U
- **35** Bob's Delta Produce-P

NECTARINES
June 15 thru September 15
- **1** Pomeroy Farm-P
- **2** Dwelley Farms-P
- **3** Lopez Ranch-P/U
- **6** Slatten Ranch-P/U
- **11** Nunn Better Farms-P
- **12** Canciamilla Ranch-P/U
- **13** Calabrese Ranch-P/U
- **14** TK'S Best Produce-P
- **15** Bacchini's Fruit Tree-P/U
- **16** Moffatt Ranch-P/U
- **17** Papini Farms-P
- **20** The Gerry's Fruit Bowl-P/U
- **21** The Farmer's Daughter Prdc-P/U
- **22** The Gerry's White Peaches-U
- **23** H.L.D. Nectarine Ranch-P/U
- **27** McKinney Farms-P/U
- **31** Matteri's Peach Ranch-P/U
- **35** Bob's Delta Produce-P

OKRA
July 15 thru September 15

- 11 Nunn Better Farms-P/U
- 21 The Farmer's Daughter Prdc-P
- 33 Smith Family Farms-P/U
- 35 Bob's Delta Produce-P

ONIONS/PEPPERS

- 2 Dwelley Farms-P
- 6 Slatten Ranch-P
- 11 Nunn Better Farms-P
- 14 TK'S Best Produce-P
- 21 The Farmer's Daughter Prdc-P
- 27 McKinney Farms-P
- 33 Smith Family Farms-P/U
- 35 Bob's Delta Produce-P

PEACHES
June 10 thru September 10

- 1 Pomeroy Farm-P/U
- 2 Dwelley Farms-P
- 3 Lopez Ranch-P/U
- 6 Slatten Ranch-P/U
- 11 Nunn Better Farms-P
- 12 Canciamilla Ranch-P/U
- 13 Calabrese Ranch-P/U
- 14 TK'S Best Produce-P
- 15 Bacchini's Fruit Tree-P/U
- 16 Moffatt Ranch-P/U
- 17 Papini Farms-P/U
- 18 Farias'-P/U
- 19 Peter A. Wolfe-P/U
- 20 The Gerry's Fruit Bowl-P/U
- 21 The Farmer's Daughter Prdc-P/U
- 22 The Gerry's White Peaches-U
- 23 H.L.D. Nectarine Ranch-P/U
- 27 McKinney Farms-P/U
- 31 Matteri's Peach Ranch-P/U
- 32 Harris Apples & Fruit Pies
- 33 Smith Family Farms-P
- 35 Bob's Delta Produce

PEARS/ASIAN PEARS
June 10 thru September 10

- 2 Dwelley Farms-P
- 6 Slatten Ranch-P/U
- 11 Nunn Better Farms-P
- 15 Bacchini's Fruit Tree-P/U
- 20 The Gerry's Fruit Bowl-P/U
- 21 The Farmer's Daughter Prdc-P
- 25 Frog Hollow Farms-P/U

PLANT NURSERIES

- 10 Dell's Nursery
- 36 Perez Nursery

PLUMS

- 2 Dwelley Farms-P
- 3 Lopez Ranch-P/U
- 6 Slatten Ranch-P/U
- 11 Nunn Better Farms-P
- 12 Canciamilla Ranch-P/U
- 13 Calabrese Ranch-P/U
- 14 TK'S Best Produce-P
- 15 Bacchini's Fruit Tree-P/U
- 17 Papini Farms-P/U
- 19 Peter A. Wolfe-P/U
- 20 The Gerrys' Fruit Bowl-P/U
- 21 The Farmer's Daughter Prdc-P/U
- 23 H.L.D. Nectarine Ranch-P/U
- 27 McKinney Farms-P

SQUASH

- 2 Dwelley Farms-P
- 6 Slatten Ranch-P
- 11 Nunn Better Farms-P/U
- 14 TK'S Best Produce-P
- 21 The Farmer's Daughter Prdc-P
- 27 McKinney Farms-P
- 33 Smith Family Farms-P/U
- 35 Bob's Delta Produce-P

STRAWBERRIES
April 10 thru July 30

- 11 Nunn Better Farms-P
- 14 TK'S Best Produce-P
- 17 Papini Farms-P/U
- 21 The Farmer's Daughter Prdc-P
- 27 McKinney Farms-P
- 34 Pease Ranch-P/U
- 35 Bob's Delta Produce-P

TOMATOES
July 15 thru September 15

- 2 Dwelley Farms-P/U
- 6 Slatten Ranch-P
- 11 Nunn Better Farms-P/U
- 14 TK'S Best Produce-P
- 21 The Farmer's Daughter Prdc-P
- 27 McKinney Farms-P
- 33 Smith Family Farms-P/U
- 35 Bob's Delta Produce-P

WALNUTS
September 20 thru January 10

- 1 Pomeroy Farm-P
- 4 Brentwood Ranch Eggs-P
- 6 Slatten Ranch-P
- 15 Bacchini's Fruit Tree-P
- 30 Gursky Ranch-P/U
- 32 Harris Apples-P
- 33 Smith Family Farms-P/U

HARVEST TIME MEMBERS' LISTING

1. POMEROY FARM
Picked & U-Pick Bing, White Rainier & Brooks Cherries on Marsh Creek Rd. west of Walnut Blvd. (Vasco Rd.) starting approximately May 20 to June 25. Picked & U-Pick sparkling June Nectarines Springcrest & Flavercrest Peaches on the east end of Eureka Ave. June 15 to July 10. Picked Patterson & Westley Apricots. Walnuts & Walnut meats available. Phone 510-634-3080

2. DWELLEY FARMS
Apples, Berries, Cherries, Apricots, Plums, Pluots, Peaches, Nectarines, White Peaches and White Nectarines, Asparagus, Squash, Onions, Green Beans, Wax Beans, Romano Beans, White and Yellow Sweet Corn, Black-eyed Peas, Tomatoes, Cukes, Dill, Basil, Peppers, Eggplant, Bell Peppers. Garlic, Melons and other fruits and vegetables. Honey and Eggs. Picnic area. Groups must call in advance. Phone 510-634-6508 for availability and conditions. Delta Rd. Between Hwy 4 & Sellers Ave. Open every day in season.

3. LOPEZ RANCH
U-Pick and Fresh Picked Sweet Bing Cherries, White Rainier Cherries, Sweet White Peaches, Freestone Peaches, Plums, Nectarines, Apples to include Mutsu, Gala, Granny Smith and Fuji varieties. Open daily. Phone 510-634-4433. Visit us at Marsh Creek Rd., 1 1/4 miles west of Walnut Blvd. Season begins May 20 thru September.

4. BRENTWOOD RANCH EGGS
EGGS--Brown or white, LAYING HENS & ROOSTERS--several breeds. All ages. CUSTOM RAISED POULTRY--Rock Cornish Cross, Red & Black Cornish Fryers, Roaster. Custom dressing available. DUCKS, GEESE AND TURKEYS. Thanksgiving and Christmas Turkey. Call for details. PURINA & FARMERS FEEDS for horses, sheep pigs, rabbits, etc. Complete line of dog and cat food. RANCH & FARM supplies & equipment. Phone 510-634-0404, 300 Balfour Road. Open year round Mon-Sat 10:00 am to 6:00 pm. Closed Sunday.

5. MAGGIORE CHERRY RANCH
Picked & U-Pick Bing Cherries. Available May 23 to June 13, approximately. Call first. Phone 510-634-4176. Corner of Fairview and Apricot Way, Brentwood. Open Daily: 8:00 am to 5:00 pm during Season.

6. SLATTEN RANCH
Fresh Fruits and Vegetables in season. Gift Baskets. Dried Fruits & Nuts at ranch and shipped nationwide. Send for our price list. Phone 510-634-3488. 6294 Lone Tree Way, Brentwood. January through April: Open Sat and Sun, 9:00 am to 5:00 pm. May thru December: 9:00 am to 5:00 pm daily. During Fresh Fruit season: Open daily 8:00 am to 6:00 pm

9. DC'S EXTRAORDINARY CHERRIES Formerly G. Nunn's
U-Pick cherries: Bing, Utah Giant, Sweet Anne, Rainier (White), Van and more. Unique European style planting makes them EASY TO PICK. No ladders to climb. Lots of off-street parking. Toddlers and handicapped can pick here. Phone 510-516-4495. One mile west of Walnut Blvd. on Marsh Creek Rd. Open every day including Memorial Day, 8:00 am to 5:00 pm during season. (May 15 to June 25)

10. DELL'S RETAIL NURSERY OUTLET
Wholesale growers of ground covers and bedding plants. Large selection of perennials, shrubs, trees, roses and more. Phone 510-634-9962. Located at 1400 Sunset Rd. Open every day 8:00 to 4:30.

11. NUNN BETTER FARMS
Picked: fresh garden vegetables including corn, bell peppers, okra, tomatoes, eggplant and more. Sold by the box only. U-Pick: cherries starting mid-May. NUNN BETTER Apple Juice and our apple juice gift boxes available year round. Please call for current crops and availability. Apple packing shed tours. Call early to reserve a tour date. We are located at 830 Sunset Road, 1 mile east or Hwy 4. Phone 510-634-1649.

12. CANCIAMILLA RANCH
Picked and U-pick peaches, nectarines and plums beginning App. May 20. Spring Gold, Springcrest, Babcock (white peaches). Nectarines--Juneglo, Fire Bright, Independence and Fantasia. Plums--Satsuma, Santa Rosa. Phone 510-634-5123. 401 Eureka Ave. (next to Seko Ranch). Open every day from May through August 8:00 am to 6:00 pm.

13. CALABRESE RANCH
U-pick & picked: Bing Cherries; May. Peaches: Redtops, Babcocks & Elbertas; early July. Nectarines: Whiterose, Fantasia, Goldmine (White); July. Plums: Greenage; early July. Fig (1st come 1st served); mid-June-Aug. Various vegetables. Registered Organic! Phone 510-634-5684. 2250 Concord Av. Open 8am-6pm. Please call ahead.

14. TK'S BEST PRODUCE
PICKED ONLY: Sweet corn, tomatoes, peppers, melons, summer squash, cabbage, Chinese cabbage, onions, daikon, cucumbers, green beans, etc. Also already picked in season: strawberries, cherries, apricots, peaches, plums and nectarines. Phone 510-634-1271. NO U-PICK. Southeast corner of Marsh Creek Rd. & Walnut Blvd. (Vasco Rd.) Open Daily 8:00 am to 5:30 pm May to November.

15 BACCHINI'S FRUIT TREE
Fruits: U-Pick & picked cherries: Bing, Brooks, Utah Giants, Lamberts and Rainier (white cherries) May and June. Olallie, blackberries and boysenberries May and June. Apricots May to July. Nectarines June to July. Peaches: White Early Babcock, Red Top, Suncrest, Flame Crest, O'Henry and Clings June to August. New Crop Walnuts "picked only" Nov 1 to Dec 1. Please call ahead for ripeness and availability. Phone 510-634-3645. Corner of Walnut Blvd. & Concord Ave. Open every day in season 8:00 am to 5:00 pm.

16 MOFFATT RANCH
Picked & U-Pick Freestone Peaches: Suncrest, Faye Elberta, O'Henry, Rio Oso. Nectarines, also. Please call ahead for ripeness and availability. Bring containers. Phone 510-634-3049. 1870 Walnut Blvd. just north Marsh Creek Rd. Open daily mid-July to mid-August 8:00 am to 5:00 pm.

17 PAPINI FARMS
U-pick and picked fruit: Strawberries followed by early variety Springcrest peaches and early apricots (app. May 25) followed by other varieties of peaches. Mid-June nectarines, white peaches, Santa Rosa plums and apricots. Early July Queen Rosa Plums. Flavorgiant nectarines and Gala apples at end of July. We supply buckets for picking and boxes for your fruit. Phone 510-516-1391 (call 8:00 am to 6:00 pm). Sellers Ave. (Marsh Creek Rd.) Open every day 8:00 to 5:00 pm.

18 FARIAS'
Picked Tilton apricots on Eureka Ave. 1/4 mile west of Walnut Blvd. (mid-June). Picked & U-pick Suncrest & Faye Elberta Peaches on Walnut Blvd. between Balfour Rd. and Eureka Ave. (early July). U-pick cherries on Concord Ave. (call for directions). We supply buckets for picking, you supply containers for ranch to home transport. Phone 510-634-4289. Open daily 8:00 am to 5:00 pm.

19 PETER A. WOLFE
Picked apricots starting middle of cherry season lasting app. 5 wks. (all varieties). Picked & U-pick Fay Elberta peaches & Black Friar plums at the west end of Payne Ave. End of July. Hand-cut dried apricots year-round. Ranch honey from our bees. Phone 510-634-1308. e-mail pwolfe@prodigy.com. 700 Creek rd. (3/4 mile north of Concord Ave. Open daily 9:00 am to 4:30 pm.

20 THE GERRYS' FRUIT BOWL
Picked & U-pick apricots June to July, Freestone peaches July 1 to August 15 (Red Top, Suncrest, Elegant Lady, O'Henry, Elberta). Plums late June. Nectarines July. Cling peaches early July & early August. Summer Rose apples mid-July. ASIAN PEARS mid-July to mid-August. Please call ahead for ripeness and availability. Phone 510-634-3155. Corner of Marsh Creek Rd. & Walnut Blvd. (Vasco Rd.). Open daily 8:00 am to 5:00 pm.

21 THE FARMER'S DAUGHTER PRODUCE & DRIVE-THRU COFFEE BAR
U-pick & picked: cherries, apricots, cling and freestone peaches, nectarines, plums and a wide selection of other picked fruits and vegetables, melons, sweet white corn, grapes & berries. Also dried fruits, nuts and fresh roasted coffee beans. Enjoy farmstyle hotdogs, fresh fruit smoothies and other refreshments in our picnic areas. Phone 510-634-4827. Located on the Northwest corner of Walnut Blvd. and Marsh Creek Rd. Open 7 days a week 8:00 am to 6:00 pm.

22 THE GERRYS' WHITE PEACHES
U-pick Freestone WHITE peaches & nectarines. Eight peach and nectarine varieties from early June to August. Call ahead for ripeness and availability. Phone 510-634-3155. Marsh Creek Rd. & Orchard Lane. Open daily 8:00 am to 5:00 pm.

23 H.L.D. NECTARINE RANCH
Picked & U-pick, May 15 thru Sept. 15. Nectarines, peaches, plums, apricots, Bing cherries, grapes. Phone 510-634-6637. Payne Ave., between Walnut & Sellers. Open Tuesday thru Sunday 8:00 am to 5:00 pm. Closed on Monday. We supply buckets for picking.

24 TIDRICK RANCH
U-pick & picked Bing cherries, refreshments, local dried fruits & nuts and firewood. Phone 510-634-5115. 1800 Orchard Lane. Open every day 7:00 am to dusk from Memorial Day to June 30, app. Call first.

26 SEKO RANCH CHERRIES
Burlap and Mono cherries picked, Bing cherries picked & U-pick. Phone orders accepted. Phone 510-634-3771. Eureka Ave., off Walnut Blvd. Open every day during season 8:00 am to 5:00 pm

27 McKINNEY FARMS
U-PICK & FRESH PICKED fruits in season. WHITE PEACHES Freestone and Cling peaches. Blenheim and Katy apricots, nectarines, white nectarines and plums. In our FRUIT STAND we have fresh picked VEGETABLES and MELONS in season. DRIED FRUITS and refreshments. Phone 510-634-7350. 25221 Marsh Creek Rd. (3/4 mile west of Hwy 4) or right on Marsh Creek from Vasco Rd. Open app. late May thru mid-August 8:00 amd to 5:00 pm every day as long as the fruit is ripe. PLEASE CALL FIRST to check on fruit availability.

30 GURSKY RANCH

DRIED FRUITS, NUTS, GOURMET GIFTS. U-pick walnuts and ten other kinds of nuts either in-shell or meats. Delicious candied fruits and nuts, chocolate-dipped and yogurt-coated items, too! All your favorite dried fruits are here along with an extensive display of other gourmet nut and fruit-related items. Gift basket and boxes galore! Ship nationwide using UPS, accept MC, VISA phone orders. Leave your name & address for new price list (app. Oct 19) by calling 1-800-576-NUTS. Phone 510-634-4913, located at 1921 Apricot Way. Open daily from October 18th to December 24th, then open weekends only. Closed from February to mid-October.

31 MATTERI'S PEACH RANCH

Picked & U-pick Freestone peaches, several varieties of nectarines. Call ahead for availability. Phone 510-625-0115. Located on Delta Rd. 1/4 mile east of Sellers Ave. Open daily late May to early September.

32 HARRIS APPLES & FRUIT PIES

Picked Fuji apples, U-pick Red Delicious, Granny Smith apples. U-pick Thompson Seedless grapes, White peaches and nectarines. Fuji blend apple juice, 64 or 44 oz., Nut and dried fruit gift packs. Apple/fruit pies made in our own bakery. Walnuts, almonds, pistachio nuts, olives, pickled garlic, jams and honey. Variety of fresh vegetables in season. Phone 510-625-5950. 1241 Delta Rd., 500 yrds. east of Sellers Ave.

33 SMITH FAMILY FARMS

U-picked & picked: over 20 varieties of tomatoes including Roma, Beefsteak and Gold. Large variety of hot & sweet peppers, cucumbers, and squash. Picked basil, peaches, melons, white corn, cherries, onions, apples and walnuts. Delivery of tomatoes available to restaurants & stores. Open daily 8:00 am to 5:00 pm. HALLOWEEN PUMPKIN HARVEST: October 4-31. Hayrides to Pumpkin Patch, live entertainment, farm animals, scarecrow display and picnic area. Farm tours for school children April, May & October. Please call for a reservation. Open Mon thru Fri 8:00 am to 2:00 pm. Saturday & Sunday 8:00 am to 4:00 pm Phone 510-634-4739 or 625-3544. Sellers Rd. between Delta & Sunset Rd., Knightsen.

34 PEASE RANCH

Different varieties of cherries, strawberries, boysenberries and olallieberries. U-pick, picked by advance request. Phone 510-634-4646. Marsh Creek Rd. (1 mile west of Hwy 4). Open app. mid-April thru June, 8:00 am daily.

35 BOB'S DELTA PRODUCE

Strawberries picked, PUMPKINS & Gourds, apples, bananas, grapes, cherries, apricots, plums, peaches, asparagus, nectarines, squash, onions, green beans, sweet corn, black-eyed peas, okra, tomatoes, cucumber dill, eggs, lettuce, greens, broccoli, cauliflower, oranges, garlic & melons. Open ever day. Located on the corner of Hwy 4 & Marsh Creek Rd. Phone 510-634-4007.

36 PEREZ NURSERY

Quality plants at an affordable price. Large selection of trees, shrubs, perennials, bedding plants and ground covers. Wide variety of citrus trees and fruit trees such as cherries, peaches and nectarines. We also have statuary and beautiful hand-carved fountains from Mexico. 201 Sunset Rd. Phone 510-516-1052. Open 7 days a week 8 am to 7 pm.

El Dorado County

El Dorado Farm Trails

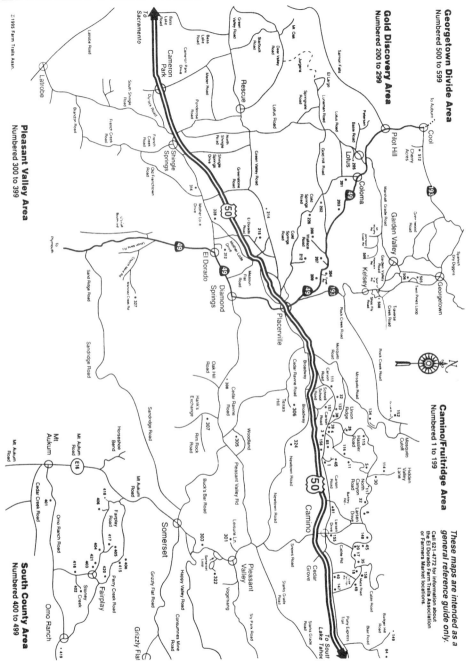

These maps are intended as a general reference guide only.
Call 621-4772 for information about the El Dorado Farm Trails Association or Farmer's Market locations.

Credit: El Dorado County Farm Trail Association

HARVEST CALENDAR

Season, varieties and availability vary... please call ahead for accurate harvest details!

APPLES

Gravenstein	1st Aug thru end Sept
McIntosh	1st Sept thru end Dec
Golden Delicious	early Sept thru end Dec
Jonagold	early Sept thru end Dec
Gala	mid thru late Sept
Jonathan	early Sept thru end Nov
Red Delicious	mid Sept thru end Oct
Empire	mid Sept thru mid Oct
Mutsu	late Sept thru mid Oct
Granny Smith	early Oct thru end Dec
Red Rome	1st Oct thru mid Dec
Winesap	mid Oct thru end Dec
Braeburn	mid Oct thru end Dec
Fuji	mid Oct thru end Dec

CHERRIES

Burlat	late May
Bing	June
Van	mid June
Rainier	mid June
Montmorency	mid to late June
Lambert	end June thru early July

NECTARINES

Snow Queen	late July
Sungold	late July thru early Aug
Summer Grand	late July thru mid Aug
Fantasia	mid Aug
Red Gold	mid thru end Aug
Royal Giant	1st thru mid Sept
Flaming Red	mid thru late Sept
Fairlane	mid Sept thru mid Oct

PEACHES

Springcrest	late June
Flavorcrest	late July
Redhaven	late July thru early Aug
Suncrest	late July thru early Aug
Fay Alberta	early to mid Aug
Cresthaven	late Aug
O'Henry	late Aug thru late Sept
Cal Red	late Aug thru late Sept
Fairtime	late Sept thru late Oct

PEARS

Bartletts	late July thru late Sept
Red Sensation	mid Aug thru mid Sept
Bosc	mid Sept thru mid Oct
Comice	1st Oct thru late Nov
ASIAN PEARS	
Kikisui	mid Aug thru end Dec
Hosui	mid Aug thru end Dec
Kosui	mid Aug thru end Dec
Yali	mid Aug thru end Dec

PLUMS

Santa Rosa	mid July
Friar	late July thru mid Aug
Kelsey	mid Aug thru mid Sept
Freedom	late Aug thru mid Sept
Empress	1st thru late Sept
President	1st thru late Sept
Autumn Rosa	late Sept thru mid Oct

MISCELLANEOUS CROPS AND LIVESTOCK

Beef, etc.	Year Round
Berries	early May thru end Dec
Citrus	1st Oct thru end Mar
Christmas Trees	mid Nov thru late Dec
Corn	mid July thru end Oct
Honey	Year Round
Pumpkins	mid Sept thru late Nov
Tomatoes	1st July thru mid Nov
Vegetables	1st June thru end Nov
Walnuts	1st Nov thru end Jan
Wine	Year Round
Wine Grapes	1st Sept thru end Oct

EL DORADO COUNTY ALPHABETICAL MEMBERS' LISTINGS

Numbers below correspond to ranch numbers on map.

Abel's Apple Acres 38	The Holly Grove 156
Andersen's Hidden Valley Farm 114	Hooverville Orchards 206
American River Cherry Co. 204	Indian Rock Tree Farm 117
Argyres Orchard 22	Irving Apple Barn 4
Attic Treasures Orchard 214	Jacquier Ranch 157
Barsotti Ranch 30	Jodar Vineyard and Winery 152
Bavarian Hills Orchard 11	Kids Inc. 5
The Big Apple 40	Marvin Larsen Ranch 49
Bill's Apples 35	Latcham Vineyards 401
Bluebird Haven Iris Garden 406	Lava Cap Winery 26
Boa Vista Orchards 3	Madrona Vineyards 46
Boeger Winery 32	Mandarin Ridge ....
Bolster's Hilltop Ranch 45	Marchini's Pear-A-Dice Ranch 203
Bountiful Lilies 322	Marmot Meadows Farm 509
Brookshire Gardens 312	Martinelli Ranch ....
Candy Apple Tree Farm 155	Meyer Ranch 209
Carson Ridge Evergreens 85	Mining Brook Ranch 324
Caswell Ranch 212	Charles B. Mitchell Vineyards 402
Charlie's Choice Xmas Tree Farm 115	Mother Lode Orchards 8
Chateau Rodin Vineyard & Winery 305	Noel Christmas Trees 404
Coalwell's Red Shack 207	North Star Tree Farm 508
Mo Daly 205	O'Halloran's Apple Trail Ranch 18
El Dorado Ranch 512	Oliver Vineyards 417
Falls Lode Farm 327	Perron Orchards 111
Fancher's Christmas Tree Farm 419	Perry Creek Vineyards 415
Fausel Ranch 307	Plubell Family Orchards 20
Fitzpatrick Winery & Lodge 403	Santa's Acres 81
Forty Mile Ranch 314	7 Up Bar Guest Ranch 416
The Front Yard Nursery 328	Sierra Apples 158
Thr Fruit Tree 147	Sierra Vista Winery 301
Ghost Mountain Ranch 149	Silver Forest Tree Farm 418
Goldbud Farms 39	Single Leaf Vineyards and Winery 421
Gold Hill Nursery 202	Smokey Ridge Ranch 133
Gold Hill Vineyard 201	Split Rock Ranch 420
Graham's Shed 226	Sundance Tree Farm 215
Grandpa's Cellar 17	Tomary Tomatoes 308
Granite Hill Vineyards 134	Twin Pines Christmas Tree Farm 506
Granite Springs Winery & Vineyards . 405	Up Country Ranch 303
Harris Tree Farm 84	Whittington Farm 505
Harvest Lane 148	Windmill Hill Orchards ....
High Hill Ranch 1	Windwalker Vineyards 408
Hillside Tree Farm 116	

PRODUCT INDEX

IMPORTANT: Because El Dorado County ranches are at different elevations and in different microclimates, ripening times vary. Please **call ahead** to check product availability.

Ranch Numbers	Area
1 - 199	CAMINO/FRUITRIDGE
200 - 299	GOLD DISCOVERY
300 - 399	PLEASANT VALLEY
400 - 499	SOUTH COUNTY
500 - 599	GEORGETOWN DIVIDE

APPLES: 1, 3, 4, 5, 8, 11, 17, 18, 19, 29, 22, 30, 35, 38, 39, 40, 45, 49, 84, 111, 133, 147, 148, 157, 158, 203, 206, 207, 209, 214, 226, 324
APPLE JUICE, CIDER: 1, 3, 8, 11, 17, 20, 30, 35, 39, 40, 45, 49, 84, 147, 148, 203, 206
APRICOTS: 3, 111, 203, 206, 214
AVOCADOS: 206, 226
BAKED GOODS: 1, 3, 5, 11, 17, 20, 38, 40, 84, 111, 115, 147, 203, 206, 314, 324
BED & BREAKFASTS: 403, 416
BEEF & CATTLE: 209, 512
BERRIES:
  BLACKBERRIES: 206
  BLUEBERRIES: 45, 314
  BOYSENBERRIES: 204, 206, 314
  OLALLIES: 204, 314
  RASPBERRIES: 204, 206, 214, 314
  STRAWBERRIES: 206
CANDIES: 37
CHERRIES: 18, 39, 111, 133, 134, 158, 204, 206, 212, 214, 226, 303, 307
CHRISTMAS TREES: 5, 49, 81, 84, 85, 86, 111, 115, 116, 117, 147, 155, 156, 215, 308, 327, 404, 418, 419, 406, 508
CHESTNUTS: 3, 133, 147, 158
CITRUS: 206, 207, 226
COOKED FOODS: 1, 45, 403
CORN: 111
DRIED FRUIT: 3, 11, 17, 20, 206
FIGS: 45
FIREWOOD: 508
FLOWERS: 156, 205, 214, 312, 314, 327
GIFT PACKS/BASKETS: 3, 8, 17, 26, 38, 39, 45, 115, 314, 508
GOATS: 406
GRAPES: 8, 22
HERBS: 205

HONEY: 11, 17, 20, 35, 50, 49, 147, 314
IRIS: 406
JAMS, JELLIES, PRESERVES: 1, 3, 8, 17, 20, 38, 40, 45, 84, 147, 203, 206, 312, 314
LAMBS: 114
LILIES: 322
MEAT CUTTING: 512
NECTARINES: 3, 8, 9, 39, 111, 203, 206, 207
NURSERIES: 202, 322, 328
ORGANIC: 509
PEACHES: 3, 8, 18, 39, 84, 111, 133, 156, 157, 203, 206, 207, 214, 226, 303, 307, 324, 505
PEARS: 1, 3, 5, 8, 11, 18, 20, 30, 39, 84, 133, 148, 203, 206, 207, 209, 324
PEARS, ASIAN: 3, 8, 49, 203, 206, 207, 209
PERSIMMONS: 1, 3, 8, 49, 147
PLUMS: 3, 5, 8, 11, 18, 20, 39, 111, 133, 156, 157, 206, 303, 505
PUMPKINS: 5, 8, 11, 17, 18, 20, 30, 45, 206, 209, 214, 324, 404
RECREATION: 1, 5, 18, 38, 46, 81, 84, 149, 415, 506, 508
SHIPPING: 3, 17
SPINNING/WEAVING INSTRUCTION: 114
U-PICK: 3, 17, 22, 111, 305
VEGETABLES: 111, 133, 206, 305, 308, 324, 327
WALNUTS: 3, 49, 84, 114, 147, 158, 226, 312, 420
WINE: 8, 26, 32, 46, 152, 201, 301, 305, 401, 402, 403, 405, 408
WINE GRAPES: 8, 38, 39, 134, 152, 201, 402, 417, 421, 505
WINE TASTING: 26, 32, 46, 152, 201, 301, 305, 401, 402, 403, 405, 408, 415
WOOL: 114
WOOD PRODUCTS & HANDSPUN YARN: 114

CAMINO/FRUITRIDGE 1-199

1 HIGH HILL RANCH
2901 High Hill Rd, Placerville. 644-1973
Apples, pears, Fuyu persimmins, apple wine, jams, jellies, pie, hamburgers, BBQ chicken trout fishing, Labor Day-Christmas Eve, daily 8-6. Bus, picnic, hay rides, pony rides.

3 BOA VISTA ORCHARDS
292 Carson Rd, Placerville. 622-5522
(U-pick; cherries & pumpkins.) Apples, apricots, peaches, plums, nectarines, pears, Asian pears, persimmons, walnuts, chestnuts. Apple cider, dried fruits, bake shop, no-sugar fruit conserves and fruit preserves. Fruit and cider tasting, fruit gift packs, shipping. Open year-round 9-5. Bus, picnic.

4 IRVING APPLE BARN
2620 Carson Rd, Placerville.
622-9444 / 622-3079 Call for information.

5 KIDS INC.
3245 N. Canyon Rd, Camino. 622-0084
Apples, pears, plums, pumpkins, Christmas trees, pie shop. Nature trail. Sept 15 - Nov 14 every day; Nov 15 - Dec 19 Thurs-Sun, 9-4. Farm animals, picnic.

8 MOTHER LODE ORCHARDS
4341 N. Canyon Rd, Camino.
644-1914 / 644-5101
Apples, pears, Asian pears, cider, wild pumpkins, Semillon wine, Semillon wine grapes, peaches, nectarines, plums, persimmons, jams, jellies. Gift packs. Sept-Oct, daily 9-4. Nov-Dec weekends only 9-5.

11 BAVARIAN HILLS ORCHARD
3100 N. Canyon Rd., Camino. 642-2714
Apples, plums, pears. Quality Arts & Crafts Fair, pie shop. Sept-Dec, Fri, Sat, Sun & holidays. Live music weekends in Oct, call. Bus, picnic.

17 GRANDPA'S CELLAR
2360 Cable Road, Camino, 95709. 644-2153
Apples, U-pick apples, juice/cider, pumpkins, dried fruit, honey, sugar-free specialties, jams, jellies, syrups, sauces, vinegars. Gift shop, gift boxes and baskets shipped anywhere year-round. Bake shop, group tours. Call or write for mail order brochure and calendar of events. Quality Arts & Crafts Fair. Bus, picnic. Daily Sept-Dec.

18 O'HALLORAN'S APPLE TRAIL RANCH
2261 Cable Rd, Camino. 644-3389
Pears, plums, apples, cherries, peaches, pumpkins. Nature trail, picnic area. Bus parking available. Sept-Nov all day, every day.

20 PLUBELL FAMILY ORCHARDS
1800 Larsen Dr, Camino. 644-1761
Apples: Reds, Goldens, Romes, Granny Smith, Early Blaze. Empress plums. Pumpkins, cider, bake shop, jams & jellies. Weekends only Sept-Nov 9-5. Picnic area.

22 ARGYRES ORCHARD
4220 N. Canyon Rd, Camino. 644-3862
U-pick apples. Apples, Concord grapes. Sept-Oct weekends 9-5 or by appt. Come see our daffodils in March.

26 LAVA CAP WINERY
2221 Fruitridge Rd, Placerville. 621-0175
Premium wine tasting and sales. Jan-Dec 12, 11-5 daily except major holidays. Picnic area, sundeck, gifts.

30 BARSOTTI RANCH
2239 Hidden Valley Ln, Camino. 622-4629
Pears, apples, pasteurized cider, fresh cider, pumpkins. Wholesale.

32 BOEGER WINERY
1709 Carson Rd, Placerville. 622-8094
Premium table wines. Wine tasting and picnic tables. Open daily year-round, 10-5. Closed major holidays.

35 BILLS APPLES
2234 Cable Rd, Camino. 644-5283
Apples, apple juice, honey, dolls and crafts. Open Labor Day thru Thanksgiving.

38 ABEL'S APPLE ACRES
2345 Carson Rd, Placerville. 626-0138
Apples, bake shop, horse & pony rides, BBQ, gift, jams & butters. Labor Day-Christmas, 7 days a week, 9-5.

39 GOLDBUD FARMS
2501 Carson Rd, Placerville. 626-6521
Apples, pears, cherries, plums, peaches, nectarines, wine grapes, cider, extra-fancy gift packs. Jun-Dec, daily 10-5. Annual Cherries Jubilee Festival June 19-20. Bus, picnic.

40 THE BIG APPLE
4567 Pony Express Trail, Camino. 644-4670
Apples, fresh apple cider, bake shop, apple butter, jams, jellies, nuts, herbal vinegars, honey chutneys, biscotti. Sept-Dec 9:30-5 daily. Picnic.

45 BOLSTER'S HILLTOP RANCH
2000 Larsen Dr, Camino. 644-2230
Apples, pumpkins, berries, blueberries, figs, apple cider, hard cider, jams, jellies, Jun-Aug by appt. Sept 1-Dec 15, daily 10-5. Picnic gift shop. Food weekends, press your own cider.

46 MADRONA VINEYARDS
High Hill Rd, Camino. 644-5948
Five miles east of Placerville off Carson Rd, through High Hill Ranch. Premium wine tasting and sales. Year-round, daily 11-5. Picnic.

49 MARVIN LARSEN RANCH
Corner of Crystal Springs & Mace Rds, Camino. 644-2475 / 644-1396
Apples, pears, apple cider, walnuts, honey, persimmons, Christmas trees. Late Sept-mid-winter.

81 SANTA'S ACRES
2921 Barkley Rd, Camino. 644-2141
Choose & cut Christmas trees. White fir, Douglas fir, Silver Tip, holly, Sequoia, Pine, Cedar. Beautiful place to walk, picnic. Straw pile for children. Friday after Thanksgiving thru Christmas 9-4:30. Closed Mondays. You're welcome to visit year-round to enjoy the view and peaceful surroundings.

84 HARRIS TREE FARM
2640 Blair Rd, Pollock Pines. 644-2194
Apples, pears, peaches, apple cider, apples pies, Christmas trees, wreaths, jams, jellies, walnuts. Aug-Dec, daily 9-5. Picnic, hiking.

111 PERRON ORCHARDS
1901 Carson Rd, Placerville. 622-5526
Cherries, U-pick, apricots, peaches, nectarines, plums, apples, fresh corn, vine-ripe tomatoes. Fresh vegetables in season, fresh fruit pies all season. Christmas trees. Open daily 9-6, June 1 'til New Years.

114 ANDERSEN'S HIDDEN VALLEY FARM
2088 Hidden Valley Ln, Camino. 622-8458
Walnuts, reg. Romney's, Rambouillet & Romney crosses, lambs, fleeces, meat, hides, custom spinning & weaving lessons. Annual wool gathering. Arts & Crafts Fair, Oct 15-16.

115 CHARLIE'S CHOICE XMAS TREE FARM
2880 Hassler Rd, Camino. 626-4378
Open Nov 25-Dec 17, daily 9-4. Doug Fir, White Fir, Sierra Redwood & Silver Tip. Homemade cinnamon rolls, free coffee, packaging available. Herbs & Heirlooms gift shop open Labor Day-Dec 17, weekends only 9-4.

116 HILLSIDE TREE FARM
2881 N. Canyon Rd, Camino. 621-2053
Choose & cut Christmas trees. Open daily 9-4:30.

117 INDIAN ROCK TREE FARM
3800 N. Canyon Rd, Camino. 622-4087
Open daily mid Nov0Dec. White Fir, Doug Fir, Silver Tip, Cedar, Pine, Sequoia. All weather roads, packaging available. Picnic tables, wreaths, gift shop.

133 SMOKEY RIDGE RANCH
2160 Carson Rd, Placerville. 626-7940
Cherries, peaches, plums, pears, apples, chestnuts and vegetables. Jun-Nov weekends, 10-5. Weekdays, call first.

134 GRANITE HILL VINEYARDS
Call for directions. 626-9696
Cherries, wine grapes: Petite Syrah, Semillon Sauvignon Blanc, Cabernet Sauvignon. Cherries-June. Wine grapes-Sept.

147 THE FRUIT TREE
4725 Pony Express Trail, Camino. 644-3672
Apples, chestnuts, walnuts, baked goods, apple butter, caramel apples, cider, juice, jams, persimmons, grapes. Sept-Dec, 9-dusk, Sun, 10-dusk, closed Wed.

148 HARVEST LANE
2261 Harvest Lane, Camino. 644-4934
Pears in August, Apples in September. Juice and apples in October.

149 GHOST MOUNTAIN RANCH
5560 Badger Hill Rd, Pollock Pines. 644-5476
RV Campground, cabin rentals, pool, horseback riding. Please write to: PO Box 1900, Pollock Pines, 95726 for a descriptive brochure. Open all year.

152 JODAR VINEYARD AND WINERY
2393 Gravel Rd, Placerville. 626-4582
Chardonnay and Cabernet Sauvignon grapes and wine. Wine tasting weekends 12-4, year-round. 15-minute scenic drive from Apple Hill. Picnicking and fishing at nearby Finnon Lake.

155 CANDY APPLE TREE FARM
2781 Larsen Dr, Camino. 644-7519
Open daily Nov 25-Dec 19, 10-5. Craft sales on weekends.

156 THE HOLLY GROVE
3030 Carson Rd, Placerville. 644-8467
Doug & White fir, wreaths, greenery. Free hot cider and popcorn. Thanksgiving-Christmas Fri-Sun, 9:30-5. Sept-Oct: peaches, plums, dried flowers, Victorian cards & pictures. Weekends and by appt.

157 JACQUIER RANCH
2731 Jacquier Rd, Placerville. 622-0705
Apples, peaches, plums. June-Nov, daily 7-7.

158 SIERRA APPLES
2685 Mace Rd, Camino. 644-1810
Cherries in June; apples, walnuts, chestnuts Aug-Nov weekends only.

GOLD DISCOVERY 200-299

201 GOLD HILL VINEYARD
Cold Springs Rd. & Vineyard Ln, Placerville 626-6522
Wine, wine tasting, wine grapes: Chardonnay, Cabernet Sauvignon, Cabernet Franc, Merlot, Chenin Blanc, White Riesling. Year-round, weekends, 10-5. Picnic, weddings, parties.

202 GOLD HILL NURSERY
6000 Gold Hill Rd, Placerville. 622-2190
Mountain-grown nursery stock since 1958. Year-round, 9-5, closed Mon-Tues.

203 MARCHINI PEAR-A-DICE
900 Hwy 49, Placerville. 622-4578
Peaches, pears, nectarines, apricots, apples, apple cider, pies and preserves. Picnic area. July-Oct, daily 8-8.

204 AMERICAN RIVER CHERRY CO.
2240 Dias Drive, Placerville. 626-3881
(Hwy 49 to Tyrrel to Dias Dr.) Sweet cherries, raspberries, boysenberries, olallie berries.

205 MO DALY
PO Box 703, Lotus, 95651. 622-8977
Fresh flowers, herbs, perennials, shrubs, handmade floral paper, dried flowers -- available at South Lake Tahoe Farmers' Market on Tuesday. Garden Tours, propagation workshops, herbs, everlasing bamboo classes. Call or write for brochure.

206 HOOVERVILLE ORCHARDS
1100 Wallace Rd, Placerville. 622-2155
Peaches, nectarines, plums, cherries, apples, cider, pears, Asian pears: 7 varieties. Citrus: oranges, grapefruit, lemons, Mandarins. Bake shop June-Feb daily 8-8.

207 COALWELL'S RED SHACK
1560 Coloma Rd, Placerville. 622-8467
A full season's varieties of peaches and varieties of pears, nectarines, Asian pears, apples and more. June-Sept. daily.

209 MEYER RANCH
2280 Coloma Rd, Placerville. 622-5881
Beef, year-round. Polled herefords. Apples, pears, pumpkins. Open daily, daylight to dusk. Pears: Aug; Asian Pears: Aug-Oct; Apples: Sept-Nov; Pumpkins: Oct.

212 CASWELL RANCH
2457 Caswell Dr, Placerville. 622-4605
Cherries, June 1'til Mother Nature says it's over. Picked fresh daily. Sold on order only.

214 ATTIC TREASURES ORCHARD
6191 Green Valley Rd, Placerville. 626-5356
Apples, cherries, peaches, apricots, raspberries, pumpkin patch. Wedding facilities, flowers.

215 SUNDANCE TREE FARM
3541 Sundance Trail, Placerville. 622-5636
Christmas trees. The day after Thanksgiving through Christmas, daily 8 'til dark. Doug Fir, Scotch Pine. Packaging available.

226 GRAHAM'S SHED
1101 Cold Springs, Placerville. 622-2612
Cherries, peaches, apples, Mandarins, oranges, walnuts, avocados. Cherries: June. Apples: Sept-Oct. Oranges: Dec-Feb. Open 7 days when selling fruit, 9 to 6, call first.

PLEASANT VALLEY 300-399

301 SIERRA VISTA WINERY
Far end of Leisure Lane, Pleasant Valley. 622-7221
Wine, wine tasting. Daily, 10-4 year-round. Closed major holidays. Picnic.

303 UP COUNTRY RANCH
5220 Mt. Aukum Rd, Placerville. 644-6843
Montmorency (sour pie cherry) cherries: late June. Suncrest (freestone) peaches: last week of July. O'Henry (freestone) peaches: Labor Day. 5 varieties plums: late July-Sept.

305 CHATEAU RODIN VINEYARD & WINERY
4771 Green Hills Rd, Placerville. 622-6839
Featuring premium varietal wines for tasting. Picnic area for family fun, set in a spectacular view of the Sierras. Large selection of fresh fruits. Old-fashioned veg. garden; U-pick veg. & fruit. Open year-round, Tues-Sun, 10-4:30.

307 FAUSEL RANCH
Squaw Creek and Hanks Exchange Rd, Placerville. 622-4390
Cherries: mid-June. Peaches: July & Aug, call first.

308 TOMARY TOMATOES
1589 Pleasant Valley Rd, Placerville. 622-8551
Over 35 varieties of heirloom tomatoes: multi-shapes, sizes and colors. Open mid-July thru mid-October. Christmas trees (Doug Fir and White Fir), Nov and Dec. Call first for details.

312 BROOKSHIRE GARDENS
6201 North Street, El Dorado. 626-3028
Walnuts, herbs, jams and jellies, dried flowers, crafts, May-Dec, daily. Picnic area, restrooms, handcrafters gift shoppe. Closed occasionally, please try again.

314 FORTY MILE RANCH
5010 Mother Lode Dr, Shingle Springs. 677-5927
Baked goods, fresh berries, honey, jams, vinegars, Light lunches, syrups, nut butters. Custom gift baskets. Dried flowers sold by the bunch or in arrangements. Walk thru display garden and plant sales. Open Saturdays 10-5, June-Dec.

322 BOUNTIFUL LILIES
3100 Nawi Trail, Pleasant Valley. 644-7003
Potted blooming lily plants. Specializing in Asiatic and Oriental hybrids; all colors. May 6-June 26, Fridays & weekends, 10-4. Call for detailed flyer.

324 MINING BROOK RANCH
3424 Mining Brook Rd, Placerville. 626-6217
Peaches, pears, apples, pies. Fresh vegetables. Pumpkins. Crafts, picnic area. Aug-Dec, weekdays, call first. Weekends 9-6.

327 FALLS LODE FARM
5600 Martinez Creek Rd, El Dorado. 621-4930
Christmas trees. Open 9-5 weekends, Thanksgiving weekend until Christmas. Weekdays by appointment. Vegetable seedlings: May, June. Flower seedlings, herbs. Vegetables: June-Sept.

328 THE FRONT YARD NURSERY
5801 Mother Lode Dr, Placerville. 626-3494
Container stock including: raspberry, cultivars, gooseberries, blackberries, boysenberries, Josta Berry, table grapes and various ornamental trees, shrubs, perennials and bedding plants.

SOUTH COUNTY 400-499

401 LATCHAM VINEYARDS
2860 Omo Ranch Rd, Mt. Aukum.
620-6834 / 620-6642
Premium wines and wine tasting. Year-round, Wed-Sun, 11-5.

402 CHARLES B. MITCHELL VINEYARDS
8221 Stoney Creek Rd, Somerset.
620-3467 / 1-800-704-WINE
Wine tasting and sales --Award-winning wines. Oak shaded picnic area, BBQs, weddings, Wed-Sun, 11-5 year-round.

403 FITZPATRICK WINERY & LODGE
7740 Fairplay Rd, Somerset 95684. 620-3248
Premium wines of the Sierra Foothills. Year-round wine tasting and Plowman's Lunch. Weekends, 11-5. Weekdays by appt. Bed & Breakfast accommodations. Write for calendar of special events.

404 NOEL CHRISTMAS TREES
7600 Fairplay Rd, Somerset.
620-4758 / 1-800-585-NOEL
Pumpkin patch, pumpkins & gourds, Oct-Nov. Tree reservations available weekends Nov. Choose & cut trees Thanksgiving thru Christmas, daily 10-5. Douglas Fir, White Fir, Monterey & Scotch Pine, Sequoia, Incense Cedar. Fresh wreaths shipped UPS. Parking, picnic.

405 GRANITE SPRINGS WINERY & VINEYARDS
6060 Granite Springs Rd, Somerset. 620-6395
Wine tasting and sales of premium wines. Year-round, Wed-Sun 11-5 or by appt. Closed major holidays. Picnic.

406 BLUEBIRD HAVEN IRIS GARDEN
6940 Fairplay Rd, Somerset. 620-5017
Iris rhizomes, Hubian dairy goats. Iris gardens open for viewing in Spring: April 17-May 16 depending on bloom. Tues-Sun, 10-5. Iris orders dug and shipped in July. Dairy goats, year-round. Call for information. Bus, pcinic, tours.

408 WINDWALKER VINEYARDS
7360 Perry Creek Rd, Somerset. 620-4054
Fine wines of the Sierra Foothills. Wine tasting and picnic area year-round. Weekends 11-5 or by appointment.

415 PERRY CREEK VINEYARDS
7400 Perry Creek Rd, Somerset. 620-5175
Wine tasting at its finest! Mission-style winery & tasting room. Classic automobile collection at the winery. Picnic, ample parking. Weekends, 11-5 & by appt.

416 7 UP BAR GUEST RANCH
8060 Fairplay Rd, Somerset. 620-5450
A historic Bed & Breakfast with country charm, situated on 199 acres. All modern accommodations. Hearty ranch breakfast. Located in the heart of wine country.

417 OLIVER VINEYARDS
6140 Granite Springs Rd, Somerset. 620-3730
Premium wine grapes: Merlot, Cabernet Sauvignon & Muscat Caneli. By appt.

418 SILVER FOREST TREE FARM
4041 Rontree Ln, Somerset. 620-6261
Choose & Cut Christmas trees: Silver Tip, White Fir, Doug Fir. Picnic and BBQ areas for large and small groups. Easy walking trail. Candy & hot beverages. Thanksgiving-Christmas, Fri-Sun, 9 'til dusk.

419 FANCHER'S CHRISTMAS TREE FARM
6781 Omo Ranch Rd, Omo Ranch. 620-6252
Choose & Cut and pre-cut Christmas trees. 62 acres White Fir, Silver Tip, Doug Fir, Incense Cedar, Sierra Redwood & Scotch Pine. Fresh & dried wreaths. Gift shop & snack bar. Picnic area with horseshoe & fire pits. Plenty of parking. Available for weddings, reunions. Open day after Thanksgiving-Dec 22, 10 'til dusk, seven days a week.

420 SPLIT ROCK RANCH
7901 Perry Creek Rd, Somerset. 620-3597
Walnuts: Fall. Call for information.

421 SINGLE LEAF VINEYARDS AND WINERY
7480 Fairplay Rd, Somerset. 620-3545
Wine grapes: fall. Call for information.

GEORGETOWN 500-599

505 WHITTINGTON FARM
5020 Twin Pines Loop, Georgetown. 333-4886
Plums: Empress and President. Wine grapes: White Riesling, Chardonnay, Pinot Noir. Peaches, cherries. June-Oct, call first.

506 TWIN PINES CHRISTMAS TREE FARM
5150 Twin Pines Loop, Georgetown. 333-4226
Christmas trees, Doug Fir, Sequoia, White Fir. Many large trees. Picnic tables, refreshments, pond, view. Free packaging, holly, mistletoe. Thanksgiving-Christmas, daily 9-dusk.

508 NORTH STAR TREE FARM
    6000 Shoofly Rd, Kelsey. 622-3663
Christmas trees, all sizes, many varieties. Wreaths, garlands, greenery. Firewood bundles, gifts, farm-grown produce. Hiking trails, tractor-drawn hayrides. Picnic areas. Nov 26-Dec 24, daily 9:30-4:30.

509 MARMOT MEADOWS FARM
    6740 Hancock Rd, Garden Valley. 333-1550
CCOF certified organically grown fruits and vegetables in season. Call for information.

512 EL DORADO RANCH
    1600 Hwy 193, Cool. 885-8999
Home of ElDorado meats: professional, custom meat cutting. Beef, pork lamb & game. Specializing in Italian & venison sausage. Open year-round. Call for receiving hours. Also pumpkin patch in Oct. Picked or U-pick. Fall crafts, gifts & foods. Field trips by reservation. Call for brochure.

Fresno County

The Blossom Trail

In early spring, one of the nicest things that happens is the Blossom Trail. For two to four weeks starting about March 1st, all the fruit and nut trees are in bloom, and most of them are really something to see, in white and pink and (in apples) a mix of both. A trip along the Fresno County Blossom Trail can be a lot of fun for everyone. In towns like Sanger and Reedley they have special festivals and events that are part of the Blossom Trail activities. Follow the map here and enjoy!

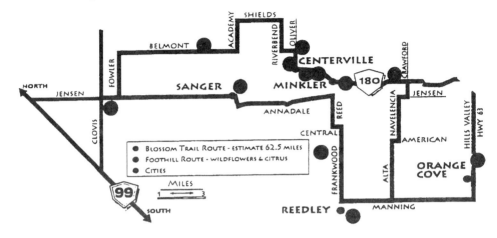

The Foothill Trail

The Foothill Trail offers an alternate route with slightly different viewing from The Blossom Trail. Many blossoming trees can be seen, but through most of the blooming season many varieties of wildflowers flourish on the rolling foothills.
Directions:

Access Jensen Ave. from Hwy 99 north or south & proceed as follows:
- turn north (L) on Flower
- turn east (R) on Belmont
- turn north (L) on Academy
- east (R) on Shields
- south (R) on Riverbend
- east (L) on Belmont
- south (R) on Oliver
- west (L) on Hwy 180
- south (R) on Crawford
- west (R) on Jensen
- south (L) on Navelencia
- west (R) on American
- south (L) on Alta
- west (R) on Manning
- north (R) on Frankwood
- west (L) on Central
- north (R) on Reed
- west (L) on Annadale
- north (R) on Academy
- and west (L) on Jensen
Return to Fresno via Hwy 99 or Hwy 99 to Hwy 41.

DID YOU KNOW?

George Washington and Abraham Lincoln both had roots deep in the country as men of the soil. Washington had large plantations and was one of the first to practice rotating crops from field to field. Literally, crop rotation; very important in most areas to help the land remain fertile and useful.

Lincoln, of course, was born in the wilderness and everyone farmed just to survive. Farmers in those days were barely able to raise enough for their own families, and hopefully have a little left over to barter or sell.

Today's Fresno County Farmer, as farmers everywhere in the nation, produce enough to feed themselves and about 130 other people: 100 in America and 30 overseas.

Credit: Blossom Trail Committee, Fresno Chamber of Commerce 209-495-4800

Harvest Calendar

Fruits and Nuts:
Almonds .... Sept/mid-Oct
Apples .... mid-Aug/Oct
Apricots .... mid-June/July
Cherries .... June
Figs .... June/Oct
Grapes .... mid-July/Oct
Kiwi .... Nov
Oranges, navel .... Nov/mid-May
Oranges, valencia .... Apr/July
Nectarines .... May/Sept
Peaches .... mid-May/mid-Sept
Pears .... Aug/mid-Sept
Pistachios .... Sept/Nov
Plums, Prunes .... June/mid-Aug
Walnuts .... mid-Sept/mid-Nov

Vegetables, Berries and Melons:
Asparagus .... mid-Apr/mid-June
Cabbage, Broccoli .... Apr/June and
    Cauliflower .... mid-Sept/Dec
Carrots .... Mar-Jun/Aug-Dec
Celery .... mid-July/mid-Oct
Sweet Corn .... mid-May/mid-Oct
Lettuce .... Apr/mid-Dec
Melons .... June/mid-Oct
Onions .... Aug/Oct
Peas, Limas and .... Feb/Apr and
    Snap Beans .... Aug/mid-Oct
Strawberries .... May/Sept
Tomatoes, Fresh .... June/mid-Aug
                                       and Sept/mid-Nov
Tomatoes, Canned ...... mid-July/mid-Nov

Field Crops:
Alfalfa and Hay .... mid-Apr/Sept
Alfalfa-Clover Seed .... mid-Sept/Oct
Dry Beans .... mid-Sept/Oct
Corn (Grain, Silage) .... Sept/Oct
Cotton .... Oct/Dec
Wheat, Oats, Barley .... May/mid-Aug
Potatoes .... June/Dec
Rice .... Sept/Oct
Safflower .... July/Aug
Sorghums (Grain) .... Sept/Oct
Sugar Beets .... mid-July/Oct

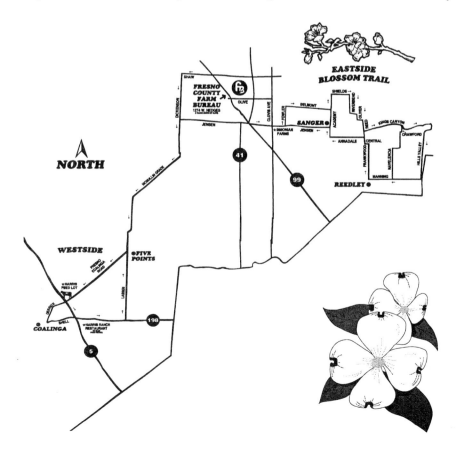

Direct Marketing:
FARM BUREAU STYLE

Andrews Ranch - FRESH FIGS
Rolland Andrews
4113 E. Copper, Clovis 93611
(4 miles north of Herndon on Minnewawa; southeast corner of Minnewawa and Copper)
209-299-4566. Bring own containers.
6/15-7/1 .... Black Mission
Aug-Oct .... Calimyrna & Missions

Angel's Produce Farms, A.R. Garcia
20117 S. Chestnut Ave, Laton 93242
209-923-4697
June-November, daily 8am-8pm
Year Round ...... Cucumbers *Armenian, others*;
Eggplant; Onions;
Peppers *Sweet, Bells & Hot Chili*;
Pickling Cukes;
Squash *Summer, Zucchini, Yellow*;
Sweet Corn; Tomatoes
7/1-11/1 .... Melons
Cantaloupe, Casaba, Crenshaw, Honeydew, Orange Honeydew, Juan Canary, Persian, Santa Claus, Watermelon

Bella Frutta, Pat Ricchiuti
Clovis (SE corner of Shepherd & Willow)
209-298-8290
All Year; Sun thru Fri 8:30am-5pm; Closed Sat
Year Round .... Almonds; Apples; Apricots;
Dried Fruit; Grapes; Nectarines;
Oranges; Peaches; Plums; Pistachios.
Candies & Nuts.

Circle K Ranch, Ronald Kazarian
8640 E. Manning, Selma 93662
209-834-1571
Mon thru Sat 7am-5pm
In Season .... Jumbo Raisins; Table Grapes
Tree Fruit; Nuts
Gift Packs available

Dean's Apples, Dean Philpott
(on Zediker, between Shields and Ashlan)
209-229-2555
7/25-10/1 .... Golden Supreme Apples
9/1-9/20 .... Fuji Apples
7/15-10/1 .... Asian Pears

DJJS Farms, David Simonian
5529 W McKinley, Fresno 93722
209-275-5529 (Call first)
Aug 10-Oct 15; daily 8am-8pm
7/20-8/1 .... Gala Apples
8/10-8/15 .... Red Delicious Apples
8/20-10/1 .... Golden Delicious Apples
8/10-8/30 .... Mutsu Apples
9/20-10/15 .... Fuji Apples
9/15-10/15 .... Granny Smith Apples
10/1-10/15 .... Arkansas Black Apples
10/10-10/20 .... Pomegranates

F & M Smith Farm, Melvin Smith
3108 S. Blythe, Fresno 93706
209-268-1890
All Year; Tues, Thur & Sat 7am-3pm
Sales at Merced & 'N' Street
As in Season .... Boy Choy; Corn; Daikon;
Eggplant; Endive;
Fava-Beans; Leeks;
Lettuce *Romaine, Red & Green Leaf*;
Melons *Cantaloupes, Honeydew*;
Okra; Parsley; Peppers *various*;
Spinach; Tomatoes & more

Pat Farley's Farm, Patrick Farley
7523 S. Kenneth, Fowler 93625
(near Hwy 99 and Clovis Ave)
209-834-3138
August 15-Labor Day: daily 7am-7pm
Grapes *Thompson Seedless and Flame*

Fresno Co-Op Raisin Growers
4466 N. Dower, Fresno 93722
209-275-3710
Year Round .... Raisins *Natural, Golden Seedless, Currants, Flames*

Giannopulos, Alex
3350 S. Indianola, Sanger 93657
209-875-5969, Mon-Sat
All Year .... Wichita Pecans *Soft Shell*

Jacobsen Farms, Robert Jacobsen
8682 E. Nebraska Ave, Selma 93662
209-896-3870
Aug 15-Sept 15, daily 8am-8pm
Thompson Seedless Grapes

Jess M. Swope
2829 Olive Street, Selma 93662
(L.A. Certified Farmers' Markets)
209-896-0505
May 15-Dec 31 .... Apricots; Cucumbers;
Grapes; Nectarines; Peaches; Persimmons;
Plums; Asian Pears; Cantaloupes

Loring Farms, Larry Loring
4381 E. International, Clovis 93612
209-299-6020
Dec-Mar, daily 7am-6pm. Call first.

Luke's Almond Acres, Lucas Nersesian
11281 S. Lac Jac, Reedley 93654
209-638-3483
Mon-Sat 8am-5pm
All Year .... Almonds; Dried Fruit; Candy Coated Almonds
Gift packs and brochures available

Magnuson's Apples, Bill Magnuson
7088 E. Jensen (corner Jensen & Temperance)
209-268-3183
Oct-Nov, Sun-up to Sun-down, 7 days a week.
Granny's & Fuji's

Marthedal's Berry Farm, Jon Marthedal
8254 S. Cedar, Fresno 93725
206-233-6553
June 1-25: Mon-Sat 8am-6pm. Call first.
Boysenberries
Look for us at Farmers' Market.

Mesple Farms, Madeleine & Paul Mesple
7443 N. Millbrook, Fresno 93720
209-439-0104
All Year, daily 9am-6pm.
61/-7/15 .... Apricots
Blenhelm, Tilton, Patterson
6/15-7/6 .... Figs *fresh*
8/1-8/15 .... Alberta Peaches
All Year .... Dried Fruit; Almonds
6/15-6/30 .... June Lady Peaches

Nonini Wineries, Gildo & Reno Nonini
2640 N. Dickerson, Fresno 93722
209-275-1936
All Year, closed Sun & Holidays.
Tours by appointment.

Pete's Egg Ranch, Peter Binz
5130 S. Orange, Fresno 93725
209-266-7630
All Year, Mon-Sat 9am-5:30pm.

Remick Farms, H. Noel Remick
10267 S. Lac Jac, Reedley 93654
209-638-3912
All Year, daily 7am-7pm.
5/1-9/30 .... Nectarines; Peaches; Plums
10/1-11/30 .... Apples
10/1-2/28 .... Lemons; Persimmons
11/1-5/31 .... Oranges
6/1 .... Apricots

Schafer Farms, Marvin & Pete Schafer
3157 N. Siskiyou, Kerman 93630
(16106 W. Shields) 209-846-8055
Raisins *Natural select: Goldens, Currants, Midgets, Chocolate Coated, Chocolate Mint, Yogurt Covered, Chocolate Fruit Coating;* Walnuts

Simonian Farms, Dennis Simonian
2629 S. Clovis Av, Fresno 93725
(SE corner of Clovis & Jensen Aves.)
209-237-2294
All Year, Summer Season, daily 8am-6pm
Winter Season, Weekdays 8am-5:30pm.
Gift packs available.
4/1 .... Strawberries
5/1 .... Nectarines; Peaches; Various Onions; Cherries; Plums
6/1 .... Coreless Tomatoes; Apricots; Plums; Bell Peppers
7/1 .... Melons
8/1 .... Grapes; Apples; Pears
10/1 .... Indian Corn; Gourds; Pumpkins; Persimmons
10/15 .... Avocados
11/1 .... Grapefruit; Oranges; Lemons; Kiwi
12/1 .... Pecans; Pistachios; Walnuts
All Year .... Thompson Raisins *Jumbo*; Dried Fruit

Soghomonian, Joe
8624 S. Chestnut, Fresno 93725
209-834-3150, 209-834-2772
July-Nov, Mon-Fri, 8:30am-5pm
8/1-8/20 .... Champagne Grapes
8/15-9/30 .... Grapes *Thompson Seedless*
9/1-10/1 .... Ribier Grapes
10/1-11/30 .... Walnuts
All Year .... Raisins *including Zante*

Sun Empire Foods, George Kenneson
1220 S. Madera, Kerman 93630
209-846-8208
Mon-Fri 8am-5:30pm, Sat 8am-12N
All Year .... Coated Fruits & Nuts
Gift packs available. Plant tours available.
Please Call.

Sunny Cal Farms
10425 S. Kings River Rd, Reedley 93654
209-638-9693
All Year ..... Apples; Grapes; Kiwi; Nectarines; Oranges; Peaches; Plums; *As in Season*

The Fruit Basket, Fred Giorgetti
Hwy 180 & Frankwood, Sanger 93657
209-787-2419
May-Sept, daily 9am-6pm
Fruits; Vegetables; Honey; Nuts

The Apple Place, Rod & Judy Taylor
54950 Hwy 245, Miramonte 93641
(one mile south of Pinehurst)
209-336-2608
Aug-Nov, daily 9am-Dusk
Apples 18 varieties;
Fresh Cider

PUMPKINS

Danny's Pumpkin Patch, Hugh Henry
6433 W. Belmont, Fresno 93722
(5 miles west of Hwy 99 & 2 miles north of Kearney Park).
209-275-3827
Oct, daily 8am-Dark.
October .... 40 acres of Pumpkins
Large & Small;
Indian Corn;
Grain Corn *Whole & Cracked;*
Corn Stalks; Gourds; Oat Hay & more;
Winter Squash

Pumpkin Valley, Allen Hovsepian
Sales at 11868 Old Friant Rd, Fresno 93720
209-434-8272
Oct 10-30, weekdays 12-6pm;
Sat-Sun 10am-6pm; School tours 9am-12pm.
October .... Corn Shocks; Indian Corn;
Pumpkins; Persimmons; Pomegranates;
Kabocha
We rent straw bales.

CERTIFIED FARMERS' MARKETS

Old Town Clovis Farmers' Market
Polasky & 4th Street, Clovis
209-298-5774
Open Friday evenings starting late May until the end of Sept 5pm.

Reedley Downtown Association
'G' Street, Reedley (between 10th & 12th)
Open Friday evenings starting in late May until the end of Sept. 4:30-7pm.

The Vineyard
500 W. Shaw, Fresno (Shaw & Blackstone Ave.)
Open Saturday mornings year-round;
Wed 3-7pm.

CHRISTMAS TREE FARMS

Brewer's Tree Farm, Bob Brewer
6879 S. Reed Av, Reedley 93654
209-638-1991
Open day after Thanksgiving, 8am-5pm.

Evelyn's Evergreens
9886 E. Belmont Av, Sanger 93657
(NW corner of Belmont & McCall Aves.)
209-251-0823
Open day after Thanksgiving; daily 10am-5pm.
Monterey Pines *Choose & Cut*

Granpa's Christmas Tree Farm, Vincent Jura
2350 Nees, Clovis 93612
209-299-4540
Open day after Thanksgiving; daily 9am-dusk.

Hillcrest Christmas Tree Farm
Melissa Bautista
6943 S. Reed, Reedley 93654
209-638-2762
Open Saturday after Thanksgiving, 10am-5pm.

Noel Tree Farm, Joseph Cassinerio
2712 W. Fir, Fresno 93711
Open day after Thanksgiving; daily 9am-dark.
#1 .... 7157 N. Willow at Herndon
#2 .... 4435 S. Elm
#3 .... Clovis & McKinley
#4 .... St. Nicks Tree Farm at D & D Ranch
38484 Ave 12, Madera
209-439-5746, 209-435-7817

Richgreen Christmas Trees
Delmer & D. Richard
4148 W. Jensen, Fresno 93706
(5 miles W of Hwy 99 on Jensen Av)
209-264-2454
Open day after Thanksgiving; daily 8am-5pm.
Monterey Pine
Gift Shop, School Tours, Santa on weekends.

Roger's Christmas Trees, Roger Brandt
40845 Road 48, Dinuba 93618
209-638-1194
Open day after Thanksgiving; daily 9am-5pm.

Santa's Forest, Bill Knowles
4125 E. Adams, Fowler 93625
209-834-3666
Open Dec 1; 10am-5pm.
Santa Claus on weekends, free refreshments.

Santa's Tree Farm, Ed Rose
725 Peach Av (between Belmont & Olive)
209-456-XMAS
Open day after Thanksgiving; daily 9am-7pm.

Shipman Tree Farm, Ira Shipman
47063 Lower Lane
(Dunlap Rd to Lower Ln, 1 mile E of Miramonte)
209-336-2539
Open day after Thanksgiving-Dec 24;
daily 10am-4pm

Steve's Christmas Trees, Steve Smith
10793 S. Pederson, Reedley 93654
209-591-7576
Open day after Thanksgiving.

Trickett's Tree Farm, Timm Trickett
(between Easton & Caruthers, 1 mile S of
Manning & 1 mile E of Hwy 41)
Open day after Thanksgiving; daily 10am-5pm.
Free Hayrides; Gift Shop.

Lake County

Lake County Farm Trails

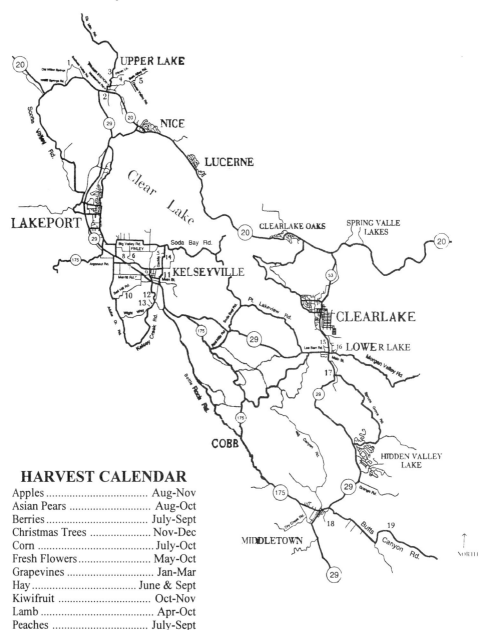

HARVEST CALENDAR

Apples	Aug-Nov
Asian Pears	Aug-Oct
Berries	July-Sept
Christmas Trees	Nov-Dec
Corn	July-Oct
Fresh Flowers	May-Oct
Grapevines	Jan-Mar
Hay	June & Sept
Kiwifruit	Oct-Nov
Lamb	Apr-Oct
Peaches	July-Sept
Prunes	Aug-Sept
Pumpkins	Sept-Oct
Strawberries	Apr-Nov
Tomatoes	July-Nov
Walnuts	Sept-Nov
Wine Grapes	Aug-Nov

ALL YEAR PRODUCE:

Wine; Honey; Wood; Native Plants; Nursery Products/Stock; Eggs; Cheese; Pigs; Chickens; Cattle; Rabbits; Goats; Wild Rice; Sheep; Herbs & Spices; and Compost.

Credit: Lake County Marketing Program 1-800-525-3743

Members' Listings

16 BRUCE ARNDT WINERY
16175 Main Street, Lower Lake; 707-995-0392
Producing reds and late harvest Muscat without chemical stabilization. No sulfite additions are made. Neutral oak aged. 700 cases produced annually. Call to arrange visit. Bruce Arndt, PO Box 509, Lower Lake, CA 95457.

14 BELL FARMS
3270 Gaddy Lane, Kelseyville; 707-263-9451
Pears, apples, peaches, walnuts, cantaloupes, tomatoes, and other miscellaneous vegetables. Call between 9am and 5pm to arrange visit. Charles and Anita Bell, 4826 Davis Drive, Lakeport, CA 95453.

5 CLOVER CREEK FAMILY FARM
10111 Sam Alley Ridge Rd, Upper Lake; 707-275-9315
We are an organic farm emphasizing sustainable farming practices. We grow fresh vegetables for direct sale at local farmers' markets and at our farm, and we have a weekly subscription program. Call between 8am and 8pm to arrange visit. Annette Durham and Thurston Williams, PO Box 637, Upper Lake, CA 95485.

3 ELK MOUNTAIN CHRISTMAS TREE FARM
10228 Elk Mountain Rd, Upper Lake, CA 95485
707-275-2075.
Choose and cut Monterey and Scotch pine trees. Various sizes. Saws and tree carts furnished. Off-road parking. Open day after Thanksgiving until Christmas. Open between 1pm and dark weekdays, and between 9am and dark weekends. John M. & Rosalie Sisevich.

1 BRUNO GRADEK FARM
4505A Old Witter Springs Rd, Witter Springs, 95493. 707-275-2122.
U-pick Kiwifruit approx. Nov 3-15. Picked kiwifruit sold through December. No pesticides or herbicides used.

19 GUENOC & LANGTRY ESTATE VINEYARDS & WINERY
21000 Butte Canyon Rd, Middletown, CA 95461
707-987-2385; Tasting Room 707-987-9127.
Historic vineyards and winery once owned by Victorian actress Lillie Langtry. Won more gold medals than any other California winery in 1993. Tasting room and picnic grounds. Open 10am-4:30 pm Thurs-Mon. Call Mon-Fri 9am-5pm for more information.

9 HANSON FARMS
3360 Merritt Rd, Kelseyville, CA 95451
707-279-4761
Bartlett and red pears in Aug; Asian Pears in Aug, Sept, Oct; kiwifruit, late Nov-May; walnuts, late Nov-Mar. Over next four years, peaches and Bosc pears to be offered. Open 8am-6pm. Gret and Chris Hanson

11 HOLDENRIED FARMS
3930 Main Street, Kelseyville; 707-279-9022.
Year-round Lake County products. Dried pears, rice, walnuts, wine, honey, salsa. Gift baskets our specialty. Open 10am-5:30pm Mon-Fri and 10am-4pm Sat. Marilyn Holdenried, PO Box 494, Kelseyville, CA 95451.

15 J'S GARDEN
9885 Lee Barr Rd, Lower lake; 707-995-3608.
Fresh herbs in season: dried herbs year-round. Moth repellents, potpourri, miscellaneous herbal products. Classes available by arrangement. Open 10 am-4pm Mon-Sat and 1-4pm Sun. Call the arrange a visit. Jeanette Grainger, PO Box 1370, Lower Lake, CA 95457.

13 KELSEY CREEK BERRY FARM
7155 Kelsey Creek Dr, Kelseyville, CA 95451
707-279-0173
A small organic family farm specializing in raspberries, boysenberries, fresh and dried flowers, and fresh fruit juices. Tree fruits, vegetables, pumpkin patch, and herbs seasonally. Call for availability. Open 7am-7pm. David & Cynthia Kimball.

12 KELSEY CREEK DONKEYS AND DAYLILLIES
6605 Kelsey Creek Dr, Kelseyville, CA 95451
707-279-9294
Rare mini-donkeys and large variety of daylillies and perennials. Sales from farm. Tour of beautiful farm garden by appointment. Wholesale prices to public. Call between 7am and 6pm during April through July to arrange a visit. Karis Webb.

7 KELSEYVILLE CERTIFIED FARMERS' MARKET
Konocti Winery, 4350 Thomas Drive, Kelseyville.
(Thomas Dr at Hwy 29) 707-279-0662
Featuring regional fruits and vegetables from more than 20 local growers and produce from out-of-county growers. Fresh baked sourdough and specialty breads, gourmet food booth, fresh eggs, goat cheese, honey, homemade fruit and nut pies, herbs, flowers and bedding plants. Weekly cooking demonstrations, mini-concerts and children's activities. Sat 8am-Noon from Memorial Day to mid-Oct. Pastry and coffee booth opens at 7:30 am. Carolyn Marchetti, Market Manager, PO Box 894, Kelseyville, CA 95451

7 KONOCTI WINERY
4350 Thomas Dr, Kelseyville; 707-279-8861
(Thomas Dr at Hwy 29)
A winery tasting room featuring 18 different wines. Beautiful lawn area available for picnics. Farmers' Market on grounds 8am-Noon Sat, Memorial Day thru mid-Oct. Open daily 10am-5pm; Sunday 11am-5pm. Konocti Winery, PO Box 890, Kelseyville, CA 95451.

10 LAKE COUNTY WALNUT
1505 Bell Hill Rd, Kelseyville, CA 95451
707-263-6887
Located south of lakeport, off Highland Springs Rd. A processor, sheller and wholesaler of locally grown walnuts. Seasonal from Oct 20 thru Jan 30. Tours and field trips by appointment. Call between 8am and 5pm Mon-Fri to arrange a visit.

4 LEHMAN'S LOLLIPOP FARM
1446 Pitney Ln, Upper Lake; 707-275-3103.
Gift shop in a quaint country setting. Handcrafted gifts. Art studio, rock shop, herbs and teas, and walnuts. Classes available. Christmas show in Nov. Open 10am-5pm Tues thru Sat, Feb thru Dec. Sunday hours in Nov. DJ Enterprises, PO Box 938, Upper Lake, CA 95485.

6 PATTY'S PLACE
2489 Big Valley Rd, Finley; 707-279-2962
All kinds and sizes of plants and ground cover. Fresh eggs, red worms and worm casting for planters. Call between 8am and 6pm weekends from mid-April thru July. Patty McCleary, PO Box 401, Lakeport, CA 95453.

8 DIETMAR RENKER
2297 Argonaut Rd, Kelseyville; 707-279-4409
Fruits, vegetables, and flowers. Open 8am-5pm. Dietmar Renker, PO box 102, Kelseyville, CA 95451.

2 SEELY STAND
80 E Hwy 20, Upper Lake; 707-275-2353.
Pears, peaches, apples, and vegetables. Open approx. Aug 1 thru Nov, 9am-6pm. Edward Seely, PO Box 218, Upper Lake, CA 95485.

17 WILDHURST VINEYARDS
11171 Hwy 29, Upper Lake; 707-994-6525.
Winery, tasting room, picnic area. Specializing in Lake County Wines. Open daily 10am-4pm. Call for additional information. PO Box 1223, Kelseyville, CA 95451.

18 CHANNING RUDD CELLARS &
MT. ST. CLAIRE ESTATE VINEYARDS
21960 St. Helena Creek Rd; Middletown
707-987-2209
Lake County's first bonded winery (1976) since Prohibition, is located high in the south county mountains. Ultra-premium wines have always been the priority. A large expansion with a tasting room on Hwy 29 was completed in 1996. Temporarily open by appointment only. Channing Rudd, PO Box 426, Miidletown, CA 95461.

Napa County

Napa County Farm Trails

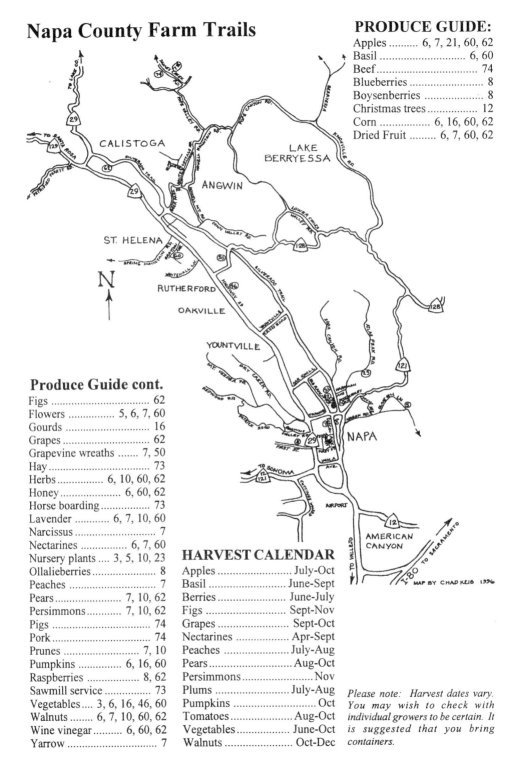

PRODUCE GUIDE:

Apples	6, 7, 21, 60, 62
Basil	6, 60
Beef	74
Blueberries	8
Boysenberries	8
Christmas trees	12
Corn	6, 16, 60, 62
Dried Fruit	6, 7, 60, 62

Produce Guide cont.

Figs	62
Flowers	5, 6, 7, 60
Gourds	16
Grapes	62
Grapevine wreaths	7, 50
Hay	73
Herbs	6, 10, 60, 62
Honey	6, 60, 62
Horse boarding	73
Lavender	6, 7, 10, 60
Narcissus	7
Nectarines	6, 7, 60
Nursery plants	3, 5, 10, 23
Ollalieberries	8
Peaches	7
Pears	7, 10, 62
Persimmons	7, 10, 62
Pigs	74
Pork	74
Prunes	7, 10
Pumpkins	6, 16, 60
Raspberries	8, 62
Sawmill service	73
Vegetables	3, 6, 16, 46, 60
Walnuts	6, 7, 10, 60, 62
Wine vinegar	6, 60, 62
Yarrow	7

HARVEST CALENDAR

Apples	July-Oct
Basil	June-Sept
Berries	June-July
Figs	Sept-Nov
Grapes	Sept-Oct
Nectarines	Apr-Sept
Peaches	July-Aug
Pears	Aug-Oct
Persimmons	Nov
Plums	July-Aug
Pumpkins	Oct
Tomatoes	Aug-Oct
Vegetables	June-Oct
Walnuts	Oct-Dec

Please note: Harvest dates vary. You may wish to check with individual growers to be certain. It is suggested that you bring containers.

Credit: *Napa County Farming Trails, Inc.*

Members' Listings

3 AMES NAPA VALLEY NURSERY
Joseph A. Ames
2664 First Street, Napa, CA 94559; 707-224-2000
Nursery plants and seasonal vegetables and fruits.
Open all year, Mon-Fri 8-6, Sat-Sun 9-5.

5 D.J.'S GROWING PLACE
Curt & Debbie Gore
1289 Olive Hill Ln, Napa, CA 94558; 707-252-6445
Specializing in annuals, perennials, flowering shrubs and hanging baskets. Retail welcome.
Open Mon-Fri 8-4, Sat 9-5, Sun 10-3.

6 NAPA DOWNTOWN FARMERS' MARKET
Laura Cole, Market Manager
West St parking lot between First & Pearl, Downtown Napa; 707-252-7142
Certified Farmers' Market, specialty foods, bakery.
Tues 7:30-Noon, May thru Nov.

7 VON UHLIT RANCH
3011 Soscol Av, Napa, CA 94558; 707-226-2844
Pears, peaches, plums, prunes, dried apricots, apples, fuyu persimmons, almonds, walnuts, grapevine wreaths, dried flowers, flowers in season.
Open all year, noon to 4.

8 NAPA VALLEY BERRY FARM
John & Marian Boyd
1945 Silverado Trail, Napa, CA 94558; 707-255-5505
Blueberries, raspberries, boysenberries, ollalieberries. No chemical fertilizers. No sprays.
Mid-May thru Oct. Open daily, hours vary.
Call ahead for availability.

10 HOFFMAN FARM
John & Margaret Hoffman
2125 Silverado Trail, Napa, CA 94558; 707-226-8938
We pick or you pick, pears, sugar prunes and walnuts. Also, sun dried prunes, persimmons. Nursery stock, herbs, perennials. *Open Aug-Dec, daily 9-5.*

12 BUCHER RANCH
John Bucher
2106 Big Ranch Rd, Napa, CA 94558; 707-224-5354
Choose and cut Christmas trees, Douglas Fir and Scotch Pine. *December, daily 9-dusk.*

16 SALSMAN PRODUCE
Sherry Paukert
1607 McKinley Rd, Napa, CA 94558; 707-226-2100
Vegetables, corn, pumpkins, gourds.
July thru Nov, Mon-Sat. Phone ahead.

21 KEIG RANCH
3165 Silverado Trail, Napa, CA 94558; 707-257-3453
Apples: Gravenstein, Golden Delicious, Red Delicious, Pippin, Jonathon. Bring containers.
Mid-July thru Oct. Daily 8:30-5:30, closed Sundays.

23 RUSSELL LEVY BONSAI NURSERY
Russell & Katherine Levy
3348 Atlas Peak Rd, Napa, CA 94558; 707-226-3963
Conifer & shade trees for oriental or western gardens. Bonsai materials, fruit trees, bare root multiple grafts in spring. 25 varieties of citrus, both dwarf and standard. *Open all year by appointment.*

46 CAKEBREAD VINEYARD PRODUCE
Jack & Dolores Cakebread
8300 Hwy 29, PO 216, Rutherford, CA 94573; 707-963-5221
Sustainable grown vegetables in season.
Open Wed-Sun 10-3. Phone for availability.

50 NAPA VALLEY GRAPEVINE WREATH CO.
Sally Wood
8901 Conn Creek Rd (Hwy 128), Rutherford, CA 94573; 707-963-8893
Hand woven Grapevine wreaths, reindeer and baskets.
Open all year, daily 11-5. Closed Tues.

60 NAPA VALLEY FARMERS' MKT
Mary Jane Franus, Market Manager
Crane Park, Grayson Av, at Hwy 29, St. Helena; 707-252-2105 Certified Farmers' Market.
Fridays 7:30-11:30, May thru Oct.

62 RANCHO MARIA LOUISA
Ben & Lynn Tanus
3911 Silverado Trail, Calistoga, CA 94515; 707-942-8182
Wine vinegar, dried fruit, seasonal garden produce, stone fruit, apples, figs, persimmons, pomegranates, pears, berries, walnuts, table grapes, honey, sweet corn. *Open all year, daily 9-6.*

73 DOUBLE D RANCH
Bo & Dede Rideout
2002 James Creek Rd, Pope Valley, CA 94567;
707-965-1451 (hay/boarding)
606-965-2887 (portable sawmill)
Livestock hay, horse boarding and portable sawmill service, specializing in post and fence boards.
Open all year by appointment.

74 WILMS RANCH
Paul & Betty Wilms
2309 James Creek Rd, Pope Valley, CA 94567;
707-965-2207
Pigs of all sizes, beef. Tours by appointment.
Please call first. *Open all year, daily 8-5.*

Nevada County
Placer County

Placer County Farm Trails

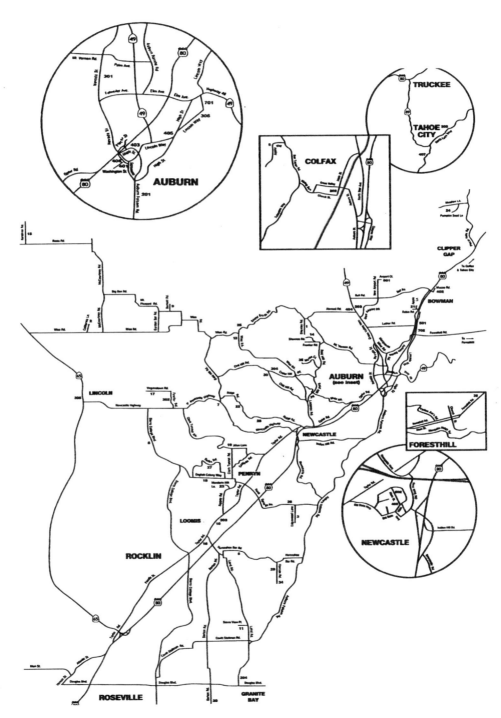

Credit: *PlacerGROWN Farm Trails, 11477 E Ave., Auburn, CA 95603*

HARVEST CALENDAR

Apples	July-Nov	Pears	Aug-Nov
Beef	Year Round	Peppers	July-Oct
Berries	May-Nov	Persimmons	Oct-June
Christmas Trees	Nov-Dec	Plums	June-Sept
Corn	July-Oct	Poultry & Eggs	Year Round
Green & Dry Beans	Year Round	Pumpkins	Sept-Feb
Herbs/Cut Flowers	Year Round	Rice	Year Round
Kiwi	Oct-June	Root Crops	Year Round
Mandarins/Citrus	Nov-Mar	Salad Greens	Year Round
Melons	July-Nov	Sheep & Wool	Year Round
Nursery Products	Year Round	Squash	June-Feb
Nuts	Year Round	Timber	Year Round
Other Livestock	Year Round	Tomatoes	June-Nov
Peaches & Nectarines	June-Sept	Winter Vegetables	Nov-May

Please note: Harvest dates vary. You may wish to check with individual growers to be certain. It is suggested that you bring containers.

PRODUCT INDEX:

Apples 4, 16, 20, 21, 25, 29, 30, 502	Onions & Garlic 10, 14, 16
Apricots 16, 21, 29, 502	Peaches & Nectarines 4, 10, 14, 16, 20, 21, 25, 29, 30, 502
Beef 6, 15	Pears & Asian Pears 14, 16, 21, 25, 29, 30, 502
Berries 1, 14, 16, 18	
Cherries 16, 21, 25, 502	Peppers 10, 14, 502
Christmas trees & Wreaths 7, 11, 16, 20, 24, 32, 303	Persimmons 14, 19, 20, 22, 23, 25, 30
	Plums 4, 10, 14, 21, 25, 29, 30, 502
Corn 10, 14, 16, 21	Poultry & Eggs 14, 16, 21, 27, 30, 35
Ducks & Geese 9, 35	Processed Foods 1, 16, 21, 201, 202, 203, 204, 501, 502, 601
Figs 29, 30	
Goats 2, 13, 35	Pumpkins 14
Grapes 16, 30	Rabbits 8, 35
Green & Dry Beans 14	Root Crops 16, 21, 27, 502
Honey 22, 502	Salad Greens 10, 14, 16, 21, 27, 502, 503
Herbs / Cut Flowers 27, 28, 306, 407, 502, 503	Sheep & Wool 2, 13, 26, 33, 35
	Squash 10, 14, 502
Kiwi 1, 4, 9, 25	Timber 302
Mandarins & Other Citrus 4, 16, 18, 19, 22, 23, 29, 31, 34	Tomatoes 1, 10, 14, 16, 20, 28, 502
	Worms 27
Melons 10, 14, 16	Farmers' Markets 201, 202, 203, 204
Nursery Stock 301, 302, 303, 304	Restaurants 401, 402, 403, 404, 405, 406, 407, 408
Nuts 1, 12, 16, 25, 31, 501	
Llamas, Emu & Wool 3, 5, 17	
Olives & Olive Oil 20, 28	

Farms, Ranches & Roadside Stands

1 AMBER OAKS RASPBERRIES
Timothy & Rhonda Boughton
2770 Shanley Rd, Auburn 95603; 885-3420
Raspberries, blackberries, chestnuts, kiwi, kiwi cider, tomatoes, rhubarb and much more. Bus parking, picnic area, tours. Groups welcome.
Open Mon, Wed, Sat 8am-2pm (or by appointment). Call first.

2 "AWAY TO ME" RANCH
Dana B. & Mark T. Hixson
3226 California Ln, Lincoln, 95648; 645-7037
Sheep & meat goats. *Open by appointment.*

3 BONNEVENTURE WEST LLAMAS
Linda & Phil Reitz
3185 Edgewood Ln, Newcastle, 95658; 663-2184
Llamas with the classic touch. Llamas, wool, fertilizer. Day hikes; birthday parties; picnic area.
Visitors always welcome. Call first.

4 BRENNER RANCH
Jim Brenner
5225 Hwy 193, Newcastle, 95658; 663-4578
Peaches, plums, apples, mandarins, kiwi. Mail order, wholesale, retail. *Open by appointment.*

5 CALIFORNIA BIG BIRDS
Chet & Mary McIntosh
1175 Alpine Way, Colfax, 95713; 346-8610
Emus. *Open by appointment.*

6 CM POLLED HEREFORDS
Ken Mackey, Barbara Crossley-Mackey, Stephanie Mahlberg
7160 Horseshoe Bar Rd, Loomis, 95650; 652-5441
Registered Polled Hereford cattle.
Open by appointment only.

7 COLE'S CHRISTMAS TREES
Ron & Joan Cole
6550 Hwy 193 (at Gold Hill Rd), Newcastle, 95658; 663-2768
Christmas Trees, wreaths, Douglas Fir Scotch Pine, Sierra Redwood, Monterey Pine.
Open after Thanksgiving until December 20, Fri-Sun 9am-5pm.

8 COTTONWOOD SPRING RABBITRY
Diana Allen
930 Sierra College Blvd, Lincoln 95648; 645-8359
(1 mile south of Hwy 193 on right hand side)
Pedigreed English Angora Rabbits for wool spinning, show, pet or breeding stock.
Open by appointment.

9 COUNTRY RANCH
Lou & Sherry Minkner
4132 Burnett Rd, Lincoln 95648; 645-1151
Kiwi fruit, kiwi plants, rare geese & ducks (Curly Frizzled Sebastopols & Crested Romans).
*Open Nov-Jan daily 8am-6pm;
Feb-Oct by appointment only.*

10 DON WOLFE'S PRODUCE @ ALICE'S
Don & Carol Wolfe
3241 Taylor Rd, Loomis, 95650; 652-3777
Fresh corn, tomatoes, peaches, plums, squash, onions, cucumbers, peppers, melons.
Open July-Oct, Wed-Sat, 9am-5pm.

11 THE FAMILY TREE
The Dowd Family
7120 Sierra View Pl, Loomis, 95650; 652-5332
Christmas trees: Douglas Fir, Scotch Pine and Sierra Redwoods.
Open first Sat in Dec until Dec 20, 10am-5pm daily.

12 FIDDYMENT FARMS, INC.
David & Dolly Fiddyment
5000 Fiddyment Rd, Roseville, 95747; 771-0800
Pistachio nuts, many flavors, many package sizes, soft drinks. *Open year round, 8am-5pm*

13 FINCA YOWEDA
Bob Holland & Virginia Dains
3371 Ayres Holmes Rd, Auburn, 95603; 888-9180
Polypay sheep, breeding stock & locker lambs, meat goats, cabritos. *Open farm visits by appointment.*

14 FOR-C-SONS ORGANIC FARM
Ron & Sue Cassar
2620 Shawnee Rd, Auburn, 95603; 885-8916
Tomatoes, green beans, squash, peppers, cucumbers, melons, corn, eggplant, pumpkins, garlic, olallie berries, raspberries, peaches, nectarines, plums, Asian pears, Fuji persimmons.
*Open June-Sept, Mon, Wed, Fri, 8am-2pm;
Sat 1pm-4pm (or by appointment).*

15 G BAR L BRANGUS RANCH
Gib & Lu Guertin
4225 Karchner Rd, Sheridan, 95681; 633-0714
Registered Brangus bulls and heifers for sale.
Open by appointment.

16 GREEN VALLEY PRODUCE
Dub & Kathy Weigand
3750 Taylor Rd, Loomis; 652-4903
Asparagus, apples, citrus, specialty melons, watermelons, sweet corn, cherries, berries, apricots, peaches, grapes, nectarines, onions, potatoes, eggs, garlic, lettuce, nuts, pears, Christmas trees, tomatoes, juices, arts-crafts. Wholesale-Retail.
Open year round, daily, 9am-dark.

17 HANKE LLAMA RANCH
Lon & Maria Hanke
2905 Virginiatown Rd, Lincoln, 95648; 645-3325
Polite, personable & beautiful llamas for sale, stud service, training, wool and consulting.
Open any time by appointment.

18 HIGHLAND ORCHARD
Tony Aguilar & Son
2170 Aguilar Ln (off English Colony), Penryn, 95663; 663-3897
Mandarins, navel oranges.
Open daily Nov-Dec 8am-5pm.
Olallie and Tay berries.
Open May-June, 8am-5pm

19 HILLCREST ORCHARD
Edmund & Steve Pilz
956 Clark Tunnel Rd, Penryn, 95663; 663-3603
Mandarins, tangerines, navel oranges, persimmons. Bring containers, packed fruit, please call first.
Open Nov 1 - Mar 15, Wed thru Mon, 8am-4pm. Closed Tue.

20 KOYAMA TREE FARM
Annie Koyama
9027 Barton Rd, Granite Bay, 95746; 791-1420 (Corner of Barton & Eureka)
Peaches, tomatoes, apples, persimmons, cured olives.
Open daily, July-Dec, Noon-dusk.
Christmas trees. *Open first Sat in Dec, 9am-4pm.*

21 MACHADO ORCHARDS
Gil, Bobbi & Gary Machado
100 Apples Ln, Bowman, 95604; 823-1393
Apples, cherries, apricots, peaches, nectarines, pears, plums, dried fruit, candy, jam, jelly, eggs, bread, local fresh veggies, corn, fresh fruit homemade pies, caramel apples, apple juice. Wholesale-retail.
Open seasonally, mid-May to end-Nov, everyday, 8am-7pm.

22 MAGNOLIA HILL ORCHARD
Loren & Barbara Lewis
7370 Ridge Rd, Newcastle, 95658; 663-3739
Satsuma Mandarin oranges, honey, persimmons.
Open Nov 10 to Dec 31, Mon-Sat, 8am until dark; Sun 1-4pm.

23 MANDARIN HILL ORCHARDS
Frank Aguilar
2338 Mandarin Hill Ln, Penryn, 95663; 633-3809
Mandarins, Algerians, navels, lemons, grapefruit, persimmons. *Open Nov-Jan, daily, 8am-5pm.*
Valencia oranges. *Open Apr-May by appointment.*

24 MEADOW VISTA TREE FARM & NURSERY
Jean von Brockdorff
1291 Meadow Vista Rd, Meadow Vista, 95722; 878-1047 / 878-7210
Choose & cut Christmas trees, wreaths, tree stands, tree baling. Varieties of trees available: Colorado, Spruce, Norway Spruce, Redwood, Douglas Fir, Scotch Pine. Picnic area.
Open year round by appointment only for container Christmas trees. Day after Thanksgiving-Dec 23 daily, 9am-5pm for everything else.

25 MT. VERNON RANCH
Herb Yamamoto
7241 Baxter Grade, Auburn, 95603; 885-6714
Cherries, peaches, nectarines, plums, persimmons (fresh & dried), Asian pears, apples, walnuts, kiwi.
Open from mid-May thru Dec.

26 MULBERRY HILL
Sue Nielsen
9115 Meadow Ln, Newcastle, 95658; 663-2552
Natural colored and White Romney-X sheep, wool and pelts, and mulberries (due in 1998).
Open by appointment.

27 THE NATURAL TRADING COMPANY
AN ORGANIC FARM. Bryan-Kaminsky
5940 Butler Rd, Penryn, 95663; 663-9568
Free-range chicken eggs, vegetables, fruits, herbs, cut flowers, worms. *Open year-round, daily, 8am-dusk.*

28 ORGASMIC ORGANIC RIDGE GARDEN
Jack Hertel & Lynn Ross
8060 Ridge Rd, Newcastle, 95658; 663-2146
Organic produce, plants, sun-dried tomatoes, basil, olive oil, veggie, flower & herb seedlings, turkey manure, tea. *Open by appointment. Call first.*

29 PINE HILL ORCHARD
The Hansen Family
4480 Hansen Rd, Loomis, 95650; 652-7556
Peaches, pears, plums, figs, apples, mandarins, Asian pears, apricots and more. *Open by appointment.*

30 SANTINI RANCH
D. Santini
7600 Chili Hill Rd, Newcastle, 95658; 885-2073
Peaches, plums, apples, pears, persimmons, grapes, figs, eggs. *Open year round, but call first.*

31 SNOW'S CITRUS COURT
Larry, Ralene, Tiffany & Tshandy Snow
Newcastle, 95658; 885-0718
Mandarins, kumquats, English walnuts.
Call to order.

32 SNOWY PEAKS TREE FARM
Charles Wilson & Jane Flickinger
6 miles past Foresthill on Foresthill Rd; 367-3766
Choose & cut Christmas trees (we furnish saws), wreaths. Free hot chocolate, coffee & candy canes.
Open day after Thanksgiving to Dec 22, daily, 9am-dusk.

33 SOUTH HAMP RANCH
Don & Bev Field
7255 S. Brewer Rd, Pleasant Grove, 95668; 991-4121
Lambs. *Open by appointment.*

34 STRUBLE RANCH
Jim & Harold Struble
4927 Hansen Rd, Loomis, 95650; 652-7503
Mandarins. *Open Nov 10 - Jan 19, 8am-5pm.*

35 SWEET HOME RANCH
Marvin & Christi Penner
2475 Moran Ct, Auburn, 95603; 823-8265
Cashmere goats and fleeces, Pygora goats and fleeces, Jacob sheep, Silkie chickens, eggs, ducks, rabbits.
Open by appointment, all seasons.

San Mateo County

Coastside Harvest Trails

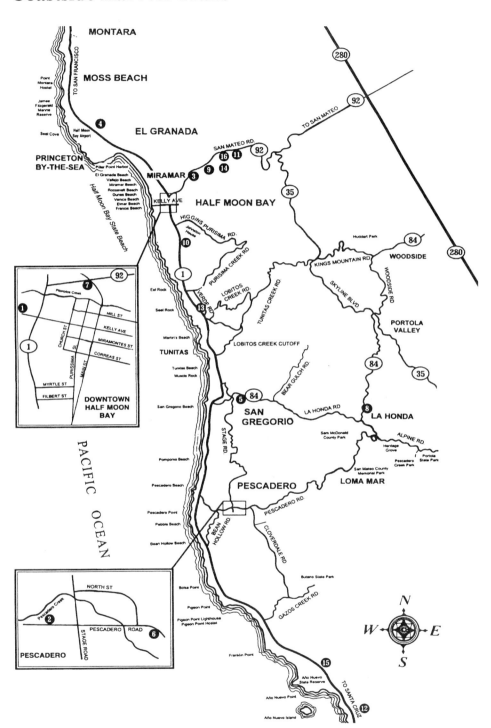

HARVEST SEASONS

Olallieberries .... June-Aug
Boysenberries .... June-Aug
Pumpkins .... Sept-Oct
Kiwi .... Nov-Dec
Christmas Trees .... Dec

Due to weather conditions, harvest dates are not exact. Please call before you visit.

HARVEST AVAILABLE ALL YEAR:
Fresh Flowers; Vegetables; Winery; Feed; Ornamental; Greenhouse Plants

FARM LISTINGS

VEGETABLES

1. ANDREOTTI FAMILY FARMS
A year round family operated business since 1926. Located in a charming barn on Kelly Ave., Andreotti Family Farms sells artichokes, Brussels sprouts (on the stock), broccoli, red wine vinegar, sugar pie, honey, Italian garlic, pumpkins and much more! 227 Kelly Ave, Half Moon Bay. Fri-Sun 10am-5:30pm. **415-726-9151**

2. ARTICHOKE JOE'S
Joe Muzzi and sons John and Dan sell fresh artichokes, sweet strawberries, peas, corn, Brussels sprouts, pumpkins and other fresh, local produce. Located in the 100+ year old Chandler Milk Barn at: 1759 Pescadero Creek Rd. Open Mar-Oct, Thur-Sun, 9am-5pm. **415-879-0371**

3. G. BERTA'S
"Shorty" G. Berta settled on this ranch in 1924 and opened his vegetable stand in 1934. The family has been known to grow cabbage weighing 15-16 lbs. which you'll find displayed outside the fruit and vegetable stand. Green beans, peas, beets, and 5 varieties of lettuce available in the summer. Sweet and tender French carrots, broccoli, cauliflower and leeks are fall specialties. Endive and escarole in winter. Half Moon Bay artichokes. Pumpkin field opens Oct. Hwy 92, 1 mile east of Half Moon Bay. Summer: daily, 9am-6:30pm. Winter: daily 10am-5pm. **415-726-4922**

4. FARMER'S DAUGHTER
In real life, Lynda Santini is the farmer's daughter. She's 3rd generation of a longtime Half Moon Bay farming family. Weekend stand with farm fresh produce. Locally grown artichokes, peas, corn, potatoes, chard, Brussels sprouts. Fruits in season. Some local organically grown produce. Honey from a local beekeeper. Pistachio nuts and more! Thousands of pumpkins in season grown by her dad. Pick your own. Warm and friendly service. 5 miles north of Half Moon Bay directly across from Half Moon Bay Airport. Open Fri, Sat, Sun 10am-dark. 7 days a week during pumpkin time. **415-728-8660**

5. N.D. MUZZI RANCH
Come try our strawberries, artichokes and other local produce fresh picked daily. Open daily from 9am-6pm, Mar-Nov. Located in San Gregorio on Hwy 84, 1 mile east of Hwy 1. **415-726-3994**

6. PHIPPS RANCH
A very special roadside market and plant nursery in a farming community. Wonderful fruits and vegetables available year round. Amazing selection of dried beans. In the nursery, ferns, succulents and herb plants. Excellent quality house and garden plants. Gourmet herb room with fruit and herbal vinegars. Dried herb and flower wreaths. Special potpourris and herb blends. In early summer, pick your own Ollallieberries and boysenberries. Picnic tables, farm animals, aviaries. 2700 Pescadero Rd. Summer: daily 10am-7pm. Winter: daily 10am-6pm. Call for berry picking times. Farm tours by appt. **415-879-0787**

7. TOM & PETE'S PRODUCE
HALF MOON BAY FISH MARKET
John Minaidis Sr., known locally as the "Pumpkin King," runs the indoor vegetable/fruit stand with his sons. Fresh flowers. Pick your own pumpkin and ask to see the roomful of exceptional pumpkins collected from all over the world. Half Moon Bay Fish Market is adjacent to Tom & Pete's Produce. Fresh fish, some local catch. Live and cooked lobsters & crabs, shell fish. Hwys 92 and 1, Half Moon Bay. Daily 9am-8pm. **415-726-2561**

8. WHITNEY RANCH ORGANIC GARDEN
A three acre market garden offering gourmet vegetables, fruits, herbs and some flowers. Sixteen different types of tomatoes and greens are just some of what you will find. All produce is grown pesticide free and 100% organic as verified by the California Certified Organic Farmers Association. The garden is open weekends and holidays 9am-4pm from May to Oct and any time by appt. We are located at 60 Fernwood Dr., La Honda.
415-747-9557 or 415-747-0846

BOB'S PUMPKIN FARM & CHRISTMAS TREES (See Pumpkins)
COASTWAYS RANCH (See U-pick Fruits)

FRESH FLOWERS/ PLANTS/NURSERIES

9. A. REPETTO NURSERY & FLORIST
"We have flowers rain or shine, even if the weather is miserable," says Doris Repetto. There's a healthy selection of plants in this light and airy greenhouse. Mini violets and self-watering violet pots are a specialty. Pick up a holiday gift; flowers in baskets, bouquets, hanging and stand-up plants. Floral arrangements and gift wrap available. Wire service and local delivery. Hwy 92, 1 1/2 miles east of Half Moon Bay, the first large group of greenhouses. Mon-Fri, 10am-5pm; Sun, 10am-4pm **415-726-6414**

10. ENOMOTO ROSES, INC.
A direct marketing company located at 2275 Cabrillo Hwy, south Half Moon Bay. (2 1/2 miles south of Hwy 92 on Hwy 1) Open Mon-Fri 7:30am-4pm. 14 different varieties of long-stemmed roses and gardenias for corsages.
415-726-4844

11. HALF MOON BAY NURSERY
1 acre of indoor and outdoor plants to select from in a country setting. Walk through the covered nursery and enjoy classical music. Specializing in coastal plants. Geraniums, fuchsias, tuberous begonias, pelargoniums. Fragrant vines and perennials. All plants grown on the property so they offer an extraordinary selection. Live Xmas trees and poinsettias in season. Hwy 92. Open daily 9am-5pm. Closed on major holidays.
415-726-5392

G. BERTA'S; PHIPPS RANCH (See Vegetables)

U-PICK FRUITS

12. COASTWAYS RANCH
Come to this scenic family farm nestled between mountains and ocean. Pick olallieberries June-July, pumpkins Oct, kiwifruit Nov-Dec. After Thanksgiving, cut your own Christmas tree (Monterey pine or Douglas fir). Bring your friends and a picnic and make a day of it! Containers & saws provided. Free recipes. Each season has its own specialties: artichokes, flowers, mini-corn, Brussels sprouts, gourds, and homemade jams. School & group tours by appt. On Hwy1, 30 miles south of Half Moon Bay, near Ano Nuevo Reservice & elephant seals. Open daily during picking season.
For specific dates, please call **415-879-0414**

PHIPPS RANCH (See Vegetables)

PUMPKINS

13. BOB'S PUMPKIN FARM & CHRISTMAS TREES
Small sugar pumpkins are only 9", but they are meatier than the Jack O'Lanterns and perfect for pies. Both are available here. Family operation with all sizes and varieties of pumpkins. Farm animals, vegetable stand. During Christmas season, thousands of Monterey pines to choose from. Cut your own. Summer: 9am-7pm. Oct: 9am-dusk. Xmas trees day after Thanksgiving, open daily. **415-726-4567**

G. BERTA'S; FARMER'S DAUGHTER; PHIPPS RANCH; TOM & PETE'S PRODUCE/HALF MOON BAY FISH MARKET; ANDREOTTI FAMILY FARMS (See Vegetables) COASTWAYS RANCH (See U-Pick Fruits)

CHRISTMAS TREES

14. 4 C'S CHRISTMAS TREES
Bring a picnic lunch and cut your own Xmas tree. Choose one of 3,000 Monterey pines. Custom flocking. Saws and help provided if necessary. "We'll even cut them down," says owner, Jim Cozzolino, a flower grower for 42 years. To eliminate fire hazards, he recommends keeping the tree in water. 2 miles east of Half Moon Bay on Hwy 92, behind Obester Winery. Seasonal. Open day after Thanksgiving 'til Xmas. Open daily during daylight hours.
415-726-4307

15. RANCHO SIEMPRE VERDE
Choose and cut your own Xmas tree overlooking Ano Nuevo Island, Douglas fir a specialty. Monterey pine, Sequoia redwood and other firs and pines. Saws available. Free boughs. Tree nets provided for ease of transportation. Picnickers welcome. Hwy 1, 5 miles south of Pigeon Point Lighthouse, between Half Moon Bay and Santa Cruz. **415-326-9103**

BOB'S PUMPKIN FARM & XMAS TREES (See Pumpkins) COASTWAYS RANCH (See U-Pick Fruits) HALF MOON BAY NURSERY (See Flowers)

WINERIES

16. OBESTER WINERY
The coastside's Obester Winery is situated in a picturesque valley surrounded by flower fields, pumpkin patches and Christmas tree farms. Obester's award-winning wines can be tasted daily at the winery and you'll find the warm and friendly tasting room a pleasant stop. Bring a lunch and enjoy the picnic area. 1.7 miles east of Half Moon Bay on Hwy 92. Open daily 10am-5pm for tasting and sales. **415-726-9463**

Santa Clara County
Santa Cruz County

Country Crossroads Farm Trails

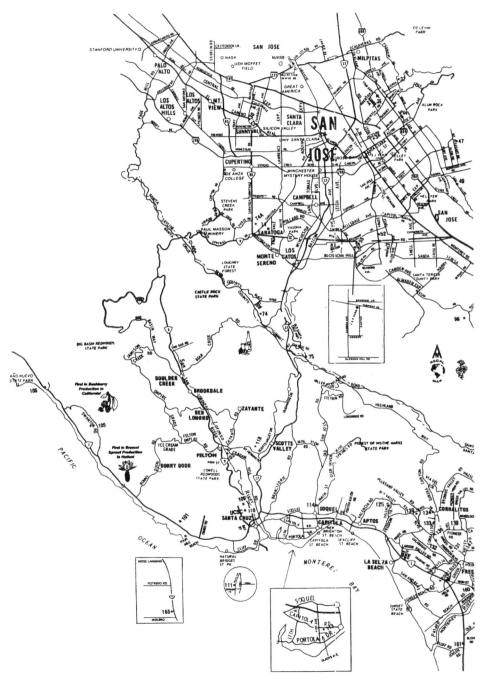

Fresh Produce Calendar

Apples, Gravenstein	July-Sept
Apples, Jonathan	Aug-Oct
Apples, Delicious	Aug-Oct
Apples, Rome	Sept-Nov
Apricots	June-July
Blackberries	June-July
Blueberries	July-July
Cherries	May-June
Corn	July-Sept
Figs	Sept-Nov
Grapes	Aug-Oct
Peaches	July-Sept
Pears	Sept-Oct
Persimmons	Nov-Dec
Plums	July-Sept
Prunes	Aug-Sept
Pumpkins	Oct-Nov
Raspberries	June-July/Sept-Nov
Strawberries	May-Oct
Tomatoes	July-Oct
Vegetables	June-Nov
Walnuts	Oct-Dec

The above calendar is only a rough guide. Dates of maturity may vary from year to year and from place to place. To be sure you may wish to phone ahead to your selected supplier. It is suggested that you bring your own containers for produce.

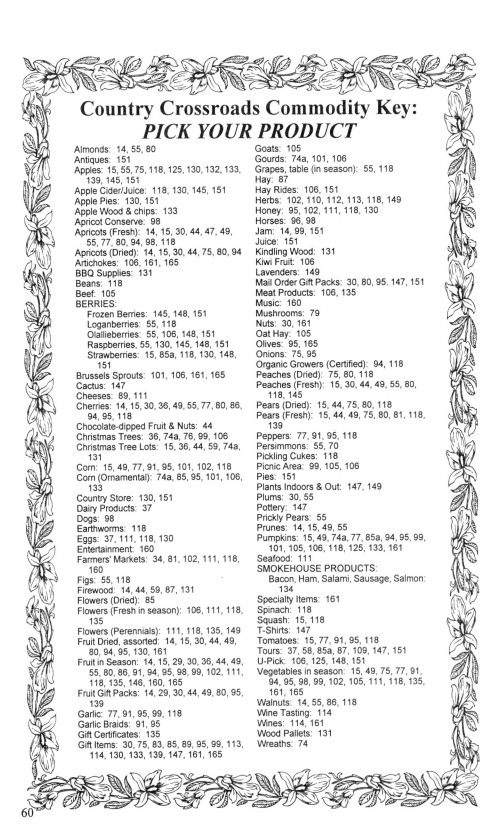

Country Crossroads Commodity Key:
PICK YOUR PRODUCT

Almonds: 14, 55, 80
Antiques: 151
Apples: 15, 55, 75, 118, 125, 130, 132, 133, 139, 145, 151
Apple Cider/Juice: 118, 130, 145, 151
Apple Pies: 130, 151
Apple Wood & chips: 133
Apricot Conserve: 98
Apricots (Fresh): 14, 15, 30, 44, 47, 49, 55, 77, 80, 94, 98, 118
Apricots (Dried): 14, 15, 30, 44, 75, 80, 94
Artichokes: 106, 161, 165
BBQ Supplies: 131
Beans: 118
Beef: 105
BERRIES:
    Frozen Berries: 145, 148, 151
    Loganberries: 55, 118
    Olallieberries: 55, 106, 148, 151
    Raspberries, 55, 130, 145, 148, 151
    Strawberries: 15, 85a, 118, 130, 148, 151
Brussels Sprouts: 101, 106, 161, 165
Cactus: 147
Cheeses: 89, 111
Cherries: 14, 15, 30, 36, 49, 55, 77, 80, 86, 94, 95, 118
Chocolate-dipped Fruit & Nuts: 44
Christmas Trees: 36, 74a, 76, 99, 106
Christmas Tree Lots: 15, 36, 44, 59, 74a, 131
Corn: 15, 49, 77, 91, 95, 101, 102, 118
Corn (Ornamental): 74a, 85, 95, 101, 106, 133
Country Store: 130, 151
Dairy Products: 37
Dogs: 98
Earthworms: 118
Eggs: 37, 111, 118, 130
Entertainment: 160
Farmers' Markets: 34, 81, 102, 111, 118, 160
Figs: 55, 118
Firewood: 14, 44, 59, 87, 131
Flowers (Dried): 85
Flowers (Fresh in season): 106, 111, 118, 135
Flowers (Perennials): 111, 118, 135, 149
Fruit Dried, assorted: 14, 15, 30, 44, 49, 80, 94, 95, 130, 161
Fruit in Season: 14, 15, 29, 30, 36, 44, 49, 55, 80, 86, 91, 94, 95, 98, 99, 102, 111, 118, 135, 146, 160, 165
Fruit Gift Packs: 14, 29, 30, 44, 49, 80, 95, 139
Garlic: 77, 91, 95, 99, 118
Garlic Braids: 91, 95
Gift Certificates: 135
Gift Items: 30, 75, 83, 85, 89, 95, 99, 113, 114, 130, 133, 139, 147, 161, 165

Goats: 105
Gourds: 74a, 101, 106
Grapes, table (in season): 55, 118
Hay: 87
Hay Rides: 106, 151
Herbs: 102, 110, 112, 113, 118, 149
Honey: 95, 102, 111, 118, 130
Horses: 96, 98
Jam: 14, 99, 151
Juice: 151
Kindling Wood: 131
Kiwi Fruit: 106
Lavenders: 149
Mail Order Gift Packs: 30, 80, 95. 147, 151
Meat Products: 106, 135
Music: 160
Mushrooms: 79
Nuts: 30, 161
Oat Hay: 105
Olives: 95, 165
Onions: 75, 95
Organic Growers (Certified): 94, 118
Peaches (Dried): 75, 80, 118
Peaches (Fresh): 15, 30, 44, 49, 55, 80, 118, 145
Pears (Dried): 15, 44, 75, 80, 118
Pears (Fresh): 15, 44, 49, 75, 80, 81, 118, 139
Peppers: 77, 91, 95, 118
Persimmons: 55, 70
Pickling Cukes: 118
Picnic Area: 99, 105, 106
Pies: 151
Plants Indoors & Out: 147, 149
Plums: 30, 55
Pottery: 147
Prickly Pears: 55
Prunes: 14, 15, 49, 55
Pumpkins: 15, 49, 74a, 77, 85a, 94, 95, 99, 101, 105, 106, 118, 125, 133, 161
Seafood: 111
SMOKEHOUSE PRODUCTS:
    Bacon, Ham, Salami, Sausage, Salmon: 134
Specialty Items: 161
Spinach: 118
Squash: 15, 118
T-Shirts: 147
Tomatoes: 15, 77, 91, 95, 118
Tours: 37, 58, 85a, 87, 109, 147, 151
U-Pick: 106, 125, 148, 151
Vegetables in season: 15, 49, 75, 77, 91, 94, 95, 98, 99, 102, 105, 111, 118, 135, 161, 165
Walnuts: 14, 55, 86, 118
Wine Tasting: 114
Wines: 114, 161
Wood Pallets: 131
Wreaths: 74

Members' Listings: SANTA CLARA

14 Novakovich Orchards   408-867-3131
14251 Fruitvale Ave, Satatoga, 95070
Fresh apricots, peaches, nectarines, Jun 20 to Aug 5; cherries May-June. All year: dried apricots & prunes. Gift boxes, pomegrante Jelly and Apricot Jam. Fresh corn & tomatoes July-Eept. Christmas gift packs and chocolate dipped Apricots, prunes, Apricot Turtles. Open all year Sun-Fri, 9am-5pm.

30 C.J. Olson Cherries   800-738-BING
Rt. 1 Box 140, El Camino Real, Sunnyvale
Famous for Bing Cherries and Blenheim Apricots since 1899. Enjoy fresh cherries, apricots, plums and other summer fruit; plus dried fruits and nuts, jams, honey and gift baskets. Visit the cherry stand "open year round." Mail orders welcome. For store hours and more information, please call. Free catalog available.

34 San Jose Japantown Farmers' Market
Japantown, San Jose, CFM **408-298-4303**
Start your week off right by strolling through our colorful Sunday morning market with fresh hot coffee, garden fresh California grown produce, cut flowers, potted plants, eggs, honey and baked goods. That's every Sunday morning 8:30 to noon, year round, rain or shine, on Jackson St. between 7th and 8th. Historic Japantown, with tofu and manju shops and Japanese grocery and gift stores, is just one block away.

35 Battaglia Ranch   408-272-0666
1410 Four Oaks Rd, San Jose 95131
(west of 680)
Cherries, Christmas trees. Open June and December.

37 Olivera Egg Ranch   408-258-8074
3315 Sierra Rd, San Jose, 95132
EGGS, milk, convenience items. Open year round, everyday, 8am-8pm. TOURS by appointment.

44 Zoria Farms   408-258-2900
234 N. Capitol Ave, San Jose, 95127
Fresh apricots, peaches, pears in season. Dry seasoned oak firewood, chocolate-dipped and extra fancy dried fruit and nuts our specialty. Open all year, Mon-Sat, 10am-5pm. Visit us on our website at www.zoria.com.

47 Del Ponte Ranch   408-274-5134
2419 Mt. Pleasant Rd, San Jose, 95148
Next door at the "Cutting Shed"
Freshly picked non-irrigated apricots. Over 25 years "Blue Ribbon Winner." Open mid-June to mid-July. Seasons vary. Family operated since 1899.

49 Cortese Brothers Orchards
408-238-2054 / 251-3730
4190 San Felipe Rd, San Jose
Santa Clara Valley's finest fresh picked fruit and vegetables: cherries, apricots, peaches, pears, prunes, sweet corn and several varieties of vegetables. Pumpkins in season. Dried fruit and nuts; gift packs. Open May-Dec. Our stand is located within the orchard so you can "see the fruit growing." Christmas trees in Dec.

55 J&P Farm   408-264-3497
4977 Carter Ave, San Jose, 95118
Farm to you fruit including some old varieties that no longer exist commercially. Twenty-five varieties peaches (some cling), nine varieties plums and prunes, seven varieties nectarines, apricots, cherries, persimmons, Olallie, Boysen and Raspberries. Table grapes, figs, almonds, prickly pears, apples and pears. Fruit sold at ranch June-Nov. Open every day 9am-dark.

74 McKenzie Ranch   408-867-5693
19970 Skyline Blvd, Los Gatos, 95030
Choose and cut Christmas trees, wreaths, 18 acres Douglas Fir and White Fir. Saws and twine provided. Tree baler available. Open day after Thanksgiving-Dec 24, 8am-5pm daily.

74a McKenzie Ranch Retail Lot
408-867-5693
13030 Saratoga-Sunnyvale Rd, Saratoga
(next to Argonaut Shopping Center)
Local grown pumpkins, gourds, ornamental corn. Open 1st weekend in Oct thru Halloween, 12 Noon to 6pm. Christmas trees from our ranch, Douglas Fir and White Fir, wreaths, custom stands and netting. Open Friday after Thanksgiving thru Dec 23, 12 Noon to 6pm.

75   J&P Farm
Summit Rd & Old Santa Cruz Hwy.
Golden Delicious, Old Fashion Red Delicious, Granny Smith, Fujis, Galas, Bartlet Pears. Open Sun-Fri, Aug-Nov.

77   High Rise Farms   408-463-0564
Palm & Santa Teresa Blvd, Coyote Valley
Specializing in field fresh fruits and vegetables, we feature our own cherries, apricots, sweet corn, tomatoes, garlic and peppers. Pumpkin patch opens Oct 1, includes giant "prize winner" pumpkins. Bulk orders for canning taken in advance. Open 10am-6pm daily, May-Oct.

79   Royal Oaks Mushrooms   408-779-2362
15480 Watsonville Rd, Morgan Hill 95037
We are a mushroom grower and shipper. Year round operation. Open Mon-Fri from 8am-4pm. Sat 8am-Noon. We sell mushrooms and compost.

80   Mariani Orchards   408-779-5467
1615 Half Rd, Morgan Hill, 95037
Freshly picked daily, many old, new and rare varieties of cherries as well as Bing & Rainier, orange and white-fleshed freestone peaches including rare Chinese flat types, clingstones, white and yellow nectarines, plums, plumcots, Fuyu and Maru (Chocolate) persimmons. Large variety of dried fruits. Store open all year Mon-Fri, 9am-5pm. Sat until noon.

81   Downtown Morgan Hill Farmers' Mkt
3rd St between Monterey Rd & Depot St
Now in its fifth exciting year, the market features farmers from the immediate area and throughout Northern California. Just minutes from San Jose, historic downtown Morgan Hill features a variety of unique shops located adjacent to the market. Market runs each Saturday from May 31 thru Nov, 8:30am-12:30pm. For more information, call 408-779-9444.

85   Aviva Designs   408-776-1284
14485 Monterey Rd, San Martin, 95046
Large selection of dried flowers and Indian corn. Open Sat-Sun 10am-3pm. Pumpkin patch open in Oct.

85a Uesugi Farms Pumpkin Patch & Strawberry Stand   408-779-2078
14485 Monterey Rd, Morgan Hill, 95037
Fresh strawberries May-July. Pumpkin Patch open in Oct, includes pumpkins, train ride, video, picnic area, arts and crafts. A family adventure.
Uesugi Farms Bolsa- Strawberry Stand
1020 State Hwy 25, Gilroy 95020
Fresh strawberries May-July.

86   Peter V. Giordano   408-779-3618
1625 Fisher Ave, Morgan Hill, 95037
Walnuts. Open Oct 1 thru Nov, 9am-4:30pm. Call first.

87   Loma Linda Ranch   408-779-2404
16180 Uvas Rd, Morgan Hill, 95037
Locally grown hay. Oak firewood. Open 7 days a week, 9am-5pm

91   LJB Farms   408-842-9755
585 Fitzgerald Ave, San Martin, 95046
Bartlett pears, corn, tomatoes, peppers, garlic, garlic braids. Vine ripened and picked fresh every day. Open July 1 to Dec 24; 7 days a week. Take the Masten Ave turnoff on Hwy 101.

94   Van Dyke Ranch   408-842-5423
7665 Crews Rd, Gilroy, 95020
Fresh and dried apricots and cherries. Fresh cherries May 20 thru June 20, fresh apricots June 1 to Aug 1. Dried fruit, sulphured and unsulphured. Available year round, some seasonal vegetables. Certified Organic Grower.

95   Garlic World   800-537-6122
4800 Monterey Hwy, Gilroy, 95020
Open daily, all yar, 9am-7pm Summers; 9am-6pm Winters. Featuring fresh garlic braids, wreaths, gourmet foods & gifts. We grow our own garlic, cherries and sweet corn. We also have local dried fruit, nuts, honey and wines. Free catalog available. UPS shipping service available.

96   Calero Ranch Stables   408-268-2567
1/2 mile south of McKean & Bailey,
San Jose, inside Calero County Park
Recreational facility of Santa Clara County. Full equestrian services: guided rental trail rides, equestrian boarding, riding lessons, and summer horsemanship camp for children.

Members' Listings: SANTA CRUZ

98 Something Special   408-637-0963
6111 Pacheco Pass Hwy 156, N of Hollister
Think July 4th for your Blenheim Apricots. Extra fancy, excellent for drying. Open June-Sept for farm grown fruits and veggies. Our very own apricot conserve available all year. Also raised on farm, Jack Russell Terriers and the German Trakehner Sport Horses.

**99 Hoey Ranch Country Mart
408-847-4639**
2480 Hecker Pass Hwy (152W),
Gilroy 95020
Historic Hoey Ranch est. 1853. Gilroy garlic and garlic products, fresh produce, homemade Hoey Ranch preserves. Unique gift items in our 100 year old barn, pumpkin patch, U-cut Christmas trees, picnic area. Close to local wineries. Open Apr-Dec, 9am-6pm daily.

101 U-Pick-Em Pumpkins   408-426-6438
Hwy 1, N of S.Cruz beyond 4 Mile Beach
Santa Cruz County's largest pumpkin patch. Many varieties to choose, including sugar pies for cooking, Indian corn, gourds, sweet corn and fresh Brussels sprouts. Open every day til Halloween. Sept 28-Oct 31.

**102 Felton Certified Farmers' Market
408-335-9364**
Presbyterian Church, 6090 Hwy 9, Felton
Open mid-May thru Halloween, 2:30pm-7pm Tuesdays. Fresh fruit & vegetables, cut flowers, herbs and honey.

105 Swanton Pacific Ranch   408-427-1718
299 Swanton Rd, Davenport 95017
The 3,200 acre diversified ranch is owned and operated by Cal Poly University, San Luis Obispo. School and private group tours by appointment. Pumpkins, Oat Hay, Spanish meat goats, grass fed beef and a variety of vegetable crops available. Group picnic area with large barbecue available for weddings or private gatherings.

106 Coastways Ranch   415-879-0414
Hwy 1, 20 miles N of S.Cruz
Open daily during the following seasons: Olallieberries (June-July); Pumpkins, gourds, Indian corn (Oct); Kiwifruit and Christmas trees (Nov-Dec). Fresh artichokes and Brussels sprouts if available. Picnic tables. Please call for details. See us online at http://www.well.com/user/dmsml/coastways.

109 UCSC Farm & Garden   408-459-3248
CASFS, 1156 High St, S.Cruz 95064
The 25 acre farm and 4 acre garden at UCSC offers free tours of its facilities. Learn about small scale bio-intensive gardening, organic farming techniques, composting and more. Groups welcome. Public tours: Thur at Noon & Sun at 2pm. Reservations encouraged for groups over 10. Call 459-4140 for directions and a calendar of events.

**111 Santa Cruz Community Farmers' Mkt
408-423-4614**
Corner Lincoln & Cedar Streets
Year round market runs Wed 2:30pm-6:30pm. Features a bounty of fresh-picked fruits, vegetables, flowers and freshly caught seafood, eggs, honey and cheeses.

113 Florabunda   408-462-0202
1030 41st Ave, Santa Cruz 95062
Display herb gardens, group tours (by appointment). Herb Nursery with 250 varieties: culinary, medicinal, fragrance, ornamental and bird & butterfly plants, Unique home & garden accessories, large selection herb books, gifts for gardeners, aroma therapy lotions and potions. Year round, 7 days a week. Call for hours.

114 Bargetto Winery   408-475-2258
3535 N. Main St, Soquel
Open daily. Wine tasting of Santa Cruz Mountains Wines overlooking Soquel Creek. Also tasting room: Monterey. 700 Cannery Row, Ste L.

118 Monterey Bay Area Cert. Farmers' Mkt
Cabrillo College, lower parking lot
Open Saturdays only, 8am-12Noon year round. More than 25 farmers from coastal and valley farms offering a wide variety of vegetables, fruit, eggs, honey and cut flowers. Excellent values and selection. Bulk purchases available.

Other Monterey Bay Area Certified Farmers' Markets not listed on the map are:

SALINAS, *Open Sun, 8am-12Noon year round. Located in the Central Parking Lot of Hartnell College. 25 farmers participate.*

MONTEREY, *Open Thur, 2:30pm-6pm year round. Located at Monterey Peninsula College, lower parking lot next to Fremont. 25 farmers participate.*

SCOTTS VALLEY, *Open May-Oct, Tues 3pm-7pm to the Old Skypark Airport.*

125 Valencia Ranch   408-684-0400
2760 Valencia Rd, Aptos
Five varieties of apples. U-choose pumpkin patch, gourds. Self-serve Oct 1-31.

130 The Apple Barn   408-724-8119
Hames Road, Aptos
Eighteen varieties of fresh apples during season. Fresh cider, berries, honey, eggs and gifts. Open daily 8:30am-5pm, Aug 9-Nov 9.

131 Pacific Firewood   408-722-9663
2536 Freedom Blvd, Watsonville 95076
Top quality firewood with dependable service guaranteed. Wood pellets, hardwood kindling and other products for heating your home and all of your barbecue needs. Delivery available or customer pickup. Also specializing in Noble Fir, Douglas Fir and Grand Fir Christmas Trees. Trees are displayed in our warehoue and kept in water. The freshest trees around! Warehouse hours vary depending on the season. Call for more information.

132 Mann's Apples   408-722-2464
2838 Freedom Blvd, Watsonville 95076
Family operated farm raising apples for 70 years. Grower, packer and shipper of varieties such as McIntosh, Red Delicious, Newtown Pippin and Fuji. Our harvest season begins in September and continues thru November. Mann's offers orchard fresh apples by the box or bag. Eat more of Mann's apples!

133 Jensen Pride   408-724-4666
463 Corralitos Rd, Corralitos 95076
Several varieties of apples including Fuji & Jon-O-gold. Season runs Sept 1-Jan 1. We also specialize in gift packs, apple wood, apple wood chips, Halloween pumpkins & Indian corn. Open Mon-Sat 10am-4pm. Call or FAX advance orders.

**134 Corralitos Market & Sausage Co, Inc.
408-722-2633**
569 Corralitos Rd, Corralitos 95076
Smokehouse products: ham bacon, sausages, salmon. Open year round, 7 days a week, 8am-6pm. 9am-5pm on Sun.

135 Stellar Farms   408-726-1184
PO Box 1736, Freedom 95019
We grow a large selection of potted and cut flowers as sell as organic vegetables and fruit. We also offer subscription vegetable and flower sales. We offer gift certificates and are happy to ship your order. Open 10am-6pm, Tue-Sun.

139 Prevedelli Farm   408-724-9282
375 Pioneer View, Watsonville 95076
Gravenstein apples, July 25-Sept. Fuji, Gala and many other varieties of apples until Jan. Asian & Bosc pears from Aug-Dec. Apple & pear gift packs available, Nov-Dec. Open daily 8am-6pm.

145 The Apple Bin   408-724-3637
1907 E. Lake Ave (Hwy 152), Watsonville
Thirteen varieties of apples, fresh-pressed natural apple juice, peaches (Elberta), raspberries (fresh and frozen). Open 7 days a week, 8am-6pm June 1-April 1. Basich family operated since 1926.

147 Desert Theatre   408-728-5513
17 Behler Rd, Watsonville, 95076
Desert Theatre offers a comprehensive selection of exotic cacti and succulents. Specializing in euphorbias from Africa and cacti from around the world. Offering unique gifts, pottery and T-shirts. Catalog sales; shipping available. Beautifully landscaped gardens to visit. Nursery tours available by appointment. Wholesale/Retail. Public welcome 10am-4pm Tues-Sun.

**148 EMILE AGACCIO FARMS, INC.
408-728-2009**
4 Casserly Rd, Watsonville
Fresh produce, U-pick Olallies & respberries Jun-Jul. Strawberries by the box, Apr-May. Frozen berries available Jun-Dec. Open daily, 8am-6pm.

149 Sierra Azul Nursery & Gardens
408-763-0939
  2660 E. Lake Ave, Watsonville, 95076
Extensive and unusual variety of plants for California's mediterranean climate. This includes flowering perennials, herbs, lavenders. California native, mediterranean, Australian and South African plants. Arboretum-style demonstration gardens are growing in and around the nursery. Most plants for sale in the nursery can be seen growing in the gardens. Open daily. Hours 9am-5:30pm.

151 Gizdich Ranch   408-722-1056
  55 Peckham Rd, Watsonville 95076
Pik-Yor-Self Strawberries (May-Labor Day), Olallies (June), Raspberries (July). 10 varieties apples (Sept-Dec). Fields open 8am-5pm daily. Enjoy Farm Park pies, juice, jams, antiques, frozen berries Jan-Mar (open weekends only) & Apr-Dec (open daily). Holiday Hayrides. We ship UPS.

160 Watsonville Farmers' Market
408-724-3954
  445 Main St, Watsonville, 95076
Downtown Watsonville between FW Woolworth & Chopstick Restaurant. Entertainment and crafts occasionally featured. Locally grown fruits and vegetables. Open early Spring. Sun, 10am-4pm. Call for more information.

161 Dominic's Farm Fresh Produce
408-722-0181
  Easily located on Hwy 1
Open year round, fruits & veggies of the season, pumpkin patch, artichokes and a great variety of specialty items, local wines, dried fruits & nuts. We're a stop worth making!

165 Springfield Farms   408-633-4768
  Located off Hwy 1 in Moss Landing in a converted barn.
Wide variety of farm fresh fruits and vegetables specializing in artichokes. We have a unique selection of gourmet products ranging from artichoke salsa to garlic stuffed olives. Gift baskets available too! Open 7 days a week from 8:30am-5pm.

Sonoma County

Sonoma County Farm Trails

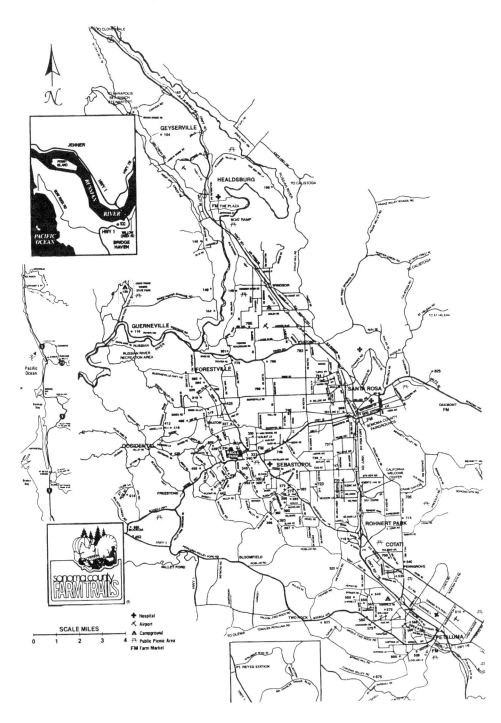

Harvest Calendar

Apples:
  Gravenstein .... July-Aug
  Jonathan .... Aug-Sept
  Delicious .... Aug-Oct
  Rome .... Aug-Nov
  Fuji .... Oct-Dec
  Granny Smith .... Nov
Azaleas & Rhodies ..... Mar-Jun
Bare-Root .... Dec-Feb
Blackberries .... May-Aug
Blueberries .... June-July
Bonzai .... Sept-Oct
Cherries .... May-June
Corn .... Aug-Oct
Evergreens/Conifers ... Jan-Dec
Figs .... Sept-Nov
Fresh Flowers .... May-Nov
Wine Grapes .... Sept-Nov
Japanese Maples .... Jan-Dec
Kiwi .... Oct-June
Orchids .... Dec-June
Peaches .... June-Sept
Pears .... Aug-Nov
Persimmons .... Oct-Dec
Plums .... June-Sept
Prunes .... Aug-Sept
Pumpkins .... Aug-Nov
Raspberries .... Aug-Nov
Strawberries .... May-Nov
Succulents .... May-Sept
Tomatoes .... July-Nov
Vegetables .... Jan-Dec
Walnuts .... Oct-Nov

Product Index

This index lists only agricultural goods produced by Farm Trails members. See numerical listing for other products sold.

ALES: 950
ALMONDS: 154
ANGORA: 372, 452
ANIMAL CORRAL: 144, 331, 435, 542, 589, 600, 625
APPLES: 100, 148, 154, 304, 305, 327, 334, 345, 352, 390, 408, 420, 425, 550, 780, 800, 825
APPLE PRODUCTS: 304, 327, 352, 425, 780
APRICOTS: 154, 157, 550
AZALEAS, RHODIES, & CAMELLIAS: 388, 412, 540, 575, 675
BAKED GOODS: 304, 310, 327, 352
BAMBOO: 370, 410
BEDDING PLANTS: 190, 340, 350, 515, 540, 575, 800, 805, 965
BEEF, CATTLE & CALVES: 550, 589
BEGONIAS: 412
BERRIES (CANE): 144, 148, 149, 154, 310, 304, 390, 705, 805
BERRIES (BLUE): 304, 310
BIRDS & FOWL, EXOTIC: 100, 370, 730
BONSAI: 337, 410
BRANDY: 116
CACTUS & SUCCULENTS: 412, 540, 560, 805
CARNIVOROUS PLANTS: 301
CARRIAGE, HAY/WAGON RIDES: 144, 395, 625, 715
CHAMPAGNE: 116
CHEESE: 572, 599, 920, 922
CHICKENS/EGGS: 100, 390, 425, 572, 589, 705, 745, 775, 825
CHRISTMAS TREES: 140, 331, 345, 356, 395, 397, 535, 542, 550, 580, 588, 600, 700, 960
CHRISTMAS TREES IN CONTAINERS: 140, 397, 540, 825
CLASSES: 319, 328, 435, 452, 575, 589, 590, 675, 705, 720, 785
CLEMATIS: 388, 540, 675
COMPOST & MANURE: 372, 525, 825
CORN, INDIAN: 144, 327, 395, 435, 625, 710, 715, 800, 955
CORN, SWEET: 144, 148, 305, 435, 550, 715, 800, 825, 955
DAYLILIES: 392, 575, 805
DOGS: 372, 785
DONKEYS: 144
DRIED FRUITS: 154, 304, 318, 327, 352, 800
DUCKS, GEESE/EGGS: 100, 589, 825
DYE PLANTS & STARTS: 450, 720, 785
EMUS/MEAT, OSTRICHES & RHEAS: 723, 730
EVENT FACILITY: 319, 352, 385, 425, 930
FEATHERS/DOWN PILLOWS, TC: 723, 775
FERNS: 388, 412, 510, 675, 783
FIGS: 148, 305, 550, 705, 775, 800, 955
FIREWOOD: 352, 780
FISH: 100, 515
FLOWERS, DRIED: 148, 328, 435, 439, 589, 955
FLOWERS, EDIBLE: 148, 350, 392, 439, 442, 450, 740, 747, 805
FLOWERS, FRESH CUT: 148, 190, 340, 395, 435, 439, 442, 450, 705, 800, 825, 955
FOLIAGE, CUT: 148, 442, 955
FRUIT TREES: 100, 334, 340, 397, 747
FUCHSIAS: 412, 540
GARLIC: 144, 148, 157, 238, 715, 794, 825, 955
GERANIUMS: 319, 412, 540, 575
GIFT PACKS: 148, 304, 310, 352, 599, 705, 780, 920, 922, 930
GOATS: 372, 428, 452
GOURDS: 144, 370, 395, 540, 589, 600, 625, 710, 715, 955

69

GRAPES/WINE: 302, 425, 780, 930, 982
HERBS: 148, 190, 305, 319, 350, 435, 442, 450, 540, 575, 705, 715, 720, 740, 747, 800, 805, 825, 955, 965
HONEY: 100, 148, 157, 304, 327, 352, 589, 705, 715, 800
HORSEBACK ADVENTURES: 100, 120
IRIS: 190, 388, 393, 410, 955
JAM, JELLY, CHUTNEY, CONDIMENTS & SAUCES: 149, 154, 304, 310, 327, 334, 340, 352, 425, 515, 550, 705
JAPANESE MAPLES: 388, 410, 412, 737
JUICE & CIDER: 304, 317, 345, 352, 420, 780
KITTENS, PERSIAN/ HIMALAYAN: 335
LAMB: 144, 372, 428, 550, 775
LANDSCAPE TREES & SHRUBS: 334, 340, 388, 397, 410, 540, 575, 675, 740, 783, 965
LAVENDER SPECIALTIES: 540, 575, 740, 955
LLAMAS: 385, 414
MAIL ORDER: 154, 190, 301, 304, 310, 337, 352, 372, 392, 410, 428, 452, 515, 560, 575, 590, 599, 705, 720, 794, 920, 922, 930, 955, 982
MEATS & POULTRY: 515, 745, 825
MELONS: 148, 157, 715, 825, 955
MOHAIR: 428, 452
NATIVE PLANTS: 334, 340, 388, 5475, 675, 783, 805
NURSERIES: 100, 190, 301, 319, 337, 350, 388, 392, 397, 410, 412, 450, 540, 560, 575, 675, 720, 740, 783, 800
ORCHIDS: 334, 337, 540, 792
ORGANIC PRODUCTS: 148, 154, 157, 305, 350, 390, 420, 572, 705, 715, 720, 825
PEACHES: 148, 157, 327, 550, 705, 825, 955
PEACOCKS: 730
PEARS: 148, 327, 420, 825, 955
PERENNIALS: 350, 392, 410, 450, 540, 575, 750, 783, 805, 965
PERSIMMONS: 157, 352, 710, 794, 800, 825, 955
PICNIC & PARTY AREA: 100, 190, 301, 304, 327, 334, 340, 352, 385, 395, 425, 588, 625, 715, 720, 780, 920, 930, 982
PIGS & PORK: 515, 825
PLUMS & PRUNES: 148, 157, 334, 340, 550, 825
POPCORN: 144
POTATOES: 715, 825, 955
PUMPKINS: 144, 304, 305, 327, 352, 370, 395, 435, 540, 550, 589, 600, 625, 710, 800, 825, 955
RABBITS: 372, 452, 515, 775
RASPBERRIES: 148, 149, 304, 370, 550
REDWOODS: 388, 397, 410, 575, 675
ROSES, PLANTS & FRESH-CUT: 148, 190, 540, 575, 590, 825
ROSES, MINIATURE: 410, 575
SALAD GREENS: 450, 575, 825
SAUSAGE: 515, 745, 825
SHEEP: 144, 372, 428, 452, 550, 775
SKINS, HIDES, CLOTHING & PRODUCTS: 144, 372, 428, 452
SQUASH: 144, 148, 305, 327, 395, 715, 800, 825, 955
STRAWBERRIES: 148, 383, 540, 715
TOMATOES: 148, 157. 305, 390, 550, 575, 705,. 747, 785, 825, 955
TOMATOES, DRIED: 148, 154, 705, 800, 825
TOURS: 116, 301, 304, 319, 334, 337, 340, 352, 385, 395, 397, 452, 525, 540, 589, 600, 625, 720, 730, 805, 922, 955, 982
TURKEYS: 515, 745, 825
U-PICK: 144, 383, 390, 395, 550, 625, 715, 747
VEGETABLES: 148, 157, 163, 305, 435, 450, 575, 705, 715, 800, 825, 955
VEGETABLE STARTS: 148, 190, 350, 715, 740, 800, 805, 825, 965
VINEGAR: 304, 435, 720, 747
WALNUTS: 148, 157, 352, 550, 705, 710, 730, 800
WATERPLANTS: 100, 675
WINERIES & TASTING: 116, 302, 425, 760, 780, 930, 982
WOOL & WOOL PRODUCTS: 144, 372, 385, 414, 428, 452, 705, 775
WORMS & CASTINGS: 190
WREATHS, FLORAL/ HOLIDAY: 328, 331, 356, 395, 435, 439, 442, 540, 542, 550, 580, 589, 600, 955

Members' Listings

NORTHWEST 100-299

100 Southern Cross Ranch   865-2040
9701 Hwy 1, Jenner
Beautiful setting overlooking the Russian River and the ocean. Horses, longhorn cattle, Xmas trees, exotic birds & a small hatchery. Picnic area & fishing. June-Sept, Sat-Sun 9am-5pm by reservation only.

116 Korbel Champagne Cellars   887-2294
13250 River Rd, Guerneville, 95446
Wine, champagne & brandy. Tours: cellars daily, gardens summer. Gourmet deli & picnic area. Sales & tasting all year daily 9am-5pm.

120 Armstrong Woods Pack Station
887-2939
Armstrong Redwoods State Reserve
(PO Box 970) Guerneville, 95446
Horseback adventures through giant redwoods, mountain wilderness, spectacular vistas. Trail rides, full-day lunch rides, packtrips. Excellent horses, gourmet meals. Brochure.

140 Hill Top Christmas Trees   838-7024
9040 Eastside Rd, Healdsburg, 95448
Choose & cut Christmas trees. Nov 25-Dec 23 Daily 10am-dark.

144 Westside Farms   431-1432
7097 Westside Rd, Healdsburg, 95448
Put a little farm in your life! U-pick Olallieberries & Boysenberries (June). October on the Farm celebration: hayrides, farm animals, activities, large selection fall harvest food and decorations. Call for seasonal hours.

148 Middleton Farm   433-4755
2651 Westside Rd, Healdsburg, 95448
Certified organic fruits, vegetables, herbs & flowers in a beautiful farm setting. Charming farm store. Sun-dried tomatoes, garlic braids, asparagus, strawberries, peaches, plums, pears, melons, tomatoes, sweet corn, sweet onions & root vegetables. Apr-Oct Mon-Sat 9am-5:30pm; Sun 1pm-5pm. Closed Wed. Call first rest of year.

149 Bucher Dairy Farms   433-2916
5285 Westside Rd, Healdsburg, 95448
Raspberries, tayberries, jam. Fresh berries May-Oct. School & group farm tours. Milking parlor viewing room. Please call for appt.

154 Timber Crest Farms   433-8251
4791 Dry Creek Rd, Healdsburg, 95448
Dried fruits, nuts & dried tomatoes: bulk, consumer packages, gift packs & mail order. Tours on request. Organic. All year Mon-Fri 8am-5pm, Sat 10am-4pm.

157 Dry Creek Peach & Produce   433-7016
2179 Yoakim Bridge Rd, Healdsburg, 95448
Organic tree-ripe peaches, nectarines, apricots, plums, melons, tomatoes, Walla Walla sweet onions, garlic, honey & more. June-Labor Day, Tue-Sun 11am-6pm.

163 Hope-Merrill & Hope-Bosworth Houses
857-3356
21253 & 21238 Geyserville Av, Geyserville
Fresh fruit chutneys, grape jelly & vegetables. Antiques, bed & breakfast. All year daily 9-5.

190 Misty Hills Farm   433-8408
5080 W. Soda Rock Ln, Healdsburg, 95448
Over 3 acres of iris, rebloomers, plants, fresh-cut flowers, worms. Tours & lectures by request, art groups welcome. Open during bloom (Apr-May). Call for times.

WEST 300-499

301 California Carnivores   838-1630
7020 Trenton-Healdsburg Rd, Forestville
Specializing in insect-eating plants. 350 varieties on display. Many for sale. "Arresting assemblage"-SF Examiner. "A botanical museum!"-NY Times. Mail order. Picnic spot. All year 10am-4pm. Please call ahead in winter.

302 Topolos at Russian River Vineyards
887-1575
5700 Gravenstein Hwy N, Forestville
100% Sonoma County gold-medal, dry farmed, organically grown wines. Tasting room. (Restaurant, indoors & outdoors) Mail order. Open daily 11am-5:30pm.

304 Kozlowski Farms   887-1587
5566 Gravenstein Hwy N (116), Forestville
Visit the farm and sample our products: berries & organic apples in season, over 60 gourmet products to choose from: jams, 100% fruit spreads, espresso bar, picnic area. Write or call for free mail order catalog. Open daily, all year 9am-5pm.

305 Foxglove Farm 887-2759
5280 Gravenstein Hwy N, Sebastopol
Organically grown vegetables & fruits including green beans, corn, tomatoes, basil, squash. Gravenstein & other apples, figs. Victorian gifts & country crafts. July-Oct, Mon-Sat 10am-6pm, Sun 12-6pm, closed Wed. Nov-Dec, Thurs-Sat 11am-5pm; Sun 12-5pm.

310 Green Valley Blueberry Farm 887-7496
9345 Ross Station Rd, Sebastopol 95472
Blueberries, boysenberries, jam, pies, muffins, tarts, ice cream & plants. June 15-July 31 daily 9am-6pm or at Farmers' Markets.

319 Vintage Herbs 823-7100
9753 Green Valley rd, Sebastopol, 95472
Herb & scented geranium nursery. Send for schedule of herb classes. Personalized wedding flowers and site for ceremony. Call for hours. Open beginning Mar 1. E-mail: herbman@sonic.net.

327 Hallberg's Apple Farm 829-0187
2500 Gravenstein Hwy N, Sebastopol
Apples: 48 varieties, U-pick from orchard bins. Peaches, nectarines, pears & Asian pears. Fresh cider, processed juice & cider. Grav. apple pies, turnovers & strudel. Dried apples, picnic area. Local jams, jellies & honey. Aug 1-Oct 31 daily 10am-6pm.

328 Bennett Valley Farm 887-9557
6797 Giovanetti Rd, Forestville, 95436
Dried flowers & herbs, garlic, wreaths & wreath-making classes. Tours available. Open Fridays. Please call before coming.

331 Victorian Christmas Tree Ranch 823-0831
1220 Gravenstein Hwy N, Sebastopol
Choose & cut Christmas trees, wreaths, garland, ornaments, complimentary refreshments, lanterns. Picnic area. Open Thanksgiving Day - Dec 24.

334 Dot's Pots-Orchids-Apples-Aprons 823-0645
9275 Ferguson Ct, Sebastopol, 95472
Cymbidiums, Gravenstein apples. Kitchen accessories, aprons, bread bags & towel sets. All year 9am-5pm by appointment.

335 Tuleburg Cattery 824-1210
1575 Hurlbut Ln, Sebastopol, 95472
Persian & Himalayan kittens for pet, breeding or show. Grand champion lines. All year, please call ahead.

337 Koala T Orchids 829-7933
7800 Bodega Ave, Sebastopol, 95472
Orchids: over 100 varieties of hybrids & species. Consulting services, repotting & boarding. DYNA-GRO products. All year Wed-Sat 10am-5pm, Sun Noon-4pm, add'l hours by appt.

340 Luther Burbank's "Gold Ridge" Experiment Farm 829-6711
7781 Bodega Av, Sebastopol
Registered National Historic Place #78000803, Western Sonoma County Historical Society. Docent or self-guided tours of the farm and cottage. Sales of Burbank's plant and fruit creations. Apr-Oct, please call ahead.

345 Early's Tree Farm 823-2410
232 Pleasant Hill Rd, Sebastopol, 95472
U-cut pine & fir Christmas trees. Pre-cut noble firs. Trees individually priced. Handcrafted ornaments & gifts. Thanksgiving to Christmas.

350 Shoestring Nursery 829-0751
7680 Elphick Rd, Sebastopol, 95472
Plants for kitchen gardens. Specialty & heirloom vegetables, culinary herbs, edible flowers. Many hard-to-find varieties, CCOF certified organic. All year, call for appt. Sat, Santa Rosa Farmers' Market.

352 Twin Hill Ranch/Darolyn's Pies 823-2815
1689 Pleasant Hill Rd, Sebastopol, 95472
Apples, almonds, walnuts, persimmons, dried fruits, firewood. Apple products: juice, pies & bread. Tours. Picnic & play area. All year, Mon-Sat. Every day Thanksgiving to Christmas 8:30am-5pm

356 Country Christmas Tree Farm 823-3309
1751 Bollinger Ln (off Elphick), Sebastopol
20 acres of firs, pines, redwoods. Beautiful precut Noble fir & silvertips. Hayrides, baby animals, 50ft pole swing. Thanksgiving to Christmas 9am-8pm (precut area lighted).

370 Outhouse Art Gallery Gifts & Farm **823-4580**
5874 Lone Pine Rd, Sebastopol, 95472
Gift shop & picnic area (Frontier town), raspberries, gourds, pumpkins, agapanthus, corkscrew willow, wreaths, U-dig bamboo & exotic parrots. Weekends 10am-5pm all year.

372 Spinners Wheel **823-0245**
6264 Fredricks Rd, Sebastopol 95472
Jacob's sheep, lambs, English, French & Satin Angora rabbits. Spinning equipment & repair. Wood: hand spun yarn, custom garments. Mail order. Small fee for tours. All year by appt. only.

383 Park Avenue Turf Inc. & Strawberry Farm **823-8899**
3075 Old Gravenstein Hwy S, Sebastopol
U-pick strawberries, priced per pound, bring your own container. We also have flats at a minimal cost for your picking needs. Apr-Aug, Tue, Thur, Sat, Sun, 9am-5pm.

385 Pet-A-Llama Ranch **823-9395**
5505 Lone Pine Rd, Sebastopol
Llamas & llama products for sale; fleece & knitting yarn. Tours year round by appt only with fee. Birthday parties-you bring the cake. Open all year Sat-Sun, 10am-4pm, weather permitting in winter.

388 Sonoma Horticultural Nursery **823-6832**
3970 Azalea Ave (off Hessel & McFarland) Sebastopol, 95472
Specializing in species, hybrids & dwarf Rhododendron. Evergreen, exbury & native Azaleas. Rare ornamental trees & shrubs. Featuring 5 acres of mature display gardens. Open daily 9am-5pm Mar-May. Thur-Mon, 9am-5pm Jun-Feb.

390 Kokopelli Farm **829-8185**
Shepherd Bliss Cunningham Rd, Sebastopol
Organic U-pick or we-pick boysenberries mid-June to mid-July. Blackberries Aug-Sept. Golden Delicious & Rome apples Sept-Nov. Daily, 7am-dusk. Farm tours and free range chicken eggs all year. Please call for appt. only.

392 Pic-A-Lily Gardens **823-3799**
2401 Schaeffer Rd, Sebastopol, 95472
picalily@sonic.net. Specializing in Daylilies. Choose from over 300 "field-grown" daylilies. Mar-Oct. Mail order catalog available. Peak bloom: June-July. Gardens are open May 15-Aug15, Thur-Sun 10am-4pm. Don't hesitate to call if this doesn't fit your schedule.

393 O'Brien Iris Garden **824-9223**
3223 Canfield Rd, Sebastopol, 95472
Bearded iris from yesterday, today and tomorrow. Talls & smalls, rebloomers, Dykes medalists, O'Brien introductions. Tours & lectures by arrangement. Garden open during bloom, Apr-May, Wed-Sun 10am-5pm. Call for opening date.

395 Fisher Farm **823-4817**
2870 Canfield Rd, Sebastopol, 95472
Pumpkin patch, Oct 4-30. Christmas trees, Nov 28-Dec 24. Choose & cut pines, fresh cut firs kept in water, stands, wreaths & snow flocking. Hayrides on the weekend.

397 Forever Yours Living Trees **829-5643**
5815 Blank Rd, Sebastopol, 95472
Conifer nursery. Living (potted) Christmas trees, daily Nov 29-Dec 22. Landscape trees (redwood, pine, fir, spruce, cedar, hemlock) all year appt. Bonsai stock. Educational tours of nursery & farm.

408 Walker Apples **823-4310**
End of Upp Rd, Sebastopol, 95444
Apples, 23 varieties. "Try before you buy" Aug 1-Nov 15 daily 10am-5pm.

410 Miniature Plant Kingdom **874-2233**
4125 Harrison Grade Rd, Sebastopol
Miniature roses, dwarf conifers, Japanese maples, Bonsai. Mail order. All year weather permitting Mon-Tues, Thur-Sat 9am-4pm, Sun Noon-4pm. Closed Wed & most holidays.

412 Occidental Nursery Company **874-3303**
4135 Harrison Grade Rd, Sebastopol
Azaleas, camellias, ferns, fuchsias, begonias, fancy leaf geraniums & pelargoniums, succulents, Japanese maples, Rhododendrons. Specializing in flowering plants for shade. All year daily 9am-4pm. Phone ahead.

414 Enjoy Ridge Llamas **874-3043**
1825 Joy Ridge Rd, Occidental 95465
We breed & raise llamas. We like to show people how great these animals are by hand-feeding & walking the llamas with visitors. All year, please call ahead.

420 Ratzlaff Ranch **823-0538**
13128 Occidental Rd, Sebastopol 95472
Fresh, Frozen apple juice all year. Apples: Grav, Golden Del, Rome Aug-Feb. Bartlett pears Aug 15-Nov 1. Daily 8am-5pm, closed Sat.

**425 Dutton Ranch/Sebastopol Vineyards
829-WINE**
8757 Green Valley Rd, Sebastopol 95472
Apples: Gravenstein, red & golden Delicious, Jonathan & Rome. Wines & wine tasting, gifts, mail order. Please call ahead for seasonal hours.

428 Cherry Ridge Ranch 823-8365
9845 Cherry Ridge Rd, Sebastopol 95472
Reg. Angora goats. Lincoln & Cormo crossbred sheep, lanbs, kids, fleece, yarn. Mail order. All year, please call ahead.

435 Pelikan Spring Farm 829-1495
320 Furlong Rd, Sebastopol 95472
Wreaths, flowers, herbs, classes. U-pick Pumpkin farm Oct 1-31. Visit our store Mon-Sun 10am-5pm. Groups welcome.

429 Devoto Gardens 823-6650
655 Gold Ridge Rd, Sebastopol 95472
20 acres field-grown flowers, cut branches, 25 varieties, apples, dry flower bouquets. Self-guided garden tour. Groups by appt. 12-4pm Mon-Sat Apr-Dec.

**442 Pooh Corner Farm Enterprises
829-2503**
2461 Burnside Rd, Sebastopol 95472
Fresh cut & dry flowers, florist services, seasonal fruits, fresh bay leaf-redwood-mixed greenery holiday decorations, wreaths & Christmas shop. Feb-Nov please call ahead. Dec: Thur-Sun 10am-5pm.

450 Linda's Garden 876-3466
17262 Bodega Hwy, Bodega 94922
Custom wedding flowers all year round. Cut flower bouquets, fresh cut herbs, herb & flower plants, hard shelled gourds. Handmade "Salmon Creek" soap. Community Supported Agriculture available-Tim Chang. May-Sept Sun 10am-4pm. Please call ahead for other times.

452 Bodega Estero Farms 876-3300
17699 Hwy 1 (PO 362), Bodega 94922
Angora rabbits & wool. Angora goats, kids & mohair. Romney, Lincoln Cormo crosses, raw wool, prepared fleece & yarn. Finished garments, blankets, custom designs. Work-shops & private lessons for spinning, kitting & wool handling in the Bed and Breakfast. Mail order. Open all year, by appt. only.

SOUTH 500-699

515 Angelo's Meats/Italian Taste 763-9586
2700 Adobe Rd, Petaluma 94954
Real beef jerky. Large variety of home-made sausage. Smoked award-winning turkey, ham & bacon. New gourmet products: Angelo's Garlic salsa & Italian mustard. All year Mon-Fri 9am-5pm, Sat 9am-2pm.

525 Sonoma Compost Company 578-5459
550 Mecham Rd, Petaluma 94952
Affordable, premium quality composts and mulches from recycled organics. On-site sales or delivered. Group tours and beautiful demonstration garden. All year. Call or hours.

**535 Sunshine Christmas Tree Farm
664-9335**
294 Palm Ave, Penngrove 94951
Choose & cut pine trees. Pre-cut Douglas fir, wreaths & stands. Thanksgiving-Christmas 8am-5pm.

540 Passanisi Nursery 792-2674
8270 Petaluma Hill Rd, Penngrove 94951
10 acre growing facility featuring annuals, perennials, bedding plants, roses, tropicals & orchids. Large variety and quantity. Pumpkin & Christmas festivals. Live potted Christmas trees. Group tours. Open all year Mon-Sat 7:30am-4pm. In Oct and from Thanksgiving-Christmas, also Sun 10am-4pm.

542 Wolf's Christmas Tree Farm 792-0602
241 Liberty Rd, Petaluma 94952
http://metro.net/christmastrees
Choose & cut Monterey pine, Douglas fir, Sierra redwood. Wreaths, garland, flame retarding, flocking. Animal corral, hay maze, free candy canes. Open Thanksgiving daily 9am-dusk.

550 McClain's Holiday Farm 664-8481
340 King Rd, Petaluma 94952
Christmas trees, choose & cut: Douglas & white firs, sequoia, spruce & small potted trees. Animal corral. Raspberries, tomatoes, apples, pumpkins, walnuts, corn, figs, plums, jam. U-pick. Lamb. By appt.

560 The Great Pelaluma Desert 778-8278
5010 Bodega Ave, Petaluma 94952
Cacti, Succulents and Cycads. Large selection from 3" to 45 gallon. Rarities galore! Fri, Sat, Sun 10am-5pm. All year.

572 Petaluma Farms   763-0921
700 Cavanaugh Ln, Petaluma 94952
Fresh eggs from our own hens, cheese & butter. Party supplies, Mon-Fri 8am-4:30pm, Sat 8am-12pm.

**575 Bioscape Nursery/Montalbano Day Spa
776-0666**
4381 Bodega Ave, Petaluma 94952
Italian garden plants, herbs, shrubs, perennials, pots & garden tools. Non-toxic pesticides for gardeners. Classes. Spa offers: facials & cellex-c skin care products. All year Tue-Sun 10am-6pm. Call ahead for spa appts: 707-429-5195.

**580 Larsen's Christmas Tree Farm
762-6317/763-4678**
391 Marshall Ave, Petaluma 94952
Choose & cut Monterey pines; fresh cut firs, wreaths, stands, garlands, flocking) Open day after Thanksgiving. Mon-Fri 10am-5pm, Sat-Sun 9am-5pm

**588 Rasmussen's Green Acres Tree Farm
762-9149**
200 Rasmussen Ln (off Marshall) Petaluma
Christmas trees, choose & cut. "Yes we have 8 & 10 ft. trees." Douglas fir our specialty. Redwood & patio tables & other woodies. Picnic area. Open day after Thanksgiving (daylight hours).

**589 Peterson's Pumpkins & Dried Flowers
765-4582**
636 Gossage Ave, Petaluma 94952
Pumpkins, dried flowers, honey. Oct 4-31, 10am-6pm. Please call ahead rest of year. School groups by appt. Animals to pet and feed.

590 Petaluma Rose Company   769-8862
581 Gossage Ave, Petaluma 94975
proseco@aol.com
Roses for the Bay Area, bareroot & potted. Antique to modern. Lovely country setting. Classes, Mail Order. All year, Mon-Sat 9am-5pm, Sun 11am-4pm. Call for directions.

599 The Creamery Store   778-1234
711 Western Ave, Petaluma 94952
"California Gold" dairy products. Mail order & cow-themed gifts. All year Mon-Fri 9am-5pm, Sat 10am-5pm.

**600 Little Hills Christmas Tree Farm
       & Pumpkin Patch   763-4678**
961 Chapman Ln, Petaluma 94952
Pumpkins in Oct. Animal corral, ornament shoppe. Santa. Choose & cut pines, fresh-cut firs, wreaths, etc. Open Nov 28; Sun-Tue 9am-5pm, Wed-Sat 9am-7pm.

**625 McClelland's Two Rock Pumpkin Farm
664-0452**
6475 Bodega Ave, Petaluma 94952
U-pick pumpkins, gourds, Indian corn & stalks. Dairy with milking barn viewing window, educational displays, farm animals, hay maze, hay rides, picnic spot. Oct daily, 9am-dark. Schools & groups by appt.

675 North Coast Native Nursery 769-1213
2710 Chileno Valley Rd, Petaluma
Native trees, shrubs, grasses and flowering perennials for landscaping and wildlife habitat. Open all year, please call ahead for hours.

NORTHEAST 700-899

**700 Christensen's Christmas Tree Farm
795-4758**
9799 Willow Ave, Cotati 94931
Choose & cut Monterey pine & Douglas fir. Fresh-cut firs, wreaths, garlands, stands. Open day after Thanksgiving, Mon-Fri 10am-5pm, Sat-Sun 9am-5pm.

705 Stonecroft Farm   584-1414
1610 Crane Canyon Rd, Santa Rosa 95404
Honey & award-winning honey products including BBQ sauce, honey-lemon nectar, honey jellies, beeswax candles, herbs, herbal cosmetics and more. All year Fri, Sat, Sun best, please call ahead.

710 Dee   795-6988
931 W. School St, Cotati 94931
Gourds, walnuts, unique pumpkins, Indian corn & country calico crafts. July-Oct Wed-Fri 10am-2pm, please call ahead.

715 Grossi Farms   664-1602
6652 Petaluma Hill Rd, Santa Rosa 95404
Organically grown, picked fresh: corn, tomatoes, peppers, lettuce, melons, squash, pumpkins & more. Halloween activities. U-pick strawberries. May-July Tues-Sat 9am-5pm, Aug & Sept Tue-Sun 9am-6pm, Oct daily 9am-6pm.

720 Mom's Head Gardens   585-8575
4153 Langner Ave, Santa Rosa 95407
Whimsical organic nursery specializing in medicinal & culinary herbs from around the world. Living history herb walk, group tours, classes & herbal gifts. Fri-Sun 10am-5pm.

723 Allen's Emu Ranch   584-3631
4099 Walker Ave, Santa Rosa 95407
Farm animals: horses, calves, goats, emus & ostrich. Craft items made with emu & ostrich feathers & eggs. Daily 9am-5pm all year by appt, weekends are the best. Please call ahead.

730 Santa Rosa Bird Farm   546-1776
1077 Butler Ave, Santa Rosa 95407
Exotic pheasants & quail, emus, emu products & meat, ostriches, rheas, swans & parrots. Walnuts in fall. Open July-Jan. Please call ahead.

737 Momiji-Japanese Maples   528-2917
2765 Stony Point Rd, Santa Rosa 95407
Exclusively Japanese maples, varieties, different sizes, propagator, custom grafting available, grower, personalized service. All year, please call ahead.

740 Jonathan's Palette   579-0633
4740 Hall Rd, Santa Rosa 95401
Naturally grown medicinal plants, culinary herbs, perennials & gourmet vegetable starts; fresh cut herbs in season; unique planters. Theme gardens. Open most weekends: Mar 15-Apr 30, Labor Day weekend-Oct 31. Visitors & tours by appt. only at other times of the year.

745 Willie Bird Turkey No 1   545-2832
5350 Hwy 12, Santa Rosa 95407
Turkey: fresh, ground, sausage, steaks, eggs. Smoked turkey & chicken. Deli on site. All year Mon-Fri 9am-5pm, Sat oam-4pm.

747 Todd Road Farms   586-3500
617 Todd Rd, Santa Rosa 95407
Large variety of herbs, edible flowers, vegetables. Herb infused, wine vinegars, available in gift packs. Mail order. All year, please call ahead.

760 De Loach Vineyards   526-9111
1791 Olivet Rd, Santa Rosa 95401
Estate bottled varietal wines: Zinfandel, White Zinfandel, Pinot Noir, Gewurztraminer, Fume Blanc, Chardonnay, Merlot & Cabernet Sauvignon. Tasting & retail sales all year daily 10am-4:30pm except major holidays.

775 Adams & Friend Farm   546-9598
3022 Trenton Rd, Santa Rosa 95401
Goose down & feather pillows cleaned. Comforters renovated. Custom designed & woven pillows. State licensed. Spinning wool, Navajo-Romney sheep, lambs, rabbits-live & dressed, chicken eggs, figs. By appt.

780 Martinelli Vineyards & Orchards   525-0570
3360 River Rd, Windsor 95492
Wines & gift packs. Apple butter, mustards, sauces, vinegars, coffees, honey, dried fruits, pumpkins, nuts. Mail order. Art gallery, wheelchair access. Picnic spot. All year daily 10am-5pm.

783 California Flora Nursery   538-8813
Somers & D Str, Fulton 95439
An extensive selection of native plants, unusual perennials, shrubs & grasses, propagated & grown on site. Mar-Nov Mon-Fri 9am-5pm, Weekends 10am-4pm. Please call for winter hours.

785 Pyr Creek Farm   838-8587
2847 Mark West Stn. Rd, Windsor, 95492
French "elephant" garlic, Fuyu persimmons, orchid species & hybrids. Mail order. All year, please call ahead.

794 Adajent Acres   575-4459
2245 Floral Way, Santa Rosa 95403
French "elephant" garlic, Fuyu persimmons, orchid species & hybrids. Mail order. All year, please call ahead.

800 Imwalle Gardens   546-0279
685 W 3rd St, Santa Rosa 95401
Fresh vegetables, nursery bedding plants. Tomatoes, corn, beans, pickling cukes, red onions, pumpkins, dill eggs, mushrooms. Since 1886 (110 years). Retail sales all year Mon-Sat 8:30am-5:30pm, Sun 11am-4pm.

805 Luther Burbank Home & Gardens
524-5445
Corner of Santa Rosa & Sonoma Aves, (PO Box 1678), Santa Rosa, 95402
Burbank's original home, green house & carriage house--a registered national historic landmark. Working garden demonstrating Luther Burbank's work, theme demonstration gardens, plant sales, tours. Gardens open year round, daily 8am-dusk. Home & carriage house museum/gift shop open Apr-Oct Wed-Sun 10-4.

825 Triple T Ranch/Rincon Valley Organics
539-8777
6265 Melita Rd, Santa Rosa 95409
Organic fruits & vegetables. Flowers, swine, ducks, & eggs. Grain-fed pork, custom-cut, weaners, roasters, local delivery. Co-ops invited. Also manure & compost. All year. Mon-Sat 9am-5pm. Call first.

SOUTHEAST 900-999

920 Sonoma Cheese Factory   996-1931
2 Spain St, "On the Plaza", Sonoma 95476
Makers of Sonoma Jack brand cheeses. Factory viewing, slide presentation on cheese-making and samples. Full deli, mail order. Picnic area. Open all year Mon-Fri 8:30am-5:30pm Sat-Sun 8:30am-6pm except for 3 major holidays.

922 Vella Cheese Co of Calif. Inc. 938-3232
315 Second St, East Sonoma 95476
1995-96 US champion Cheese Factory for aged Dry Monterey Jack. Tastings, tours (on request) & mail order. Open daily Mon-Sat 9am-6pm, Sun 10am-5pm. Closed Thanksgiving, Christmas & New Year's Day.

930 Cline Cellars   935-4310
24737 Arnold Dr, Sonoma 95476
Best known for California Rhone-style wines. The tasting room is located on historic Sonoma property in an 1850's farmhouse. Mail order, Picnic spot. Chocolate Fest-first weekend in Nov. Jan-Dec open daily 10am-6pm.

950 Humes Brewing Company   935-0723
2775 Cavedale Rd, Glen Ellen 95442
Hand-crafted, premium "Cavedale Ale" from organically grown barley & hops-the first domestic organic ale. Our ales are unfiltered & kraeusened for natural carbonation. We use returnable, refillable bottles. All year, please call ahead.

955 Oak Hill farm   996-6643
15101 Sonoma Hwy, Glen Ellen 95442
Summer produce, fresh cut & dried flowers, handcrafted household & holiday wreaths & decor for sale at the Red Barn. Jun-Nov Thru-Sat 10am-4pm, Dec Fri-Sun 10am-3pm or by appt.

960 Moon Mountain Christmas Tree Farm
996-6454
1550 Moon Mtn Dr., Boyes Hot Springs
Christmas trees. Reserving weekends in Nov. Daily after Thanksgiving 9am-5pm.

965 Sunrise Industries Nursery   938-6612
non-profit corp. on grounds of Sonoma Developmental Center; Eldridge 95431
(take Harney Rd. off Arnold Dr.)
Perennials, annuals, vegetable starts & shrubs. All year Mon-Fri 9am-3pm or by appt.

982 Benziger Family Winery   935-3000
1883 London Ranch Rd, Glen Ellen 95442
Located on Sonoma Mtn, adjacent to Jack London State Park. Wine tasting, motorized vineyard tour and picnicking. All year, daily 10am-4:30pm.

Regions of California Farmers' Markets

California Federation of Certified Farmers' Markets

AMADOR
Sutter Creek CFM
Eureka St. Municipal Lot
Sat 8am-11:30am Jun-Oct
209-296-5504
P.O. Box 1393, Jackson, 95642
Maureen Funk

BUTTE
Chico CFM, 2nd & Wall
Sat 7:30am-1pm
916-893-FARM
P.O. Box 3672, Chico, 95927
Randy Srnith, Chico CFM Association

Chico CFM, East & Pillsbury
Wed, 9am-1pm Jun-Oct
916-893-FARM
P.O. Box 3672, Chico, 95927
Randy Smith, Chico CFM Association

Paradise CFM, 6400 Clark
Tues 7:30am-12pm May-Oct
916-893-FARM
P.O. Box 3672, Chico, 95927
Randy Smith, Chico CFM Association

Oroville CFM
Myers & Bird St, Downtown
Thurs, 4pm-7pm Jun-Sep
916-893-FARM
P.O. Box 3672, Chico, 95927
Randy Smith, Chico CFM Association

CALAVERAS
Arnold-Mountain Growers CFM
Cedar Center
Sun, 10am-1:30pm, May-Sept
209-728-8864
P.O. Box 2052, Murphys, 95247
Eric Taylor

Angel's Camp CFM,
Bergantz Parking Lot
Wed, 3pm-7pm, June-Oct
209-736-4281
Rt. 2 Box 17, Angell's Camp, 95000
Duane Oneto

CONTRA COSTA
Antioch CFM, 2nd St, City Hall
Sat 8am-1pm, 510-757-6440
P.O. Box 267, Antioch, 94509
Charlene Martin

Concord CFM, Todos Santos Plaza
Sat, 10am-2pm; Tue 10am-2pm, Jun-Dec
800-949-FARM
4725 First St. #200, Pleasanton, 94566
Wendy Mattolo, PCFMA

Danville CFM, Railroad & Prospect
Sat, 9am-2pm, May-Dec,
800-949-FARM
4725 First St #200, Pleasanton, 94566
Cecil Patrick, PCFMA

El Cerrito CFM, San Pablo/Fairmont
Tues, 9am-1:30pm, 510-528-7992
307 El Cerrito Plaza, El Cerrito 94530
Judy Blue

Martinez CFM, Main St. Downtown
Thurs, 10am-2pm, 510-945-2940
P.O. Box 3241, Walnut Creek, 94598
Barbara kobsar, Contra Costa City CFMS

Pittsburg, undecided
Sun, 9am-2pm, 510-432-7301
2010 Railroad Ave, Pittsburg, 94565
Alice Love, Contra Costa Cty CFMS

Pleasant Hill CFM
City Hall, 100 Gregory Lane
Sat, 9am-2pm, May-Nov, 510-945-2940
P.O. Box 3241, Walnut Creek, 94598
Barbara Kobsar, Contra Costa City CFMS

Richmond CFM, Richmond Civic Centre
Fri, 2pm-6pm, May-Nov, 510-724-2283
P.O. Box 434, Station A, Richmond, 94808
Kinene Barzin, Contra Costa City CFMS

San Pablo CFM, Church Lane & San Pablo
Sat, 9am-1pm, 510-233-2603
P.O. Box 6204, San Pablo, 94806
Ruth W. Rockey, Contra Costa City CFMS

Walnut Creek CFM, Broadway & Lincoln
Sun, 8am-1pm, 510-945-2940
P.O. Box 3241, Walnut Creek, 94598
Barbara Kobsar, Contra Costa City CFMS

EL DORADO
El Dorado Hills CFM, Lake Forest Plaza
Sun, 9am-1pm, 916-823-6183
P.O. Box 1565, Loomis, 95650
Anne Zumalt, Foothill CFMA

Lake Tahoe CFM,
American Legion Hall, Hwy 50
Tues, 9am-1pm, 916-621-4772
P.O. Box 542, Camino, 95709
Jim Coalwell, El Dorado CFM Association

Placerville CFM,
Main Street at Cedar Ravine
Sat, 8am-Noon, 916-621-4772
P.O. Box 542, Camino, 95709
Jim Coalwell, El Dorado CFM Association

Placerville Thurs Nite CFM,
Downtown Placerville
Thurs, 5pm-8pm, Jul-Oct, 916-621-3913
858 Goldner Ct, Placerville, 95667
Danna Madison, El Dorado CFM Assn.

FRESNO
Clovis Old Town CFM, Pollasky 4th & 5th
Fri, 5pm-9pm, May-Sept, 209-298-5774
P.O. Box 1548, Clovis, 93613
Rob Van Wagoner

Coalinga CFM, Coalinga Plaza
Tues, 6pm-9pm, May-Sept, 209-935-2948
276 Coalinga Plaza, Coalinga, 93210
Kim Bell-Davis

Fresno, 100 W Shaw & Blackstone
Sat, 6am-12pm; Wed, 2pm-6pm
209-222-0182
100 W Shaw, Fresno, 93704
Rick Erganian

Fulton Mail CFM, 1250 Fulton Mall
Daily, 6am-6pm, Year Round
209-277-3641
P.O. Box 11457, Fresno, 93773
John Estrada

Kingsburg CFM, Tulare St. at 18th
Thur, 5pm-7:30pm, July-Sept
209-897-2933
P.O Box 307, Kingsburg, 93631
Sandra Staats

Reedley CFM, G & 11th, Pioneer Park
Fri, 4:30pm-7:30pm, May-Aug
209-638-5484
P.O. Box 615, Reedley, 93654
Shelley Jackson

GLENN
Orland CFM, 4th St. & Library Pk
Fri, 5pm-8:30pm, 916-893-FARM
P.O. Box 3672, Chico, 95927
Randy Smith, Chico CFM Association

HUMBOLDT
Eureka CFM, Eureka Mall
Thur, 10am-10m, Jun-Oct, 707-441-9699
P.O. Box 4232, Arcata, 95521
Jane Jackson, N. Coast Growers CFM Assn.

Arcata CFM, Arcata Plaza
Sat, 9am-1pm, May-Nov, 707-441-9699
P.O. Box 4232, Arcata, 95521
Jane Jackson, N. Coast Growers CFM Assn.

Eureke Old Town CFM,
Old Town Eureka
Tue, 10am-1pm, Jul-Oct, 707-441-9699
P.O. Box 4232, Arcata, 95521
Jane Jackson, N. Coast Growers CFM Assn.

McKinleyville CFM,
McKinleyville Gazebo
Tue, 3:30pm-6:30pm, Jul-Oct
707-441-9699
P.O. Box 4232, Arcata, 95521
Jane Jackson, N. Coast Growers CFM Assn.

Fortuna CFM
Del's Parking Lot, Fortuna Blvd
Tues 3P-6 P, Jun-Oct, 707-768-3342
P.O. Box 232, Carlotta, 95528
Toni Brengle

Garberville CFM, Locust/Church
Fri, 11am-3pm, Jun-Oct, 707-923-2613
P.O. Box 445, Garberville, 95542
Shanna Archibold

IMPERIAL
El Centro CFM, 400-500 blocks Main St
quarterly call for days/times, 619-352-3681
P.O. Box 3006, El Centro, 92244
Paul Simpson

KERN
Bakersfield East Hills Mall CFM,
Gottschalk's Court
Sun, 1pm-5pm; Tue, 3pm-6pm
805-324-1863
13901 Breckenridge Rd, Bakersfield, 93307
Charles Drew, Kern County CFM Assn.

Bakersfield Montgomery Ward,
30th & F St.
Sat, 8am-11am, 805-324-1863
13901 Breckenridge Rd, Bakersfield, 93307
Charles Drew, Kern County CFM Assn.

Bakersfield Stockdale Fashion Plaza CFM
Stockdale Hwy/Outback Steakhouse
Thur 3pm-6pm; Sat 2pm-5pm
805-324-1863
13901 Breckenridge Rd, Bakersfield, 93307
Charles Drew, Kern County CFM Assn.

Bakersfield CFM, White Lane & Gosford
Fri 3pm-6pm; Sun 10am-4pm
805-324-1863
13901 Breckenridge Rd, Bakersfield, 93307
Charles Drew, Kern County CFM Assn.

Bakersfield, Mt. Vernon & University
Tue & Fri 2pm-5:30pm, 805-873-0477
2001 Sandy Lane, Bakersfield, 93306
Larry Richardson

Bakersfield, Brimhall & Coffee
Sat, 9am-1pm, 805-873-0477
2001 Sandy Lane, Bakersfield, 93306
Larry Richardson

Kern City, Kern City Center
Thur, 2pm-5:30pm, 805-873-0477
2001 Sandy Lane, Bakersfield, 93306
Larry Richardson

KINGS
Lemoore CFM, D & Fox St.
Tue, 4pm-7pm, May-Oct, 209-924-6401
218 W. D St., Lemoore, 93245
Jill Duvall

Hanford CFM, Irwin/Douty
Thur, 4pm-7pm, Apr-Oct, 209-582-9457
116 W. 7th St., Hanford, 93230
Nancy Elliot.

LAKE
Kelseyville CFM, Konocti Winery
Sat 8am-Noon, May-Oct, 707-279-0662
P.O. Box 894, Kelseyville, 95451
Carolyn Marchetti

Middletown CFM, Calistoga & Wardlow
1st Sat of Month, 9am-4pm, Apr-Dec,
707-987-2733
P.O. Box 1648, Middletown, 95461
Rosa Raymer

LOS ANGELES
Agoura Hills, Whizen's Mall
Tue, 3pm-7pm, 818-991-7324
5699 Kanan Rd #121, Agoura Hills, 91301
Darlene McBane

Alhambra CFM
Monterey & E. Bay State Streets
Sun 9am-1pm, 818-308-0457
717 N. Cordova, Alhambra, 91801
Carolyn Hill

Azusa CFM, Dalton & Foothill
Thur, 4pm-8pm, Mar-Oct, 818-812-5280
320 N. Orange, Azusa, 91702
Lenore Gonzalez

Bellflower CFM, Simm's Park, Oak & Clark
Mon, 9am-1pm, 310-804-1424
16600 Civic Center Dr, Bellflower, 90706
Muriel MacGregor

Beverly Hills CFM
300 Block N. Canon Dr.
Sun, 9am-1pm, 310-285-1048
455 N. Rexford Dr., Beverly Hills, 90210
Gail Trachtenberg

Burbank CFM, 3rd & Orange Grove
Sat, 8am-12:30pm, 818-308-0457
717 N. Cordova, Alhambra, 91801
Carolyn Hill

Calabasas CFM, Old Town Calabasas
Sat, 8am-Noon, 818-223-8696
23504 Calabasas Rd, Calabasas, 91302
Linda Evron

Carson CFM, Carson & Bonita St.
Thur, 9am-1pm, 310-375-5900
22513 Evalyn Ave, Torrance, 90505
Tyler Thayer

Claremont CFM
Foothill & Indian Hill Blvd
Sun, 8am-1pm, 910-887-8156
P.O. Box 99, Lytle Creek, 92358
Ken& Merri Wood

Compton/Hub City CFM,
Alameda & Compton
Fri 11am-6pm, 310-537-5415
600 N. Alameda St. #116, Compton, 90221
Joe Storey

Covina CFM, 100 Block Italia St.
Fri, 9am-1:30pm, 818-858-7214
125 College St, Covina, 91723
Hamilton/Sterling

Culver City CFM, Washington/Culver/Main
Tue 3pm-7pm, 310-287-3850
9696 Culver Blvd #308, Culver City, 90232
Jozelle Smith

Encino CFM, Victory Blvd & White Oak
Sun 8am-Noon, 818-708-6611
c/o ONE 17400 Victory Blvd
Van Nuys, 91406
Stan Lubitch

Gardena CFM
Meth. Church, 13000 VanNess
Sat 6:30am-Noon, 213-731-2464
1866 W 94th Place, Los Angeles, 90047
Leroy & Ida Edwards

Glendale CFM, N. Brand & Broadway
Thurs 9:30am-1:30pm, 818-449-0179
c/o Gretchen, 363 E.Villa, Pasadena, 91101
Hamilton/Sterling

Hermosa Beach CFM, 13th & Hermosa
Fri Noon-4pm, 310-376-0951
2506 Ardmore Ave, Hermosa Beach, 90254
Mary Lou Weiss

Hollywood CFM, Ivar & Hollywood
Sun 8:30am-1pm, 213-463-3171
6855 Santa Monica #410
Los Angeles, 90038
Pompea Smith

L.A. Adams & Vermont CFM
St. Agnes Catholic Church
Wed 2pm-6pm, 213-731-2464
1866 W. 94th Place, Los Angeles, 90007
Leroy & Ida Edwards

L.A. County Fair CFM
L.A. County Fair Ag. Bldg.
Daily, 11am-10pm, Sep 9-Oct 1
213-244-9190
1308 Factory Pl, Unit 68,
Los Angeles, 90013
Southland CFMA, Marion Kalb

L.A. Mercado Alvarado CFM
McCarthur Park, Wiltshire & W. Lake
Sun, 8am-1pm, 213-385-7800
1636 W. 8th St. #215, Los Angeles, 90017
Mario Marroquin

L.A. Figueroa St. CFM
Figueroa St. between 7th & 8th
Thur, 4pm-7pm, 213-623-8446
845 E. 6th St., Los Angeles, 90021
Marianne Shannon

L.A. Walton/Crenshaw CFM
Crenshaw & Coliseum
Sun, 10am-3pm, 213-731-2464
c/o 1866 W. 94th Pl, Los Angeles, 90047
Leroy & Ida Edwards

Lomita CFM, Narbonne & Lomita
Thur, 3pm-7pm, 310-327-7110
24300 Narbonne Ave., Lomita, 90717
Charles Felix

Long Beach Downtown CFM,
Promenade & Broadway
Fri 10am-4pm, 310-433-3881
3326 Magnolia, Long Beach, 90806
Harbor Area CFMA, Dale Whitney

Monrovia CFM
Library Park @ Myrtle & Lime
Fri 5pm-9pm, 818-357-7442
1906 W. 22 St, Los Angeles, 90018
Harry Hiegel

North East Long Beach CFM
Wardlow Road & Norwalk Blvd
Sat 7:30am-11:30am, 310-433-3881
3326 Magnolia, Long Beach, 90806
Dale Whitney, Harbour Area CFMA

Norwalk CFM, Alondra & Pioneer
Tue, 9am-1pm, 310-864-8288
12133 Gridley Rd, Norwalk, 90650
Ray Crispi

Palos Verdes/Rolling Hills Estates
Peninsula Ctr, Hawthorne & Silverspur
Sun 9am-1pm, 310-375-5900
22513 Evalyn Ave, Torrance, 90505
Tyler Thayer

Pasadena CFM, Victory Park
Sat, 8:30am-12:30pm, 818-449-0179
363 E. Villa, Pasadena, 91101
Hamilton/Sterling, Pasadena CFMA

Pasadena CFM,
Villa Park Community Center
Tue 9:30am-1:30pm, 818-449-0179
363 E. Villa, Pasadena, 91101
Hamilton/Sterling, Pasadena CFMA

Pomona Valley CFM, Second at Garey
Sat 7:30am-11:30am, 909-623-1031
1753 N. Park Ave, Pomona, 91768
Harry Heigel

Redondo Beach CFM, Redondo Beach Pier
Thur, 8am-1pm, 310-318-0610
5217 Carson St, Torrance, 90503
Geraldine Watkins

San Dimas CFM, Old Town San Dimas
Wed 5pm-9pm, 909-592-3002
138W. Bonita #105, San Dimas, 91773
Joyce Wolf

San Pedro CFM, Port's O Call Village
Thur 10am-2pm, 310-433-3881
3326 Magnolia, Long Beach, 90806
Dale Whitney, Harbour Area CFMA

Santa Clarita CFM
Rockwell Rd. & Valencia Blvd.
Sun 8:30am-Noon, 805-529-6266
P.O. Box 1959, Moorpark, 93020
Karen Wetzel, Ventura Cty CFMS

Santa Monica CFMs, Arizona Ave & 2nd
Wed 9:30am-3pm; Sat 8:30am-1pm
310-458-8712
200 Santa Monica Pier,
Santa Monica, 90401
Laura Avery, Santa Monica CFMA

Santa Monica CFMs, Pico & Cloverfield
Sat 8am-1pm, 310-458-8712
200 Santa Monica Pier,
Santa Monica, 90401
Laura Avery, Santa Monica CFMA

Santa Monica CFMs, Ocean Pk & Main St
Sun 9am-Noon, 310-458-8712
200 Santa Monica Pier,
Santa Monica, 90401
Laura Avery, Santa Monica CFMA

Saugus CFM, Soledad Canyon Rd.
Sun 7am-3pm, 805-259-3886
22500 Soledad Cyn Rd,
Santa Clarita, 91350
Brad Berens

South Gate CFM
S. Gate Parkway &Tweedy
Mon 9am-1pm, 213-774-0159
600 N. Alameda, Ste 118, Compton, 90221
Fannie Coates Earl

Sylmar L.A. Mission College, Eldridge
Sun 8:30am-2pm, 818-896-6539
10626 Amboy Ave., Pacoima, 91331
John Rodriquez

Torrance CFM
Wilson Park, Carson & Sepulveda
Tues & Sat 8am-Noon, 310-618-2930
3031 Torrance, Torrance, 90503
Mary Lou Weiss

Venice CFM, Venice & Ocean Sts
Fri 7am-11am, 310-399-6690
804 Main St., Venice, 90291
James Murez

W. Covina CFM,
The Plaza, Sunset & Broadway
Sat, 8am-Noon, 818-338-8496
811 5. Sunset Ave, W Covina, 91790
Hester Teall

W. Hollywood CFM, Plummer Park
Mon 9am-2pm, 213-848-6502
8611 Santa Monica Blvd
W. Hollywood, 90069
Aron Sumii

Westchester CFM, 87th & Sepulveda
Wed 8:30am-1pm, 310-375-5900
22513 EvalynAve., Torrance, 90505
Tyler Thayer

Westwood Village CFM
Weyburn & Bullocks Store
Thur 3pm-7pm, 310-208-1984
1010 Westwood Blvd, Los Angeles, 90024
Aaron Shaprio

Whittier CFM, 12000 Bailey & Greenleaf
Fri 8am-1pm; Wed 4pm-8pm, Apr-Oct
714-526-5814
109 Miramonte Ave, Fullerton, 92635
Kae Thomas

MARIN
Novato Old Town CFM, Sherman & Grant
Tue 4pm-8pm, May-Oct; 415-456-FARM
1114 Irwin St, San Rafael, 94901
MCFMA

San Rafael-Marin Co. CFM
Civic Ctr, Hwy 101 & San Pedro
Thur & Sun 8am-1pm, 415-456-FARM
1114 Irwin St., San Rafael, 94901
Olivia Beltran, MCFMA

Corte Madera CFM
The Village Shop Ctr. P.L
Wed 2pm-6pm, May-Oct; 415-456-FARM
1114 Irwin St, San Rafael, 94901
Howard King, MCFMA

San Rafael Downtown CFM
Cijos & 4th St.
Thur 6pm-9pm, Apr-Oct; 415-457-2266
18 Mary St, San Rafael, 94901
Brigitte Moran

West Marin CFM, Pt Reyes Station
Sat, 9am-Noon, Jul-Sept, 415-662-1256
P.O. Box 664, Pt Reyes Station, 94956
Mark Sheft

MARIPOSA
Mariposa CFM, Darrah & Triangle Sts.
Wed 5pm-6pm; Sun 9:30am-11am
May-Oct; 209-966-271
4945 Hidden Springs Rd., Mariposa, 95338
Judy Sheets

MENDOCINO
Boonville CFM
Boonville Hotel Parking Lot
Sat, 9am-12pm, May-Oct; 707-743-1726
P.O. Box 68, Calpella, 95418
Renee Thompson, Redwood Empire CFMA

Fort Bragg CFM, Laurel & Franklin
Wed, 3:30pm-5:30pm, May-Oct
707-743-1726
Rella, Redwood Empire CFM

Laytonville CFM
Good Food Store Parking Lot
Sun, 2pm-5pm, May-Oct; 707-743-1726
Glo Plitt-Croom, Redwood Empire CFMS

Mendocino CFM, Howard St.
Fri, 12pm-2pm, May-Oct; 707-743-1726
Rosa Wyglendowski
Redwood Empire CFMS

Point Arena CFM, 219 Main St.
Sun 10am-1pm, 707-882-2973
15 Riverside Drive, Point Arena, 95468
Raven Earlygrow

Ukiah CFM, Orchard Plaza Parking Lot
Sat, 8:30am-12pm, May-Oct; 707-743-1726
Max Odekirk, Redwood Empire CFMS

Ukiah CFM, School & Clay St.
Tue, 3pm-6pm, May-Oct; 707-743-1726
Max Odekirk BR>

Willits CFM, City Park
Thur, 3pm-6pm; Sun, 1pm-4pm, May-Oct
707-743-1726
Sharon Crothers, Redwood Empire CFMS

MERCED
Merced Downtown Association
Main & K St.
Thur, 6pm-9pm, May-Sept; 209-722-8820
1722 Canal St, Merced, 95340
Harriet Ledford

Original Merced Cty CFM, N St. & 18th
Sat, 7am-Noon; 209-389-4652
2031 S. Burchell, Le Grand, 95333
Stephanie Marthimi

MONTEREY
Aptos CFM, Cabrillo College
Sat, 8am-Noon; 408-728-5060
P.O. Box 955, Freedom, 95019
Catherine Barr

Marina CFM, Kmart Parking Lot
Fri, 2:30pm-Dusk; 408-384-8229
211 Hillcrest Ave, Marina, 93933
Wilma McKenzie

Salinas CFM, Hartnell College
Sun, 8am-Noon; 408-728-5060
P.O. Box 955, Freedom, 95019
Catherine Barr

Old Monterey Marketplace CFM,
Alvarado St.
Tue, 4pm-8pm; 408-665-8070
499 Alvarado St, Ste. 1, Monterey, 93940
Jane Harder

Old Town Salinas CFM, 100-300 Main St.
Wed, 3pm-8pm; 408-598-2076
P.O. Box 2325, Salinas, 93902
Carl Serra

Seaside/Sand City CFM
Freemont Blvd., Playa & Ord
Sat, 9am-3pm; 408-394-6501
505 Broadway Ave, Seaside, 93955
Jacqueline Lambert

Monterey Bay Peninsula College
980 Fremont
Thur, 2:30pm-6pm; 408-728-5060
P.O. Box 955, Freedom, 95019
Catherine Barr

NAPA
Napa Chefs CFM, 1st & Coombs St.
Fri, 4pm-8pm, May-Nov; 707-252-7142
P.O. Box 3634, Napa, 94558
Laura Cole

St. Helena/Napa Valley CFM
St. Helena Railroad Depot
Fri 7:30am-11:30am, May-Nov
707-963-7343
P.O. Box 436, St. Helena, 94574
Sheila Mannix

Napa Downtown CFM
West Pearl Parking Lot
Tue, 7:30am-12pm, May-Nov
707-252-7142
P.O. Box 3634, Napa, 94558
Laura Cole

NEVADA
Grass Valley/Combie CFM
Combie & W. Hacienda
Tue, 4pm-7pm; 916-268-9125
22924 W. Hacienda, Grass Valley, 95949
Mechele Harter

Grass Valley, Mill & Main St.
Fri, 5pm-Dusk, Aug-Oct; 916-265-9495
P.O. Box 2317, Nevada City, 95959
Ray & Cheri Diggins

Grass Valley/Nevada County CFM,
County Fairgrounds, Grass Valley
Sat, 9am-12pm, May-Oct; 916-558-0401
P.O. Box 2477, Grass Valley, 95945
Mary Carlton

Nevada County CFM, Broad & Pine
Wed, 5pm-7pm; Thur, 5pm-7pm; Jul-Oct
916-265-9495
P.O. Box 2317, Nevada City, 95959
Ray & Cheri Diggins

Truckee CFM, Truckee River Regional Park
Tue, 9am-1pm, Jun-Sep; 916-823-6183
P.O. Box 1565, Loomis, 95650
Anne Zumalt, Foothill CFM Association

ORANGE
Anaheim CFM
Harbor Point Place & Broadway
Thur, 9am-1:30pm; 714-526-5814
109 Miramonte Dr., Fullerton, 92635
Kae Thomas

Costa Mesa CFM, County Fairgrounds
Thur, 9am-1pm; 714-573-0374
3172 Irvine Blvd, Irvine, 92720
Nancy Caster, Orange Cty Farm Bureau

Dana Point CFM
Dana Pt. Plaza, Coast Hwy & La Plata
Wed, 3pm-7pm; 714-361-0735
104 S. Olavista, San Clemente, 92672
Rick & Sandy Heil

Fullerton CFM, 450 W. Orangethorpe
Wed, 9:30am-2pm; 714-535-5694
P.O. Box 6093, Fullerton, 92634
Mona Amoon

Fullerton Market, Wiltshire & Pomona
Thur, 4pm-8pm, seasonal; 714-526-5814
109 Miramonte Dr., Fullerton, 92635
Kae Thomas

Garden Grove CFM, Garden Grove & Kerry
Thur, 10am-2pm, seasonal; 714-537-3157
9860 Larsen, Garden Grove, 92644
Karol Krane

Huntington Beach CFM, Main & Orange
Fri, 2pm-6pm; 714-573-0374
3172 Irvine Blvd, Irvine, 92720
Larry Nedeau, Orange Cty Farm Bureau

Irvine Valley College CFM
Irvine Center Dr. Jeffrey
Sun, 10am-2pm; 714-573-0374
3172 Irvine Blvd, Irvine, 92720
Jennifer Griffith, Orange Cty Farm Bureau

Irvine CFM, Campus & Bridge
Sat, 9am-1pm; 714-573-0374
3172 Irvine Blvd, Irvine, 92720
Nancy Caster, Orange Cty Farm Bureau

Laguna Beach
Lumberyard P.L. near City Hall
Sat, 9am-1pm; 714-573-0374
3172 Irvine Blvd, Irvine, 92720
Jennifer Griffith, Orange Cty Farm Bureau

Orange CFM, Lemon & Chapman
Sat, 9am-1pm; 714-573-0374
3172 Irvine Blvd, Irvine, 92720
Larry Nedean, Orange Cty Farm Bureau

San Clemente "Village" CFM
200 Avenida Del Mar D
Sun, 10am-2pm, Apr-Nov; 714-361-0735
104 S. Ola Vista, San Clemente, 92672
Rick & Sandy Heil

Tustin CFM, El Camino & 3rd
Wed, 10am-2pm; 714-573-0374
3172 Irvine Blvd, Irvine, 92720
Nancy Caster, Orange Cty Farm Bureau

PLACER
Auburn CFM, Sac & Wash St, Old Town
Sat, 8am-Noon; 916-823-6183
P.O. Box 1565, Loomis, 95650
Anne Zumalt, Foothill CFM Association

Colfax CFM, Main St. at City Hall
Wed, 4:30pm-7:30pm, Jun-Sep
916-346-2313
P.O. Box 702, Colfax, 95713
Will Steelewin

Granite Bay CFM
Douglas Blvd & Auburn-Folsom Rd.
Sun, 9am-1pm, Jun-Nov; 916-823-6183
P.O. Box 1565, Loomis, 95650
Anne Zumalt, Foothill CFM Association

Squaw Valley CFM, Squaw Valley at tram
Sun, 9am-1pm, Jul-Aug; 916-823-6183
P.O. Box 1565, Loomis, 95650
Anne Zumalt, Foothill CFM Association

Tahoe City CFM
Watermelon patch at Dollar Hill
Thur, 8:30am-1pm, Jun-Oct; 916-823-6183
P.O. Box 1565, Loomis, 95650
Foothill CFM Association

RIVERSIDE
Moreno Valley CFM, Moreno Valley Mall
Fri, 5pm-8pm; 619-244-2772
P.O. Box 4115, Riverside, 92514
Kathy Sappington, Inland CFMA

Old Town Temecula CFM, Old Town Plaza
Thur, 2pm-5pm; 909-699-8138
P.O. Box 1981, Temecula, 92593
Volunteers

Riverside CFM, Riverside Arlington Sears
Fri, 8:30am-Noon; 619-244-2772
P.O. Box 4115, Riverside, 92514
Kathy Sappington, Inland CFMA

SACRAMENTO
Farmer Bob Fair Oaks CFM
3571 Sunset Ave
Sun, 9am-5pm; Mon-Sat, 7:30am-8pm
916-967-6i97
8571 Sunset Avenue, Fair Oaks, 95628

Sacramento Plaza Park CEM
Plaza Park, 10th & J
Wed, 10am-2pm, May-Dec; 916-363-3663
2140 Chase Drive, Pancho Cordova, 95670
Dan & Renae Best, Sacramento CFMA

Sacramento Florin Mall CFM
Florin Mall at 65th St.
Thur, 8am-11:30am; 916-363-3663

Sacramento Roosevelt Park CFM
Roosevelt Park at 9th & P
Tue, 10am-2pm, Jun-Oct; 916-363-3663

Sacramento K. St Mall CFM
K. St. Mall at 11th & K
Thur, 5pm-9pm, May-Oct; 916-363-3663

Sacramento Sunrise Mall CFM
Sunrise Mall behind Sears
Sat, 8am-Noon; 916-363-3663

Sacramento N. Laguna Creek Park
Jacinto & Center Parkway
Sat, 8am-11:30am, Jun-Oct; 916-363-3663
Sacramento C634, Napa, 94558
Laura Cole

St. Helena/Napa Valley CFM,
St. Helena Railroad Depot
Fri, 7.30am-11:30am, May-Nov
707-963-7343
P.O. Box 436, St. Helena, 94574
Sheila Mannix

Napa Downtown CFM
West Pearl Parking Lot, 8th & W
Sun, 8am-Noon; 916-363-3663

Sacramento Country Club Ctr. CFM
El Camino & Watt
Tue, 8am-11:30am; 916-363-3663

Sacramento Elk Grove CFM
Elk Park Village
Sun, 8am-11am, Jun-Oct; 916-363-3663

Sacramento Town & Country CFM,
Town & Country Village Shop Ctr
Fri, 8am-11:30am, Jun-Oct; 916-363-3663

SAN BENITO
Hollister Downtown CFM
6th & San Benito
Fri, 2pm-6:30pm, May-Oct; 408-637-9460
1030 Sunset Drive, Hollister, 95023
Bill Weinheimer

SAN BERNARDINO
Big Bear Lake CFM
Pine Knot Ave, Downtown
Tue, 8am-1pm, Apr-Nov; 619-247-3769
P.O. Box 3585, Apple Valley, 92307
Kerri Santoro

Colton CFM, Wal-Mart Parking Lot
Mon, 9am-1pm; 909-780-1774
P.O. Box 4115, Riverside, 92514
Leslie Dellaro, Inland CFMA

Redland CFM, E. State & Orange
Thur, 6pm-9:30pm; 909-798-7548
P.O. Box 3005, Redlands 92373
William Cunningham

Upland CFM, Euclid & 9th
Thur, 5pm-9pm; 213-735-2586
1906 W. 22nd St, Los Angeles, 90018-1644
Harry Hiegel

High Desert CFM
Victor Vally College, Lower Campus P.L.
Thur, 8am-Noon; 619-247-3769
P.O. Box 3585, Apple Valley, 92307
Kerri Santoro

SAN DIEGO
Carlsbad Village CFM
Roosevelt & Carlsbad Dr.
Wed, 2pm-6pm; 619-720-9161
P.O. Box 4307, Carlsbad, 92018
Cynthia Bucker

Carlsbad CFM
Anderson's Pea Soup P.L., North End
Sat, 2pm-5pm; 619-720-9161
295 Chestnut Ave. #16, Carlsbad, 92008
Cynthia Bucker

Chula Vista CFM, 3rd & E
Thur, 3pm-6pm; 619-258-5420
355 AlBahr Rd, El Cajon, 92021
Suzanne Bendixen

Coronado CFM, 1st & B
Tue, 2:30pm-6pm; 619-424-4416
1811 Citrus Glen Dr, Escondido, 92027
Mary Hillebrecht

Coronado-Loews Bay Resort
4000 Coronado Bay Rd
Fri, 5pm-8pm; 619-424-4000
4000 Coronado Bay Rd., Coronado, 92118
Katherine Gonzales

Del Mar CFM, City Hall Parking Lot
Sat, 1pm-4pm; 619-727-1471
562 Mimosa Ave, Vista, 92083
Alan Usrey

Escondido North County CFM
across from N. County Fair
Wed, 9am-Noon; 619-967-9120
3191 Calle Osuna, Oceanside, 92056
Bud Whitney BR>

Escondido Downtown CFM
Grand & Broadway
Tue, 3pm-8pm; 619-745-8877
119 N. Broadway, Escondido, 92025
Alan Usrey

Fallbrook Village CFM,
Alvarado & Main
Fri, 9am-1pm; 619-723-8378
100 N. Main, Fallbrook, 92028
Janet Stewart

La Mesa CFM, 8300 Allison
Fri, 3pm-6pm; 619-258-5420
355 AlBahr, El Cajon, 92021
Suzanne Bendixen

Mission Valley CFM
Mission Valley Center
Thur, 2:30pm-6pm; 619-741-3763
1811 Citrus Glen Dr, Escondido, 92027
Mary Hillebrecht

Ocean Beach CFM, 4900 Newport Ave
Wed, 4pm-8pm; 619-223-3903
P.O. Box 7136, Ocean Beach, 92167
Claire Carpenter

Oceanside Downtown CFM
North Hill & 3rd
Thur, 9:30am-12:30pm; 619-258-5420
355 AlBahr, El Cajon, 92021
Suzanne Bendixen

Pacific Beach CFM
Mission Blvd & Reed Pacific Beach
Sat, 8am-Noon; 619-741-3763
1811 Citrus Glen Dr, Escondido, 92027
Mary Hillebrecht

Poway CFM
14050 Midland Rd. & Temple
Sat, 8am-11am; 619-258-5420
355 AlBahr Rd, El Cajon, 92021
Suzanne Bendixen

Ramona CFM, Main & 7th St.
Fri, 9am-Noon; 619-967-9120
3191 Calle Osuna, Oceanside, 92056
Bud Whitney

Rancho Bernardo CFM, Bernardo Winery
Fri, 9am-Noon; 619-631-0200
P.O. Box 13, Vista, 92085
Barry Koral

San Diego Hazard Ctr CFM
Friars & Frazee Rds
Thur, 3pm-6:30pm; 619-741-3763
1811 Citrus Glen Drive, Escondido, 92027
Mary Hillebrecht

San Diego El Cajon CFM
El Cajon Blvd & Marlborough
Sun, 10am-2pm; 619-258-5420
355 AlBahr Rd, El Cajon, 92021
Suzanne Bendixen

Solana Beach CFM
Lomas Santa Fe & Cedros
Sun, 2pm-5pm; 619-72~916I
295 Chestnut Ave #16, Carlsbad, 92008
Cynthia Bueker

Vista CFM, Eucalyptus & Escondido
Sat, 8am-11am; 619-726-8545
29933 Disney Lane, Vista, 92084
Margo Baughinan

Vista Main Street CFM, E. Vista & Citrus
Thur, 4pm-7pm; 619-724-8822
126 E. Vista Way, Vista, 92089
Jean Ann Mayberry

SAN FRANCISCO
San Francisco Heart of the City
Market St & 7th
Wed & Sun, 7am-5pm; 415-558-9455
1182 Market St. Ste 415, S.F., 94102
Christine Adams

San Francisco CFM, 100 Alemany Blvd
Sat, 6am-6pm; 415-647-9423
100 Alemany Blvd. San Francisco 94110
Christine Adams

San Francisco Ferry Plaza CFM
Ferry Building
Sat, 8am-1:30pm; 510-528-6987
1417 Josephine St, Berkeley, 94703
Judy Blue

SAN LUIS OBISPO
Arroyo Grande City Hall CFM
City Hall, Branch & Mason
Sat, 11:45am-3:30pm; 805-544-9570
P.O. Box 16058; San Luis Obispo, 93406
John Turner, San Luis Obispo CFMA

Arroyo Grande Oak Park Plaza
K-Mart P.L., Oak Park & Hwy 101
Wed, 9am-11:30am; 805-544-9570
P.O. Box 16058, San Luis Obispo, 93406
John Turner, San Luis Obispo CFMA

Atascadero Farmer's Outlet CFM
Factory Outlet, El Camino Real
Tue, 4pm-7pm, Apr-Nov; 805-238-5634
3760 Hwy 46 West, Templeton, 93465
Ken Jevec

Atascadero CFM
W. Mall at El Camino Real
Wed, 3pm-dark; 805-239-3200
P.O. Box 1783, Paso Robles, 93447
Pearl Munak, N. San Luis Cty CFMA

Baywood/Los Osos CFM
Santa Maria & 2nd St.
Mon, 2pm-dark; 805-239-3200
P.O. Box 1783, Paso Robles, 93447
Marcia Perez, N. San Luis Cty CFMA

Cambria CFM, Vets Memorial Hall
Fri, 2:30pm-5:30pm; 805-9274715
P.O. Box 1351, Cambria, 93428
Jane & Jack Gibson

Morro Bay CFM, 2650 N. Main
Thur, 3pm-5pm; 805-544-9570
Gary McBride, San Luis Obispo CFMA

Paso Robles CFM, 14th & Spring
Tue, 9:30am-12:30pm; 805-239-3200
Pearl Munak, N. San Lois Cty CFMA

Paso Robles CFM, 12th & Spring
Fri, 4pm-8pm; 805-238-5634
George Allen, N. San Lois Cty CFMA

Pismo Beach CFM, Main & Dolliver
Tue, 4pm-7:30pm, May-Oct; 805-544-9570
John Turner, San Luis Obispo CFMA

San Luis Gottschalk CFM
Gottschalks-Madonna & Zozobra
Sat, 8am-10:30am; 805-544-9570
Charlotte Turner, San Luis Obispo CFMA

San Luis Obispo Higuera St. CFM
Higuera St.
Thur, 6:30pm-9pm; 805-544-9570
Peter Jankay, San Luis Obispo CFMA
http://www.slonet.org/~ipslococ/farmers.html

Templeton CFM
Templeton at Park, 6th & Crocker
Sat, 9am-12:30pm; 805-239-3200
George Allen, N. San Luis Cty CFMA

SAN MATEO
Daly City CFM
Serramonte Ctr, behind Wards
Thur, 9am-1pm; 800-806-FARM
830 Navaronne Way, Concord, 945 18
Doug Hayden, CA Farmers' Mkt Assn.

Menlo Park CFM, Crane & Chestnut
Sun, 10am-2pm; 408-257-2760
20282 Carol Lane, Saratoga, 95070
Lori Hennings

Millbrae CFM, 200 Block Broadway
Sat, 8am-1pm; 415-697-7324
50 Victoria Ave Ste 103, Millbrae, 94030
Michal Morgan

Redwood City CFM
Winslow & Middlefield
Sat, 7am-Noon, May-Nov; 415-5924103
345 Middle Road, Belmont, 94002
Norman Shapiro

San Mateo CFM
Fashion Island Shop Center
Wed, 10am-2pm; Sat, 9am-1pm; May-Nov
800-949-FARM
4725 First St, #200, Pleasanton, 94566
Tom & Vince, PCFMA

SANTA BARBARA
Buellton CFM, Ave. Flags & Hwy 246
Sun10AM-3PM; 805-688-5736
491 Gay Dr, Buellton, 93427
Edward Ando

Carpinteria CFM, Linden Ave
Thur, 4pm-7pm; 805-962-5354
P.O. Box 2082, Santa Barbara, 93427
Kathy McIntosh, Santa Barbara CFMA

Goleta CFM, Calle Real Shopping Center
Thur, 3pm-7pm; 805-962-5354
P.O. Box 2082, Santa Barbara, 93120
c/o Mark Sheridan, Santa Barbara CFMS

Guadalupe CFM, 9th & Guadalupe
Sun, 11am-3pm, Jul-Nov; 805-473-4877
632 Pier Ave, Oceano, 93445
Wendy Andersen, Santa Barbara CFMS

Isla Vista CFM
Parking Lot, St. Athan Church
Wed, 3pm-7pm; 805-962-5354
Santa Barbara CFMA

Lompoc CFM, Ocean & I St.
Fri, 2pm-6pm; 805-343-2135
P.O. Box 958, Nipomo, 93444
Kathy McNay, Central City CFMA

Montecito CFM, 1200 Coast Village Rd
Fri, 8:30am-12:30pm; 805-962-5354
Santa Barbara CFMA

Orcutt CFM, Bradley & Clark
Tue, 10am-1pm; 805-343-2135
Central City CFMA

Santa Barbara CFM, Coast Village Rd.
Fri, 8:30amA-Noon; 805-962-5354
Santa Barbara CFMA

Santa Barbara Old Town CFM
500-600 blocks State St
Tue, 4pm-7:30pm; 805-962-5354
Santa Barbara CFMA

Santa Barbara CFM
Santa Barbara & Cota St.
Sat, 8:30am-12:30pm; 805-962-5354
Santa Barbara CFMA

Santa Maria CFM, Mervyns Parking Lot
Wed, 1pm-5pm; 805-343-2135
Central City CFMA

SANTA CLARA
Gilroy CFM, Monterey & 5th
Thur, 3pm-8pm, Jun-Oct; 408-842-6964
P.O Box 2310, Gilroy, 95020
Joy Duarte

Los Altos Loyola Corner CFM
901 Fremont Ave
Sat, 8:30am-12pm, May-Nov
415-949-0773
101 First St. #484, Los Altos, 94022
Kevin Kornegay

Los Gatos CFM, Downtown Park Plaza
Sun, 8am-12pm; 408-3534293
21900 Summitt, Los Gatos, 95030
SuEllen Sterling, South Bay CFMA

Milpitas CFM, Milpitas Town Center
Wed, 10am-2pm; 800-949-FARM
4725 First St. #200, Pleasanton, 94566

Mission City CFM, Homestead & Jackson
Thur, 3pm-7pm, Jun-Nov; 800-949-FARM
830 Navaronne Way, Concord, 94518
Doug Hayden, CA Farmers' Mkt Assn.

Morgan Hill CFM
Downtown 3rd & Monterey
Sat, 8:30am-12:30pm, Jun-Nov
408-779-5130
1210 Llagas Rd., Morgan Hill, 95037
Virginia Sellers

Mountainview CFM, Hope & Evelyn
Sun, 9am-1pm; 800-806-FARM
830 Navaronne Way, Concord, 94518
Doug Hayden, CA Farmers' Mkt Assn.

Palo Alto Downtown CFM,
Hamilton & Gilman
Sat, 8am-Noon, May-Nov; 415-325-2088
127 Rinconada, Palo Alto, 94301
Margaret Carroll

San Jose Blossom Hill CFM
Princeton Plaza Mall
Sun, 10am-2pm, Jun-Nov; 800-806-FARM
830 Navaronne Way, Concord, 94518
Doug Hayden, CA Farmers' Mkt Assn.

San Jose Downtown CFM
San Fernando & S. First
Thur, 10am-2pm, May-Nov
800-949-FARM
4725 First St, #200, Pleasanton, 94566
John Silveira, PCFMA

San Jose Japan Town CFM
Jackson St & 7th
Sun, 8:30am-1pm; 408-2984303
567 North 6th St, Ste G, San Jose, 95112
Cone Shaw

San Jose Town & Country
Town & Country Shopping Centre
Fri & Sun, 10am-2pm; 800-949-FARM
4725 First St. #200, Pleasanton, 94566
PCFMA

Saratoga CFM, Hwy 9 at Saratoga Ave.
Sat, 9am-1pm, Apr-Dec; 408-353-4293
21900 Summit Rd, Los Gatos, 95030
SuEllen Sterling, South Bay CFMA

Sunnyvale CFM, Murphy & Washington
Sat, 9am-1pm; 415456-3276
1114 Irwin, San Rafael, 94901
MCFMA

Willow Glen CFM
Minn. & Lincoln, Elementary School
Sat, 8am-Noon, May-Dec; 408-3534293
21900 Summit Road, Los Gatos, 95030
SuEllen Sterling, South Bay CFMA

SANTA CRUZ

Felton CFM, Felton Presbyterian Church
Tue, 3pm-7pm; 408-335-9364
6116 Hwy 9, Felton, 95018
Wendy Krupnick

Santa Cruz CFM, Lincoln & Cedar
Wed, 2:30pm-6:30pm; 408-429-8433
P.O. Box 1384, Santa Cruz, 95061
Lori Hennings

Watsonville CFM, Peck & Main
check in future, 408-724-3954
23 E. Beech St. Ste. 210, Watsonville, 95076
Jeri Hernandez

SHASTA

Redding CFM, Mt. Shasta Mall
Tue & Sat, 7:30am-Noon; 916-347-4627
P.O. Box 291, Douglas City, 96024
Susan Laurente, Shasta Growers Assn.

Redding CFM, Pine St. School
Tue & Sat, 7:30am-Noon; 916-241-5878
11235 Old Oregon Trail, Redding, 96003

SISKIYOU

Greenview CFM
Scott Valley Feed Store, Hwy 3
Thur, 5:30pm-7pm, Jun-Oct; 916-468-2603
12245 Quartz Valley Rd, Ft. Jones, 96032
Dorothy Rickey

Montague Savor N Thyme CFM
120 N. 11th St.
Sun, 11am-2pm, Jul-Oct, 916-459-5175
P.O. Box 567, Montague, 96094
Bill Long

Yreka CFM, Wal-Mart Parking Lot
Fri, 11am-2pm, Jul-Oct; 916-842-7167
4820 Schulmeyer, Yreka, 96097
Lee Gagner

Weed CFM
800 College Ave, College of Siskiyous
Thur, 4pm-7pm, Jul-Oct; 916-938-5373
800 College Ave, Weed, 96094
Peter Eddy

SOLANO

Benicia CFM
Downtown First St.between B & D
Thur, 4pm-8pm, May-Oct; 707-745-9791
831 First St, Benecia, 94510
Patti Baron

Fairfield CFM, Texas & Madison St.
Thur, 3pm-6:30pm, May-Oct
707-425-FARM
625 Webster St., Fairfield, 94533

Suisun CFM, Harbor Plaza, Main & Solano
Fri, 4pm-8pm, Jun-Sep; 707-421-7309
220 Morgan St, Suisun City, 94585
Laura Cole

Vacaville CFM, Downtown Main St.
Sat, 8am-Noon; 9am-1pm winter
800-897-FARM
1114 Irwin St, San Rafael, 94901
Howard King, MCFMA

Vallejo-Old Town CFM
Georgia & Sonoma Blvd.
Sat, 9am-1pm; 707-552-3115
3113 Camby Road, Antioch, 94509
Teresa Heltsley

SONOMA

Cloverdale CFM
Broad St. & Cloverdale Blvd.
Sat, 9am-11am, May-Nov; 707-894-4623
Franklin & S. Cloverdale Blvd.
Sun, 10am-12:30pm, June-Oct
28185 River Road, Cloverdale, 95425
Steve Ginsburg

Healdsburg CFM
West Plaza Parking Ares (North & Vine)
Sat, 9am-Noon, May-Dec; 707-431-1956
Tue, 4pm-6:30pm, Jun-Dec; 707-431-1956
555 Alexander Vly Rd, Healdsburg, 95448
Renee Kiff

Petaluma CFM
Walnut Park, Petaluma Blvd. & D St)
Sat, 2pm-5pm, Jun-Nov; 707-762-0344
P.O. Box 2835, Petalurna, 94953
Erica Burns-Gooler

Santa Rosa-Rincon Valley CFM
Rincon Vly Comm. Ctr, Montecito Blvd
Wed, 9am-Noon, May-Nov; 707-538-7023
110 Valley Oaks Dr, Santa Rosa, 95409
Hilda Schwartz, Sonoma Valley CFMS

Santa Rosa Original CFM
SR VT Memorial Bldg, Maple & Hwy 12
Sat & Wed, 8:30am-Noon; 707-523-0962
P.O. Box 3148, Santa Rosa, 95402
Linda Cornelius

Santa Rosa Thurs Nite CFM
Downtown Santa Rosa (4th & E Street)
Thur, 5pm-8:30pm, June-Sept
707-769-9145
1275 Eucalyptus Ave, Petaluma, 94952
Judy Collins

Sonoma CFM,
Arnold Field Pkg Lot, 1st Street W, Sonoma
Fri, 9am-Noon; 707-523-7023
110 Valley Oaks Dr, Santa Rosa, 95409
Hilda Schwartz, Sonoma Valley CFMS

Sonoma CFM, Sonoma Plaza, Napa St.
Tue, 5:30pm-Dusk; 707-523-7023
Hilda Schwartz

Sebastopol CFM
Downtown Plaza, McKinley & Petaluma
Sun, 10am-1pm, Jun-Oct; 707-522-9305
P.O. Box 592, Sebastopol, 95473
Rikka Rasmussen

STANISLAUS
Modesto CFM, 16th & H
Thur & Sat, 7am-Noon, May-Nov
209-632-9322
P.O. Box 3364, Modesto, 95353
Steve Christy

Riverbank CFM, Santa Fe & 2nd
Tue, 5:30pm-8:30pm; 209-869-4541
3237 Santa Fe St, Riverbank, 95367
Joe Avila-Summer

Turlock CFM, W. Main & Market
Thur, 5:30pm-9pm, May-Oct
209-667-6670
202 W. Main St. Ste. 5, Turlock, 95380
Kevin Cuningham

SUTTER
Yuba City CFM, Center & Plumas St.
Sat, 9am-Noon, May-Sep; 916-671-3346
P.O. Box 1756, Yuba City, 95992
Rose Godfrey
EMail, godfrey@jps.ns.net

Marysville CFM, D St. between 2nd & 3rd
Wed, 5pm-8pm, Jun-Aug; 916-671-3346
P.O. Box 1756, Yuba City, 95992
Rose Godfrey

TEHAMA
Red Bluff CFM, Walmart Parking Lot
Sat, 8am-12pm; Wed, 5pm-7pm; June-Sept
916-527-6220
P.O. Box 850, Red Bluff, 96080
George Peterson

TRINITY
Hayfork CFM, Hayfork Park
Wed, 10am-1pm, May-Oct; 916-628-4002
P.O. Box 1228, Hayfork, 96041
David Hodgehead

Weaverville CFM, Contel Building
Wed, 5pm-8pm, May-Oct; 916-623-6821
P.O. Box 37, Weaverville, 96093
Susan Lethbridge,
Trinity Organic Growers Assn.

TULARE
Exeter CFM, Chestnut & E
Wed, 5pm-7:30pm, May-Sept
209-592-2919
101 W. Pine, Exeter, 93221
Felix Ortiz

Visalia Tulare County CFM
Sears parking lot, Mooney & Caldwell
Sat, 8am-11:30am; 209-747-0095
15908 Ave. 264, Visalia, 93292
Mary Benton & Betty Keim

Visalia Downtown CFM, Church & Main
Thur, 5:30pm-8:30pm, May-Sept
209-747-0095
15908 Ave. 264, Visalia, 93292
Mary Benton & Betty Keim

Visalia CFM, K & Tulare
Tue, 5:30pm-8:30pm, May-Sept
209-747-0095
15908 Ave. 264, Visalia, 93292
Mary Benton & Betty Keim

TUOLUMNE
Sonora CFM, Porthouse Parking Lot
Thur, 4:30pm-6pm, Jul-Aug; 209-599-4960
22844 S. Frederick Rd, Ripon, 95366
Dale Kuehl

Sonora CFM, Theall & Stewart
Sat, 8am-12pm, May-Oct; 209-599-4960
22844 S. Frederick Rd, Ripon, 95366
Dale Kuehl

VENTURA
Camarillo CFM, 2220 Ventura Blvd
Sat, 7am-1pm; 805-482-1507
525 San Clemente, Camarillo, 93010
Bob Trainer

Channel Islands Harbor CFM
2810 S. Harbor Blvd, Harbor Landing
Sun, 10am-2pm; 805-985-4852
3810 W.Channel Isl. Blvd Ste. G
Oxnard, 93035
Thomas Jackson

Ojai CFM, 300 E. Matilija
Sun, 10am-2pm; 805-646-4444
802 Mercer Ave, Ojai, 93023
Cynthia Korman

Oxnard CFM, Downtown Plaza, 5th & B
Thur, 10am-10m; 805-483-7960
715 S. "A" Street, Oxnard, 93030
Desiree Ventura

Thousand Oaks CFM
Village Square Center
Thur, 4pm-7pm; 805-529-6266
P.O. Box 1959, Moorpark, 93020
Karen Wetzel, Ventura Cty CFMA

Ventura Downtown CFM
Santa Clara & CA St
Sat, 8:30am-Noon; 805-529-6266
P.O. Box 1959, Moorpark, 93020
Karen Wetzel, Ventura Cty CFMA

Ventura Midtown CFM
Main & Mills Montgomery Ward
Wed, 10am-1pm; 805-529-6266
P.O. Box 1959, Moorpark, 93020
Karen Wetzel, Ventura Cty CFMA

Ventura State Beach CFM
Ventura State Beach Parking Lot
Fri, 9:30am-1:30pm; 805-654-4679
901 San Pedro St, Ventura, 93001
Brian Cox

YOLO
Davis CFM, Central Park, 4th & C
Sat, 8am-12pm, Year Round; 916-756-1695
Wed, 2pm-6pm, Nov-Apr
4:30pm-8:30pm, May-Oct
P.O. Box 1813, Davis, 95617
Randii MacNear, Davis CFMA

Woodland CFM
County Fair Mall Parking Lot
Tue, 5pm-8pm; Sat, 8am-Noon; Summer
916-661-6018
38868 C.R. 18, Woodland, 95695
Ed & Janet Eckhoff

Alameda CFM, Central Ave & Webster
Tue, 9:30am-1pm, May-Nov
800-949-FARM
4725 First St, #200, Pleasanton, 94566
Tom Nichol, PCFMA

Berkeley CFM, Center & MLK Way
Sat, 10am-2pm; 510-548-3333
2530 San Pablo Ave, Berkeley, 94702
Clem Clay, Berkeley CFM Assn.

Berkeley CFM, Derby & MLK Way
Tue, 2pm-7pm, Summer; 510-548-3333
2530 San Pablo Ave, Berkeley, 94702
Clem Clay, Berkeley CFM Assn.

Berkeley CFM, Haste & Telegraph
Sun, 11am-3pm, May-Nov; 510-548-3333
2530 San Pablo Ave, Berkeley, 94702
Clem Clay, Berkeley CFM Assn.

Fremont CFM, Bay & Freemont Blvd.
Sun, 9am-1pm, Jun-Nov; 415-456-3276
1114 Irwin St, San Rafael, 94901
MCFMA

Hayward CFM, Main & B St.
Sat, 9am-1pm, May-Nov; 415-456-3276
1114 Irwin St, San Rafael, 94901
MCFMA

Oakland CFM, Jack London Square
Sun, 10am-2pm; 800-949-FARM
4725 First St, #200 Pleasanton, 94566
Wendy Mattolo, PCFMA

Old Oakland CFM,
Downtown 9th & Broadway
Fri, 8am-2pm; 415-456-3276
1114 Irwin St, San Rafael, 94901
MCFMA

Pleasanton CFM, W. Angela & Main
Sat, 9am-1pm; 800-949-FARM
4725 First St, #200, Pleasanton, 94566
Hohn Silveira, PCFMA

San Leandro CFM, Bayfair Mall
Fri, 10am-2pm; 800-806-FARM
830 Navaronne Way, Concord, 94518
Doug Hayden , CA Assn. CFM

Travel Notes
CALIFORNIA

Date   **Place**   **Comments**

Oregon State
Seasonal Guides & Farm Trail Maps

154 Oregon Farms
and
32 Farmers' Markets
Featured

Oregon Farm Facts:
37,000 farms
18 million acres of farm land
473 acres average per farm
Toll Free Travel Info:
1-800-547-7842

State Fair:
Salem
Late August - September

Oregon is a beautiful state with a bountiful harvest. From the Hood River Valley along the scenic, world famous Columbia River Gorge where apples, cherries, peaches, pears, berries and other fruits and vegetables are grown, to the Willamette Valley with a view of spectacular Mt. Hood and its famous Marionberries, apples, cherries, hazelnuts, and other delicious farm grown produce. Oregon farmers grow almost every variety of fruit and vegetable you can think of that can be grown in the Northwest.

Source: 1995 World Almanac and Book of Facts, *Funk & Waganalls*

Clackamas County
Multnomah County
Washington County

Farms in Clackamas, Multnomah, & Washington Counties

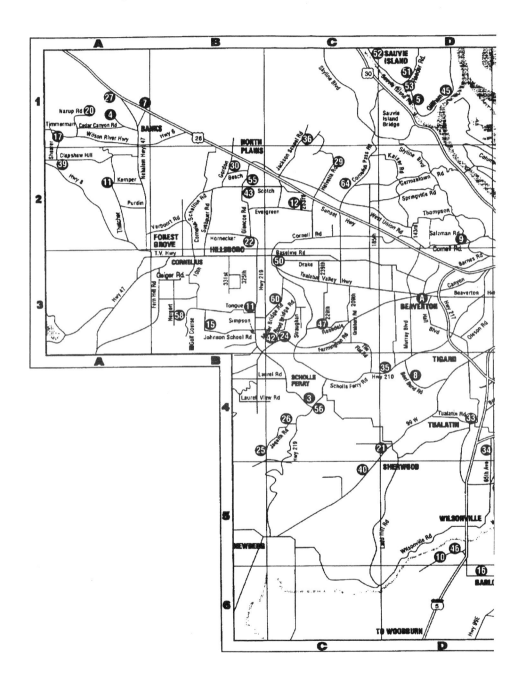

Credit: Tri-County Farm Fresh Produce

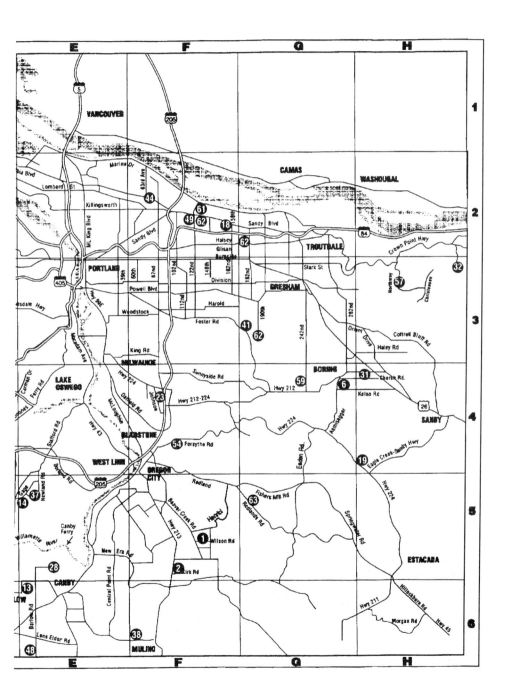

SEASONAL GUIDE

Apples ... July-Nov	Dry Onions ... Sept-Dec
Apricots ... July-Aug	Filberts ... Oct-Dec
Asparagus ... May-July	Herb Plants ... Apr-July
Beans ... July-Sept	Marionberries ... July-Aug
Bedding Plants ... Apr-July	Peaches ... July-Sept
Beets ... July-Oct	Pears ... Aug-Oct
Blackberries ... July-Sept	Peppers ... Aug-Oct
Blueberries ... July-Sept	Plums/Prunes ... Aug-Sept
Boysen-Logan ... June-July	Potatoes ... July-Dec
Broccoli ... July-Oct	Pumpkins ... Oct-Nov
Cabbage ... July-Nov	Raspberries ... June-Sept
Cauliflower ... Aug-Nov	Rhubarb ... Apr-July
Cherries ... June-July	Squash ... July-Dec
Corn ... Aug-Oct	Strawberries ... June-July
Christmas Trees ... Nov-Dec	Tomatoes ... July-Oct
Cucumbers ... July-Sept	Walnuts ... Oct-Dec

Produce Reference Guide
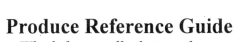
Which farms sell what products.
The 64 farms in the tri-county area are listed in alphabetical order following this guide.

APPLES: 1, 5, 14, 15, 16, 21, 23, 27, 30, 34, 35, 36, 40, 43, 45, 47, 49, 53, 54, 55, 56, 58, 61
APRICOTS: 5, 15, 16, 23, 34, 45, 53, 56, 61
ASPARAGUS: 5, 15, 16, 23, 34, 53, 61
BASIL: 10, 14, 16, 18, 21, 23, 54, 56, 61, 64
BEANS: 1, 5, 10, 13, 14, 15, 16, 18, 21, 23, 27, 34, 38, 45, 49, 53, 54, 55, 61, 64
BEDDING PLANTS: 12, 13, 16, 21, 23, 25, 34, 38, 48, 55, 61
BEETS: 10, 13, 15, 16, 18, 21, 23, 28, 34, 38, 45, 49, 54, 55, 56, 61
BERRY PLANTS: 16, 32, 34, 55
BLACKBERRIES: 1, 6, 15, 16, 21, 23, 24, 34, 35, 53, 55, 56, 60, 61, 62, 64
BLACKCAPS: 13, 15, 16, 34, 38, 60, 62, 64
BLUEBERRIES: 1, 5, 6, 7, 8, 9, 15, 16, 19, 20, 21, 23, 24, 27, 31, 32, 34, 35, 37, 41, 45, 46, 50, 51, 52, 53, 55, 56, 57, 59, 61
BOYSENBERRIES: 1, 2, 6, 15, 16, 21, 23, 24, 27, 34, 35, 44, 53, 55, 56, 59, 62, 64
BROCCOLI: 1, 10, 13, 14, 16, 18, 38, 45, 49, 53, 59, 61
BRUSSELS SPROUTS: 16, 18, 53, 61
BULBS: 16, 53, 55

CABBAGE: 5, 10, 13, 16, 18, 21, 23, 28, 34, 38, 49, 53, 61
CANNING SUPPLIES: 5, 53, 61
CARROTS: 10, 15, 16, 18, 21, 23, 34, 45, 49, 54, 56, 61
CAULIFLOWER: 10, 13, 16, 18, 21, 34, 38, 45, 49, 53, 59, 61
CHERRIES: 1, 5, 6, 15, 16, 21, 23, 27, 34, 40, 43, 45, 53, 55, 56, 60, 61
CHESTNUTS: 16, 18, 21, 34, 55, 56, 61
CHRISTMAS TREES: 12, 13, 16, 25, 34, 38, 55, 58, 63
CIDER: 3, 13, 16, 21, 23, 27, 34, 38, 40, 43, 45, 47, 53, 55, 56, 58, 61
CORN: 1, 5, 10, 13, 14, 15, 16, 18, 21, 23, 24, 27, 28, 33, 34, 38, 43, 44, 45, 49, 53, 54, 55, 56, 59, 61
COUNTRY STORE: 1, 12, 13, 16, 25, 27, 34, 36, 38, 40, 43, 53, 55, 56
CUCUMBERS: 1, 5, 10, 11, 13, 14, 15, 16, 18, 21, 23, 27, 34, 38, 44, 45, 49, 53, 54, 55, 56, 61, 64
CURRANTS: 16, 64
DILL: 10, 15, 16, 23, 27, 28, 34, 45, 53, 54, 55, 61, 64

DRIED FRUIT: 16, 34, 40, 53, 55, 63
EGGPLANT: 10, 15, 16, 18, 21, 28, 34, 55, 61
EGGS: 16, 27
FENNEL: 16
FIGS: 16
FLOWERS, DRIED: 12, 16, 21, 23, 25, 27, 34, 55
FLOWERS, FRESH: 10, 12, 13, 16, 21, 23, 27, 28, 34, 35, 38, 40, 43, 53, 55, 56, 64
GARLIC: 5, 10, 15, 16, 18, 21, 23, 27, 34, 35, 40, 45, 49, 53, 54, 55, 56, 61, 64
GIFT PACKS: 13, 16, 18, 34, 36, 38, 40, 55, 56
GOOSEBERRIES: 5, 55, 56, 61, 64
GOURDS: 3, 13, 16, 21, 23, 25, 33, 34, 38, 43, 45, 49, 53, 55, 59, 61, 64
GOURMET FOODS: 13, 16, 36, 38, 40
GRAPES: 1, 14, 15, 16, 23, 27, 34, 43, 55, 56
GREENS: 16, 34
HANGING BASKETS: 13, 16, 21, 23, 34, 38, 48, 55, 56, 61
HAY RIDES: 3, 13, 16, 34, 43, 53
HAZELNUTS: 15, 16, 17, 23, 30, 34, 40, 43, 55, 56, 61
HERBAL PRODUCTS: 16, 25
HERBS, PLANTS/CUTTING: 16, 21, 25, 28, 48, 55
HONEY: 3, 5, 15, 16, 18, 21, 27, 34, 35, 40, 43, 53, 55, 56, 60, 61
INDIAN CORN: 3, 13, 16, 21, 23, 25, 33, 34, 38, 43, 45, 49, 53, 55, 56, 59, 61, 64
JAMS, SYRUPS, ETC.: 5, 13, 16, 21, 27, 34, 36, 38, 40, 43, 55, 56, 60
KIWI: 16
KOHLRABI: 16, 61, 64
LEEKS: 16, 18, 64
LETTUCE: 14, 16, 18, 23, 34, 53, 61
LOGANBERRIES: 2, 6, 15, 16, 21, 27, 34, 44, 53, 62, 64
MARIONBERRIES: 1, 2, 5, 6,15, 16, 21, 23, 24, 27, 34, 35, 44, 52, 53, 55, 56, 59, 61, 62, 64
MEAT: 15
MELONS: 10, 16, 23, 34, 55, 61, 64
NECTARINES: 1, 4, 16, 23, 28, 40, 61
NURSERY STOCK: 16, 32, 48, 55, 63
ONIONS: 10, 13, 15, 16, 18, 21, 23, 24, 34, 38, 45, 49, 53, 54, 55, 56, 61
ORGANIC FARMS: 14, 23, 58
PARSLEY: 10, 16, 56, 61

PARSNIPS: 16, 18
PEACHES: 1, 4, 5, 13, 15, 16, 17, 21, 22, 23, 27, 28, 30, 31, 34, 35, 38, 39, 40, 42, 45, 47, 52, 53, 54, 55, 56, 61
PEARS: 1, 13, 15, 16, 21, 23, 27, 30, 34, 38, 39, 40, 43, 45, 47, 49, 53, 54, 55, 56, 61, 63
PEAS: 14, 16, 27, 34, 35, 45, 53, 54, 61
PEPPERS: 10, 13, 14, 15, 16, 18, 21, 23, 27, 28, 34, 38, 45, 49, 53, 54, 55, 56, 61
PERENNIALS: 24, 48
POPCORN: 15, 16, 18, 49
POTATOES: 10, 13, 16, 18, 21, 23, 34, 38, 49, 53, 54, 55, 56, 61, 64
PRUNES/PLUMS: 14, 15, 16, 17, 21, 23, 27, 40, 43, 45, 47, 54, 55, 56, 61, 63
PUMPKINS: 1, 3, 10, 13, 15, 16, 18, 21, 23, 27, 33, 34, 35, 38, 40, 43, 45, 49, 53, 55, 56, 59, 61
RASPBERRIES: 1, 2, 5, 13, 14, 15, 16, 21, 23, 24, 27, 34, 35, 38, 44, 45, 52, 53, 55, 56, 59, 60, 61, 62, 64
RASPBERRIES, FALL: 1, 14, 15, 16, 56, 64
RADISHES: 16, 49, 61
RESTAURANT DELIVERY: 40
RHUBARB: 15, 16, 34, 49, 53, 55, 61, 64
RUTABAGA: 16, 18, 61
SHALLOTS: 16, 18
SPECIAL EVENTS/TOURS: 15, 16, 34, 40, 43, 53, 55, 56
SPINACH: 14, 16, 49, 61
SQUASH: 3, 10, 13, 14, 16, 18, 23, 27, 28, 33, 34, 38, 43, 45, 49, 53, 54, 55, 56, 59, 61
STRAWBERRIES: 1, 2, 5, 6, 10, 13, 15, 16, 20, 21, 23, 24, 26, 27, 29, 33, 34, 35, 38, 45, 52, 53, 55, 56, 59, 61, 62, 64
TOMATOES: 1, 10, 11, 13, 14, 15, 16, 18, 21, 23, 27, 28, 34, 38, 43, 44, 49, 53, 54, 55, 56, 59, 61, 64
TREES, FRUIT: 16, 55
TREES, ORNAMENTAL: 55
TURNIPS: 16, 18, 49, 61
WALNUTS: 15, 16, 18, 21, 23, 30, 34, 40, 43, 45, 53, 55, 56, 61
WREATHS: 13, 16, 25, 34, 38, 55, 56
ZUCCHINI: 10, 13, 16, 18, 23, 27, 34, 38, 49, 53, 54, 55, 56, 61, 64

Farm Listings
U-pick available for some produce

1. **ALBEKE FARMS** *F-5
   Doug & Becky Albeke   632-3989
   16107 S. Wilson Road, Oregon City 97045
   Season: Jun-Oct.
   Hours: Mon-Fri, 9-7; Sat 9-5; Sun 12-5.
   10 minutes from I-205. Take Park Place (exit 10) onto Hwy 213 to Beavercreek Rd.; turn left, go 3 miles to Wilson Rd. Call ahead for availability.
   U-pick/ready picked: Strawberries, raspberries, apples, marions, boysens, blueberries, peaches, cukes, tomatoes, beans, pumpkins, Concord grapes. Also at farm stand: Broccoli, corn, cauliflower, apricots, pears, apples, cherries, country crafts and more.

2. **B&B BERRY FARM** *F-5
   Doris Rousett-Shively   632-3445
   15211 S. Kirk Rd., Oregon City 97045
   Season: June-Aug. Open: Call for hours and days for U-pick. Ready picked by phone order only. Bring your own containers for U-pick.
   Take Hwy 213 south 3 miles past Clackamas Community College, left on Kirk.
   Strawberries, Marions, Logans, Boysens, & Raspberries.

3. **Baby Gotter's Pumpkin Patch** *C-4
   Jane Gotter   628-1366
   24375 SW Scholls Ferry Rd
   Hillsboro, 97123
   Season: Oct.
   Open: Call for weekdays/time. Sat- Sun, 9-5:30.
   In Scholls (between two stores) nine miles west of Washington Square on Scholls Ferry Rd. (Hwy 210).
   Pumpkins, gourds, Indian corn, winter and Turban squash, cider, honey, corn stalks. Picnic area, flower gardens, hayrides, farm animals, cash prizes for pumpkin contest & turkey drawing.

4. **BAYS FARM** *A-1
   Anna, Jim & Randy Bays   324-0261
   14550 NW Bays Dr, Banks 97106
   Season: July to early Sept. Hours: 9-7.
   Call for availability. U-pick.
   At the north end of Banks, go west on Cedar Canyon Rd. 1/2 mile and at the base of first hill drive straight up gravel road for another 1/2 mile.
   Nectarines: Harko, Hardired, Fantasia & more. Peaches: Suncrest, Veterans & many other varieties. Plums: Shiro.

5. **THE BERRY BASKET** D-1
   David & Vicki Egger   621-3155
   15318 NW Sauvie Island Rd, Ptld, 97231
   Season: June-Aug. Open: 9-7 daily, closed Sunday. Farm produce stand. Ready pick and pick on order, phone ahead.
   On Sauvie Island Rd 1/4 mile from bridge.
   Strawberries, raspberries, marionberries, blueberries, peaches (for pick your own, see Sauvie Island Farms #52), apples, apricots, asparagus, beans, cabbage, canning supplies, cherries, corn, fresh herbs, honey, onions/garlic, peas, pears, potatoes, tomatoes, watermelon and more.

6. **BITHELL FARMS** *G-4
   Bob & Mary Bithell   663-9335
   28355 SE Kelso Rd, Boring 97009
   Season: June-July. Hours: 7 days a week, 8-6.
   U-pick only, bring your own containers.
   Go east on Hwy 26, turn right on SE Kelso Rd, go 2 1/2 miles, see berry signs on right.
   Strawberries, marionberries, blueberries, loganberries, boysenberries, blackberries, pie cherries. Gazebo shelter and picnic area.

7. **BLUEBERRIES OF BANKS** *A-1
   Robert & Bernice Dietlein   324-4411
   16220 NW Sellers Rd, Banks, 97106
   Season: July-Aug. Hours: Daily 8-6; Sun 12-6. U-pick or ready picked by order. Containers furnished. Easy picking. Stop by with your family on the way to the coast.
   We are right on Hwy 26, on the North side at Sellers Rd, 2 1/2 miles west of Hwy 6 and Hwy 26 junction. Easy Access.
   Blueberries. Picnic area.

8. **BLUEBERRY HILL FARM** *D-4
   590-1525
   16997 SW Beef Bend Rd, Sherwood, 97140
   Season: July 1-July 30.
   Hours: 8-8, Mon-Thur; 8-5, Fri-Sat; 10-5, Sun.
   7 acres, U-pick & ready pick. Call ahead.
   From Washington Square: travel west on Scholls Ferry Rd, app. 4 miles, turn left on Beef Bend Rd, travel 1/4 mile on Beef Bend and we are on the left.
   Blueberries: Early Blue and Blue Crop varieties.

9. BONNY SLOPE BLUEBERRIES *D-2
Joan Gunness & Family   645-1252
3565 NW South Rd, Portland, 97229
Season: July 1-Sept 1. Hours: 9-6, Mon-Sun or by appointment. Bring own containers, some provided. U-pick, ready pick on order.
Close to Beaverton, follow signs along West Union Rd, NW Skyline or Cornell Rd. in Cedar Mill to Thompson Rd, follow signs to South Rd.
Unsprayed Blueberries. Clean fields, easy picking, families welcome. Call for availability.

10. JOE CASALE & SON *D-5
Joe Casale & Jennie Casale   682-1760
13116 NE Denbrook Rd, Aurora, 97002
Season: June strawberries; July 15 veggies; season ends Nov 1. Hours: Mon-Sat, 9-6; closed Sun. U-pick, ready pick, farm produce stand, call for availability, bring containers.
I-5 South to Charbonneau dist. exit 282 B or northbound Canby exit 282.
Beans, cabbage, cauliflower, corn, tomatoes, carrots, beets, cukes (slicers, picklers), peppers, dill, squash, garlic, broccoli, potatoes, onions, basil, flowers.

11. CLEARWATER GROWERS A-2/B-3
Mark Hansen, Rod Sandoval,
Mel & Ginger Hansen   357-4146
6225 NW Kansas City Rd, Frst Grv, 97116
Season: Oct-July. Open: daily, dawn-dusk. Future farming at its best in Washington County. The Clearwater family offers greenhouse-grown hydroponic produce at the peak of flavor, insecticide free and vine ripened. Wholesalers welcome. Come see us at our "garden under glass" in Forest Grove & at Dad's place, 31045 SW Tongue Lane, Cornelius, 648-2711. Tours available by appointment.
Tomatoes & European Cucumbers.

12. COUNTRY GARDENS C-2
Carol & Ray Haag   648-1508
4825 NW 253, Hillsboro, 97124
Season: Year round. Hours: 9-6, Mon-Sat; 1-5, Sun. Specializing in hybrid lilies, blooms, bulbs, florist/gift shop (books and gift items to enhance and inspire), appointments to plan weddings. Photograph display gardens, 1890 setting.
West of Portland on Sunset Hwy 26, Exit 61, S. to Evergreen, right 1/3 mile to 253rd.
Country/Victorian shop, fresh & dried flowers, bedding plants, Christmas trees, ornaments & gifts.

13. THE DAIRY GARDEN E-6
Hoffman Family Farms   266-4703
6815 S. Knightsbridge Rd, Canby 97013
Season: Apr-Dec.
Hours: 9-6, Mon-Sat; 10-5, Sun.
I-5 to Canby exit & follow signs.
Picked to order & ready picked farm fresh produce: strawberries, blackcaps, raspberries, beans, cole crops. Pumpkin patch, hayrides, bedding plants, fuschia baskets, Christmas trees, wreaths & country gift shop.

14. DENNIS ORGANIC FARM *E-5
Dale & Margaret Dennis   638-4211
25006 SW Gage Rd, Wilsonville, 97070
Season: May-Nov. Hours: Tue-Sat, 9-6.
U-pick.
Take I-5 to Stafford exit east on Elligsen Rd. 1 mile, follow signs.
Produce strictly organic. Pole peas (shelling, snap), lettuce, spinach, cucumbers, corn, beans, broccoli, peppers, squash, tomatoes, apples, plums, basil, grapes, raspberries, red & Golden, early & late types.

15. DUYCK'S PEACHY-PIG FARM *B-3
Gary, Sally & Family   357-3570
34840 SW Johnson School Rd
Cornelius, 97113
Season: May-Dec. Open: Daily 9-dark; Sun 12-dark. U-pick & we pick. Bring containers, children & food stamps welcome. See & touch animals. Tours May thru Oct: schools, birthday parties, pumpkins in patch, etc.
4 m. S of Hillsboro on Hwy 219. R on Simpson Rd. R on Johnson Sch. Rd. go 3 m. or take 10th St. out of Cornelius 3 m. L at golf course, R on Johnson Sch. Rd. 1 m.
Custom filbert harvesting. Apples, apricots, asparagus, beans, beets, berries (black, blue, blackcaps, Chehalems, logan, marion, rasp, straw, young), carrots, cherries, cukes (reg & lemon), corn, dill, eggplant, filberts, freezer hogs, garlic, honey, onions (reg & Walla Walla), peaches, pears, peppers (Bell & hot), popcorn, prunes, plums, pumpkins, rabbits, rhubarb, tours, tomatoes, walnuts, weaner pigs, grapes & golf balls. Picnic area, panoramic view, natural well water.

16. **FIR POINT FARMS** *D-6
    Ed & Judy Stritzke   678-2455
    14601 Arndt Rd, Aurora, 97002
Season: Apr-Dec. Hours: 9-6 daily.
U-pick or ready picked.
Go I-5 southt to Canby exit 282A. Turn left on Arndt Rd.
Everything country fresh from apples to zucchini. Corn picked fresh daily, vine ripe strawberries & cantaloupe, tree ripe peaches, small & giant pumpkins, fresh cut trees, handcrafted gifts, 2 acres U-cut flowers. Gourp tours, special holiday fun & free picnic area. For family fun, enjoy our new farm trail; see our giant oxen & visit with friendly farmers. UPS available.

17. **GILES FARM** *A-1
    Ken & Lora Giles   357-3944 / 771-8320
    12670 NW Shearer Rd, Forrst Grove, 97116
Season: July-Oct. Hours: Call for open hours and availability of crop. U-pick, ready pick on order. Bring your own containers for U-pick. Also ready-pick on order in Eastmoreland, 6812 SE 30th, Portland.
5 miles west of Banks on Hwy 6 (Wilson River Hwy), turn left at Timmerman Rd, turn left at Shearer Rd, 1/2 mile.
Red Haven peaches, Brooks prunes, hazelnuts.

18. **GIUSTO FARMS** F-2
    Augie & Dominic Giusto   253-0271
    3518 NE 162nd Ave., Portland, 97230
Season: July-Feb. Hours: 10-6, closed Sundays.
Farm fresh ready picked produce.
One block south of Sandy Blvd.
Basil, beans, beets, broccoli, Brussels sprouts, cabbage, carrots, cauliflower, sweet corn, cucumbers, eggplant, garlic, leeks, shallots, lettuce, onions, peppers, parsnip, potatoes (red, yellow, white), pumpkins, rutabagas, tomatoes, turnips, winter squash (5 varieties), zucchini, chestnuts, nuts, popcorn, holiday fruit baskets, honey, fruit and more.

19. **GLOVER'S CENTURY FARM** *H-4
    Clifton Glover   637-3820
    29177 SE Hwy 224, Eagle Creek, 97022
Season: July. Hours: 8am-dark.
U-pick. Call ahead for availability. Clean field, parking and water, sanitary service. Bring containers.
13 miles toward Estacada from I-205 Clackamas Exit. 6 miles north of Estacada.
Unusually large, flavorful blueberries.

20. **GORDON'S ACRES** *A-1
    Doug & Barthene Gordon   324-9831
    48360 NW Narup Rd, Banks, 97106
Season: every day June-Sept. Hours: 8-dark.
U-pick, ready-picked, picked to order. Children welcome.
3 miles west of Banks. Take Hwy 6 to milepost 46, turn north on Cedar Canyon Rd and follow signs 0.7 mile. Call day or evening.
Strawberries, blueberries.

21. **GRAMMA'S PLACE** *D-4
    Don & Margaret Wachlin   625-7104
    21235 SW Pacific Hwy, Sherwood, 97140
Season: Strawberries to Pumpkins.
Hours: 10-6. Closed Sun June-July only.
Bedding plants, hanging baskets, strawberries, corn, garlic, peaches, pears, onions, potatoes, pumpkins & harvest adventures, apples, u-pick flowers and much more. Bunnies to llamas, fall hayrides and family fun. Fall school tours welcome.

22. **TOM GREGG FARM** *B-2
    Tom & Donna Gregg   693-8775
    31660 Hornecker Rd, Hillsboro, 97124
Season: July-Sept. Hours: 9-7. U-pick or ready pick on order. Bring containers, some available.
1 1/2 mile NW Hillsboro at Hornecker and Leisy Rd, from Portland west on Hwy 26, left on Jackson Rd to Evergreen, then right to Glencoe and turn left, past Glencoe High cross railroad tracks on right, then right on Hornecker 1 mile to Leisy Rd, right turn to orchard driveway 1/4 mile. See signs.
Peaches, Red Haven (early), Veteran (mid), Elberta (late) varieties.

23. **HARTNELL FARMS** *F-4
    Larry & Jeff Hartnell   655-1297
    15000 SE Johnson Rd., Milwaukie, 97267
Season: May-Oct. Hours: 8-6. Closed Sun.
U-pick, fresh-picked.
Farmer-owned produce stand 1/2 mile S of Hwy 224 on Johnson Rd.
Raspberries, pole beans, cucumbers, tomatoes. Ready-picked strawberries, blueberries, peaches, pears, apples, squash, corn, boysens, logans, carrots, beets, salad veggies, other fruits & veggies, pumpkin patch.

24. **DAVE HEIKES FARMS, INC.** C-3
    Dave & Cheryl Heikes   628-7226
    9400 SW Heikes Rd, Hillsboro, 97123
Season: June 1 thru end of Oct. Hours: Mon-Sat, 10-7; closed Sun. Ready picked produce stand. Call for large orders.
On Farmington Rd between Hwy 219 and River Rd. Follow signs.
Hood strawberries, red raspberries, blueberries, marionberries, boysenberries, Later, Jubilee sweet corn, onions.

25. HOUSE OF WHISPERING FIRS B-4
Kathy & Richard Thompson   628-3695
20080 SW Jaquith Rd, Newberg, 97132
Season: Year round.
Open: 9-dusk. Closed major holidays.
Follow signs from Hwy 219 & Mountain Top Rd.
Herb, vegetable & bedding plants, scented geraniums, dried flowers, Indian corn, gourds, Christmas greens, trees, wreaths. Victorian country gift shop, herbal crafting classes, books, fresh dried botanicals, essential oils and walking gardens.

26. JAQUITH STRAWBERRY FARM *C-4
Kenneth Jaquith   628-1640
23135 SW Jaquith Rd, Newberg, 97132
Season: Late May-mid July. Hours: 8-8, Mon-Sat; closed Sun. U-pick or ready picked on order.
2 1/2 miles SW of Scholls on Jaquith Rd.
Early and late season strawberries: Hoods, Shukson, Bentons. Clean field and scenic drive.

27. JIM DANDY FARM MARKET *A-1
Ginger Davis
Ray & May Trussell   324-3954
45770 NW Sunset Hwy, Banks, 97106
Season: June-early Nov. Hours: 9-dusk.
Hwy 26 at Manning.
Strawberries, corn, tomatoes, honey, brown eggs, jams & jelly, peaches, pears, etc. by pound or box. Collectible corner, U-pick beans, cukes, tomatoes & flowers.

28. JOHN'S PEACH ORCHARD *E-5
Bertram John Fawver   266-9466
7335 S. Fawver Rd, Canby, 97013
Season: June-Oct. Hours: Mon-Sat 8-7; Sun 1-7. U-pick, ready-picked on order. Bring your own containers. Home grown, sold by family.
Peaches, nectarines, tomatoes, peppers, squash (Danish, butternut, hubbard, sweetmeat), eggplant, dill, beets, sweet corn, cabbage, cut flowers, perennials & herbs.

29. DAVE JOSSI & SON *C-2
Dave & Joanie Jossi 647-2158 / 647-5641
10490 NW Groveland Rd, Hillsboro, 97124
Season: June. Hours: 9-7, closed Sunday.
U-pick. Call for availability.
Take Helvetia Rd exit from Sunset Hwy, north 2 1/2 miles to Bodertscher Rd (first right past Helvetia tavern), watch for U-pick signs.
Shuksan strawberries.

30. JOSSY FARMS *B-2
Bob Jossy   647-5234 / 647-5668
31965 NW Beach Rd, Hillsboro, 97124
Season: July, Aug & Nov. Hours: Call for open hours and availability of crop. U-pick, ready-pick on order. Bring your own containers.
1/8 mile S of Sunset Hwy at North Plains exit, turn west on Beach Rd 1/4 mile.
Peaches (Veterans, Red Haven & others), pears, Gravenstein apples, hazelnuts and walnuts.

31. KELSO BLUEBERRIES *H-4
Diane Kelso   663-6830
28951 SE Church Rd, Boring, 97009
Hours: 8-8 Fri-Sun. U-pick, ready-picked. Please call for availability and directions. Recorder on, messages returned promptly during open hours.
Blueberries, Suncrest peaches (ripe app. Aug 20).

32. KLOCK FARM *H-3
Clair & Beverly Klock   695-5882
931 NE Salzman Rd., Corbett, 97019
Season: mid-July to late Aug. Hours: 10-6 Thur-Sun only. Call for availability. U-pick and orders taken. Bring own containers.
Crown point Hwy 2 miles E of Corbett to Larch Mt Rd, 2 blocks to Salzman Rd. Turn R 1/4 mile.
Blueberries (fresh & frozen), blueberry plants, nursery stock.

33. KOCH FARM *D-4
Ron & Kay Koch   692-5749
11350 SW Tualatin-Sherwood Rd
Tualatin, 97062
Season: June-Nov Call for hours & availability. U-pick or ready-picked on order. Bring your own containers.
Tualatin-Sherwood Rd. near Avery Rd. Look for signs.
Strawberries, sweet corn, pumpkins, Indian corn, gourds, squash & straw.

34. LEE BERRY FARM ON 65th   *D-4
    Larry, Craig & Heidi Lee   638-1869
    21975 SW 65gh Av, Tualatin, 97062
Season: March-Christmas. Hours: vary with seasons, 7 days a week. Call ahead U-pick and ready-picked. Call to place orders. Country store opens with Daffodil crop. Featuring farm fresh produce & unique gifts. Pumpkin Festival last three weekends in Oct. Festivals include hayrides, see & touch animals & special events each weekend. Bring the whole family, picnic area available. "Family farming in Tualatin since 1869."
1 mile south of Meridian Park Hospital.
Bedding plants, hanging baskets, strawberries, raspberries, marionberries, boysenberries; produce, peaches, apples, cider, U-cut flowers, u-pick pumpkin & jams. Group tours, hay maze, hayrides, Christmas trees (2-20ft.), wreaths, country store.

35. LOLICH'S BERRY FARM   *D-4
    Frank, Dina & Erin Lolich   628-1436
    18407 SW Scholls Ferry Rd
    Beaverton 97007
Season: Strawberries only in June; Blues start July 4th; Raspberries, marions, boysens, blacks, peaches, pumpkin patch with the works in Oct. Hours: 8:30 to dusk for U-pick Blues.
5 miles west of Washington Square.
Oregon's premier blueberry farm. The largest bushes & the most varieties: ten on 12 scenic acres. Our berries are irrigated with deep pure well water, not filthy pond or river water. Please bring containers. We provide a very relaxing environment, a nice time for all ages & a very clean restroom.

36. MASON HILL ORCHARD   C-1
    Mark & Pat Susbauer   647-5669
    13145 NW Mason Hill Rd, Hillsboro 97124
Season: Aug 9-Oct 26. Hours: 9-6 daily. Call ahead for availability. Ready-picked only.
From Sunset Hwy (26) turn north onto Jackson School Rd, go 2 1/2 miles, turn right onto Mason Hill Rd, go 1000 feet to 2nd house on left. Signs are posted.
Apples: Gravenstein, Gala, Jonagold, Mutsu, Melrose, Criterion. Gourmet foods: Apple & Pumpkin Butter, jams & jellies are all produced here.

37. McKNIGHT'S BLUEBERRY FARM
                                                        *E-5
    John & Linda McKnight   638-4989
    24275 SW Nodaway Ln, Wilsonville, 97070
Season: July to mid-Aug. Hours: 8-5 daily; Sun 10-5; closed Mon-Tue. U-pick or ready picked, call ahead for availability. Containers furnished. Clean fields with ample parking and sanitary facilities.
Easily reached off I-5 or I-205 via Stafford Rd. Follow signs.
Blueberries.

38. MULINO PLANT & PRODUCE   F-6
    Hoffman Family Farms   829-4710
    26600 S. Hwy 213, Mulino 97042
Season: Apr-Oct.
Hours: 9-6 Mon-Sat; 10-5 Sun.
Exit 10 at I-205, south on Hwy 213 to Mulino.
Picked to order and ready-picked: strawberries, blackcaps, raspberries, beans, corn, cole crops, tomatoes, blueberries, farm fresh vegetables & fruits available at produce stand.

39, NORMANDIN ORCHARDS   *A-2
    357-2351 / 357-7000
    50500 NW Clapshaw Hill Rd
    Forest Grove, 97116
Season: Aug-Sept. Hours: 8-7.
Quality guaranteed. Bring containers.
Straight through Forest Grove, take Hwy 8 to Gales Creek. Drive 1/4 mile, right to Clapshaw Hill Rd, 1 mile to the finest freestone peaches and clean No 1 pears.
Bartlett pears; Red Globe and Harken Peaches.

40. OLIPHANT ORCHARD   *C-5
    Richard & Patricia Oliphant   625-7705
    23995 SW Pacific Hwy, Sherwood 97140
Season: July-Oct when fruit is available.
Hours: 9-6 or until sold out, 7 days a week. Call ahead, orders taken. U-pick, ready-pick. Bring your own containers, some supplied. School groups welcome!
Apples, cherries (sweet & pie--u-pick, we pit!), peaches, plums, prunes, pears, pumpkins, apple cider, flowers.

41. OTT'S BLUEBERRIES   *G-3
    Richard & Charlotte Ott   665-3567
    17632 SE McKinley, Portland, 97236
Season: July 15-Aug 31.
Hours: Mon-Sat 8-7; Sun 8-4. U-pick, ready picked orders taken. Call for availability. Bring containers. Clean fields, ample parking.
In SE Portland, go east on Powell to 182nd (Highland Dr). Turn right & go south about 1 1/2 miles. Turn right on Giese Rd & follow signs.
Blueberries.

42. **PAULSON'S PEACH PHARM** C-3
John & Colleen Paulson 648-6359
29000 SW Burkhalter Rd, Hillsboro
Season: July-early Sept. Hours: 9-5.
Call for availability.
South on Hwy 219 from Hillsboro app. 4 miles, left on Burkhalter Rd, past Oak Knoll Winery 1/2 mile.
Veterans, Reliance and Red Haven peaches.

43. **PETERSON FARMS** B-2
   APPLE COUNTRY
Frank & Pat Peterson 640-5649
4800 NW Glencoe Rd, Hillsboro 97124
Season: Aug-Dec. Hours: 10-dusk, Wed-Sun. Call for crops in season. Apple/Pumpkin Harvest Festival last three weekends in Oct. Country store, orchard tours, draft horses/hayrides, our farm or wherever all year, including Christmas caroling and weddings.
Midway between Hwy 26 and Hillsboro.
Apples (45 varieties), cider, jellies, apple butter, honey, pears, grapes, plums, cherries, pumpkins, squash, tomatoes, corn, nuts, gourds, U-cut flowers.

44. **PULOS FARMS** *F-2
Thomas M. Pulos 281-0751
6912 NE 63rd Ave, Portland, 97218
Season: mid-June to end of July on U-pick berries. Mid-July to end of Sept on ready picked vegetables. Hours: Mon-Fri 8-6; Sat-Sun 8-5. Call ahead for availability. Bring own containers.
Columbia Blvd to NE 63rd Av, 1/2 mile north on 63rd.
Raspberries, marions, boysen & loganberries. Corn, cucumbers & tomatoes.

45. **PUMPKIN PATCH**
    PRODUCE MARKET *D-1
Bob & Kari Egger 621-3874
16511 NW Gillihan Rd, Sauvie Isl., 97231
Season: June-Nov. Hours: 9-6 daily.
Fresh picked produce, Pumpkin Cottage Gift Shop, Patio Cafe.
Loop under bridge, straight 2 miles.
U-pick berries, apples, peaches, tomatoes, flowers, pumpkins. Fall animal barn, free hayrides, corn maze, hay maze, barbecue. All your fall decorations, field trips & festivals. Fresh corn (yellow, bi, white), beans, squash, gourds, cole crops, garden needs.

46. **RILEY & SONS OREGON**
    BLUEBERRIES *D-5
Rick & Marie Riley 678-5852 / 678-5842
26022 NE Butteville Rd, Aurora 97002
Season: July 1-Aug 17.
Hours: Mon-Sat 8-7; Sun 10-7. U-pick and ready pick on order. Bring your own containers. Please order 24 hours in advance. Large size berries, clean fields, easy picking. Blueberries.

47. **ROSEDALE ORCHARDS** *C-3
Ray & Millie Vandegrift 649-7354
23100 SW Rosedale Rd, Beaverton 97007
Season: July 15-Dec. Call for picking dates.
Hours: weekdays 8-dark; weekends 10-6. Some containers supplied.
Corner of Rosedale Rd & 229th, between Farmington Rd & TV Hwy.
U-pick & ready-picked apples (8 varieties), ready-picked peaches, pears, prunes & apple cider.

48. **ROSS NURSERY** E-6
Erric Ross 266-4485
26851 S. Barlow Rd, Canby 97013
Season: April to July.
Hours: Mon-Fri 10-6; Sat 9-5; closed Sun.
From Canby, proceed S on 99E to traffic light at Barlow. Turn left and proceed a little over 2 miles on Barlow Rd to nursery on west side of road. Look for Tri-County Farm Fresh sign.
Specializing in hanging baskets, perennials and 4 in. color spots. Fuschias, Begonias, Geraniums, Petunias, Impatiens & more.

49. **ROSSI FARMS** F-2
   253-5571
3839 NE 122nd Ave, Portland, 97230
Season: Aug 1-Jan 1. Hours: 9-6 Mon-Sat.
20 acres in Portland, corner of 122nd Av and NE Shaver. Ready picked produce stand on farm.
Beans, beets, broccoli, cabbage, carrots, cauliflower, cucumbers, garlic, corn (super sweet, white & yellow), tomatoes, peppers, onions, spinach, potatoes (red, white, blue & yellow), squash (10 varieties), radishes, pumpkins, mini pumpkins, popcorn, corn stalks, Indian corn, gourds, zucchini, turnips, rutabagas & more. We sell Hood River apples and many varieties of pears & Asian pears.

50. **SARA'S BLUEBERRIES** *C-3
Sara Ackerman 649-6000
24375 SW Drake Ln, Hillsboro 97123
Season: July 5-Aug 15. Hours: 8:30-8.
U-pick & ready-picked on order. Call recording for crop availability. Clean field with plentiful picking, children welcome, shady picnic area. Come enjoy the farm animals.
East of Hillsboro, turn north from Tualatin Valley Hwy at 239th and follow blue/white signs 1 mile.
Blueberries: 5 varieties.

**51. SAUVIE ISLAND
BLUEBERRY FARM** *D-1
Anne K. Jones 621-3332
15140 NW Burlington Court
Sauvie Island, Portland, 97231
Season: mid-June to mid-Aug. Hours: 7 days a week 8-5. U-pick and ready-pick on order. Containers supplied for picking and transferred to bags at checkout. Your containers welcome. Clean fields, plentiful picking.
Take Sauvie Island Rd to Reeder Rd, follow the white and blue signs 2 1/2 miles from bridge, close to tennis courts, school church, Bailey Nursery.
Blueberries: wide selection of varieties.

52. SAUVIE ISLAND FARMS *D-1
David & Vicki Egger 621-3988
19818 NW Sauvie Isl. Rd, Portland 97231
Season: App. June 1-Sept.
Hours: 8-7, closed Sun. PICK YOUR OWN. Containers supplied or bring your own.
3 1/2 miles from bridge on Sauvie Island Rd, follow signs. Already picked produce available at our retail stand (The Berry Basket, #5).
Strawberries, raspberries, marionberries, peaches, blueberries.

53. SAUVIE ISLAND MARKET *D-1
Denny & Nancy Grande 621-3489
17100 NW Sauvie Island Rd, Portland 97231
Season: May to Nov 7.
Hours: 7 days a week 9-6:30. U-pick and ready-pick family-owned farm with fresh fruits, vegetables and u-cut flowers. Aug 17 Flower Festival. Oct activities include u-pick pumpkins, hayrides, animal barn & food.
Take Hwy 30 to Sauvie Island. Cross bridge and continue straight ahead 1 1/2 miles.
Strawberries (June), raspberries, marions, boysens, blues, apricots, peaches, pears, apples, asparagus, beans, beets, broccoli, cauliflower, carrots, corn, cukes, dill, garlic, herbs, onions, melons, peppers, tomatoes, potatoes, pumpkins, winter squash & u-cut flowers: tulips Apr; peonies May.

54. SERRES FARM *F-4
Dan & Pattie Serres 655-0938
14620 S. Forsythe Rd, Oregon City 97045
Bedding plants season: Apr-June. Hours: 10-6. Produce season: Aug-Oct. Hours: 8:30-6:30.
PLEASE NO PETS.
Take Park Place exit #10 off I-205, turn left at 1st light, Clackamas River Dr. to Forsythe Rd turn right, follow signs.
U-pick beans, tomatoes. Ready-picked beans, tomatoes, pickling cukes, corn, dill, carrots, potatoes, onions, garlic, Bell/hot peppers, beets, zucchini, winter squash. Fresh fruits: peaches, apples, pears, prunes, plums. Basil by order.

55. SIMANTEL'S FARM/NURSERY B-2
Marcus & Marilyn Simantel 648-0925
31665 NW Scotch Church Rd
Hillsboro, 97124
Season: Open year round.
Hours: Mon-Fri 8-6; Sat 9-5; Sun 11-5.
1 mile south of the Sunset Hwy (US 26). Take exit 57 (Glencoe Rd).
Fruits & veggies in season, fresh cut and dried flowers, perennials, annuals, herbs, bulbs, shrubs & trees. Hazelnuts, walnuts, gift packs. Christmas greens and wreaths. Shipping available.

56. SMITH BERRY BARN *C-4
Ralph & Sue Smith 628-2172
24500 SW Scholls Ferry Rd, Hillsboro 97123
Season: May 23-Dec 21. Hours: May-Aug, 9-7; Sept-Oct, 9-6:30; closed Sun. Christmas season Nov-Dec. Call for hours. U-pick, ready-pick, produce stand. Bring containers, or we furnish. Apple Festival Oct 18.
Scholls Ferry Rd 10 miles SW of Washington Square in Scholls.
Raspberries, boysenberries, marionberries, cukes, corn, tomatoes, table and juice grapes, Bartlett & Asian pears, varietal apples, many other fruits, vegetables and nuts, honey, jam & more. Handcrafts at The Barn Boutique.

**57. SUNRISE BERRIES
LARSON BLUEBERRY FARM** H-3
Peter D. Moldovan 695-2756
1428 SE Christensen Rd, Corbett 97019
Season: June 25-Sept 10.
Hours: 8-6, closed Sun.
Ready pick or order, farm stand.
From Crown Point Hwy in Springdale, take right on Northway 1/2 mile and right on Christensen Rd 1/2 mile. Follow signs.
Blueberries.

58. SUNSHOWER ORCHARD *B-3
Ted & Beth Schlapfer 357-6423
5010 SW Hergert, Cornelius, 97113
Season: Aug.-Dec. Hours: Call ahead.
Organic (Tilth Certified), U-pick, we-pick, bring containers.
From Cornelius, go south on 10th Ave to Blooming Fernhill Rd. Turn right to blinker, left on Hergert Rd, 200 yeds.
Apples (12 varieties), Noble & Grand fir Christmas trees.

59. THOMPSON FARMS *G-4
Larry & Betty Thompson 667-9138
24727 SE Bohna Park Rd, Boring 97009
Season: June-July, Sept-Oct. Hours: 8-6, closed Tue. U-pick, ready-picked farm produce stand. We grow it! Please call for daily updates.
5 miles south of Gresham on SE 242nd or 1 mile north Hwy 212 on SE 242nd.
Strawberries, raspberries, blues, marion, boysen, pumpkins, fall produce & decor.

60. TOMLIS FARM *C-3
Tom & Lissa Radomski 640-0885
4950 SW Minter Bridge Rd, Hillsboro 97123
Season: June-Sept. Hours: days & hours depend on crop availability. Call ahead.
TV Hwy, 2 miles south on Minter Bridge, 1st driveway on left after bridge.
Blackberries, blackcaps, summer & fall raspberries, sweet cherries (ready-pick only), jam, syrup & honey.

61. TRAPOLD FARMS (THE BARN) *F-2
253-5103
5211 NE 148th Av, Portland, 97230
Season: June-Dec. Hours: 9-6, closed Sun.
Food stamps welcome.
Strawberries, raspberries, honey, salad vegetables, tomatoes, carrots, sweet corn, pickling cukes, spices, jars, vinegar, salt, everything to make pickles, evern recipes. Green and shell beans, potatoes, cabbage, broccoli, cauliflower, Brussels sprouts, summer and winter squash, fruit in season, U-pick strawberries, eggplant, peppers, peas, tomatoes, flowers. Pumpkings available to large and small groups, free hayrides on weekends.

62. VAN BUREN FARMS *G-2, F-2, G-3
253-7459 Office / 252-7102 info
301 NE 148th Av, Portland, 97230
Season: June-July. Hours: call info line
Bring containers.
Strawberries, raspberries (u-pick at 147th & Sandy), Logans, cascades, marions, Fairview raspberries, boysens, blackcaps (u-pick at 6300 SE 190th Dr.)

63. VANCIL-POLEHN FARM *G-5
Lois & Annette Vancil 631-2311
19594 S. Redland Rd, Oregon City 97045
Season: late Aug-Dec. Hours: open all year
Visit our 95 year old family farm. Bring containers.
I-205 to exit 10, right to Redland Rd, from signal 7 miles on right (2 miles past Fisher Mill Rd).
U-pick Bartlett pears (late Aug); Italian, Brooks prunes (Sept), Brooks dried prunes (year round), Noble fir Christmas trees (Nov-Dec), nursery stock.

64. WEST UNION GARDENS *C-2
Jeff & Cheryl Boden 645-1592
7775 NW Cornelius Pass Rd
Hillsboro, 97124
Season: June-Sept.
Hours: Mon-Fri 8-8; Sat 8-5; closed Sun.
After Labor Day, open 8-5 Mon-Sat. Our farm stand is full of fresh wholesome berries and vegetables. U-pickers and children welcome in the berry fields.
Close and easy to find, 1.7 miles north of Sunset Hwy (26) on Corneluis Pass Rd.
Hood strawberries, summer & fall raspberries, boysenberries, blackberries (early & late), marionberries, loganberries, tayberries, gooseberries, Roma/canning tomatoes, basil, garlic, flowers and lots more.

Hood River County

Hood River Fruit Loop

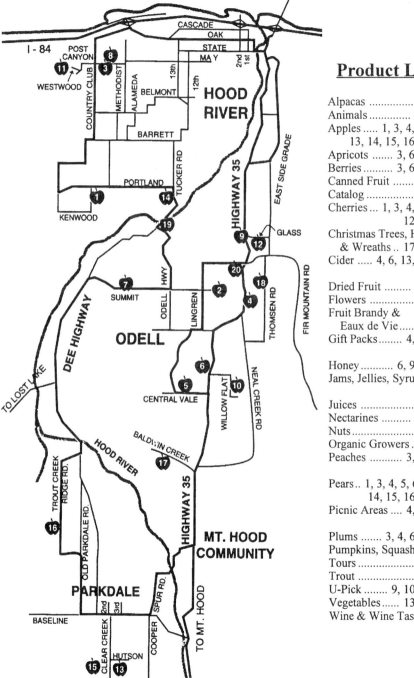

Product Listing

Alpacas 2
Animals 2, 9, 15, 19
Apples 1, 3, 4, 5, 6, 9, 10, 13, 14, 15, 16, 18, 19, 20
Apricots 3, 6, 18, 19, 20
Berries 3, 6, 18, 19, 20
Canned Fruit 5, 19
Catalog 19
Cherries ... 1, 3, 4, 5, 6, 9, 10, 12, 18, 19, 20
Christmas Trees, Holly & Wreaths .. 17, 18, 19, 20
Cider 4, 6, 13, 14, 15, 16, 18, 19, 20
Dried Fruit 5, 6, 19, 20
Flowers 6, 18, 19
Fruit Brandy & Eaux de Vie 7
Gift Packs 4, 5, 6, 9, 18, 19, 20
Honey 6, 9, 14, 19, 20
Jams, Jellies, Syrups 6, 9, 18, 19, 20
Juices 5, 6
Nectarines 3, 6, 10, 20
Nuts 6, 19, 20
Organic Growers 5, 19
Peaches 3, 4, 5, 6, 18, 19, 20
Pears .. 1, 3, 4, 5, 6, 9, 10, 13, 14, 15, 16, 18, 19, 20
Picnic Areas 4, 7, 8, 9, 11, 12, 17, 19
Plums 3, 4, 6, 16, 19, 20
Pumpkins, Squash .. 4, 13, 18
Tours 5, 7, 9, 19
Trout 17
U-Pick 9, 10, 12, 18, 19
Vegetables 13, 18, 19, 20
Wine & Wine Tasting .. 8, 11

Credit: Hood River Grower-Shipper Association

HARVEST SEASON

JUNE	**Strawberries**	June 15-25
JULY	**Cherries**	July 4-25
	Apricots	July 15-25
AUGUST	*PEACHES*	
	Red Haven	Aug 5-15
	Alberta	Aug 15-30
	PEARS	
	Bartlett	Aug 15-Sept 10
	APPLES	
	Gravenstein	Aug 10-Sept 10
SEPTEMBER	*PEARS*	
	Anjous	Sept 15-Nov 1
	Bosc	Sept 15-Nov 1
	APPLES	
	Golden Delicious	Sept 15-Oct 1
	Red Delicious	Sept 15-Oct 1
OCTOBER	**Newtown Pippin**	Oct 1-Nov 15

Dates may vary depending upon weather.

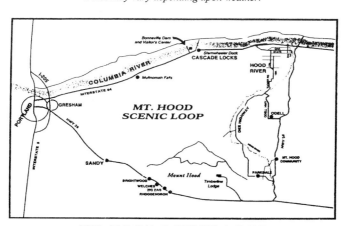

MT. HOOD SCENIC LOOP

For spectacular scenery any time of the year, you will enjoy traveling the loop around beautiful Mt. Hood. Whether you start at Hood River, Sandy or Gresham, you are sure to experience a trip of a lifetime.

Members' Listings

1 A & J ENTERPRISE
4600 Kenwood   541-386-1974
July 1-Nov 30; 7am-6pm daily
PEARS: Anjou, Asian, Bartlett, Bosc, Comice, Red Anjou, Stark Crimson. CHERRIES: Bing, Lambert, Rainier, Van. APPLES: Golden Delicious, Gravenstein, McIntosh, Pippin, Red Delicious.

2 ALPACAS of DOUBLE DUTCH FARMS
3057 Lingren Road   541-354-6262
March 1-Dec 1; 11am-4pm Mon-Sat.
Appointments appreciated.
The DeGroot family invites you to join them for a tour of their beautiful ranch. Alpacas... the earth friendly farm animal. Personality, poise and easy care, Alpacas are mainly used for their fleece, which is known for its cashmere-like feel, superb strength and warmth. Double Dutch Farms is proud to have both types of Alpaca breeds in their herd: the Suri, which has a lustrous fine fibre (in a dreadlock fashion); and the Luacaya, which is known for its crimp or wavy quality that enhances its use in spinning. Come up the hill for a visit and see why Alpacas are the huggable investment.

3 BERRY BRIER
4257 Post Canyon Drive   541-386-5920
June-Sept; 8am-9pm daily.
Phone orders accepted to reserve available fruit.
BERRIES: Strawberries, Raspberries, Tayberries, Marions, Blueberries, Katada Blackberries. APRICOTS: Tomcots, Rivals, Tiltons. CHERRIES: Bing, Lamberts, Rainiers. PEACHES: Red Havens, Hale Havens, Elbertas, Hales, Early Glows, HaleBertas. APPLES: Gravenstein, Red Delicious, Yellow Delicious, Winesap. PEARS: Bartletts, Yellow, Red. Nectarines, Plums, Tomatoes, Corn.

4 BLUE CHIP FARM
3187 Hwy 35   541-354-5858
July-Oct; 10am-6pm daily
Cider, picnic area, gift baskets. APPLES: Red Delicious, Golden Delicious, Rome Beauty, Gala, Jonagold, Gravenstein, Pippin, Lodi. PEARS: Anjou, Comice, Bartlett, Asian. Cherries, Plums, Peaches, Pumpkins.

5 COLUMBIA GORGE ORGANIC FRUIT
3610 Central Vale Rd   541-354-1066
July 20-April 1; 8am-5pm, Mon-Sat.
Organic grower, tours welcome, packing house. APPLES: Empire, Golden Delicious, Granny Smith, Pippin, Red Delicious, Jonagold, Liberty. CHERRIES: Lambert, Van, Sam's. PEARS: Stark Crimson, Red Bartlett, Anjou, Asian, Bartlett, Red Anjou, Bosc, Comice. PEACHES: Fair Haven, Red Haven. CANNED FRUIT: apricots, cherries, pears, peaches. JUICES: fresh apple, apple-pear, apple-pear-cherry, pear juice concentrate. Dried fruit and gift packs, compost.

6 COUNTRY FAIRE FRUIT MKT
3900 Hwy 35   541-354-1189
May-Nov; 9:30am-6pm daily.
Fresh fruit & vegetable juice daily, old fashioned ice cream. APPLES: Lodi, Early Gold, Gravenstein, Golden Delicious, Gala, Red Delicious, Striped Delicious, McIntosh, Spartan, Pippin, Rome, Winter Banana. PEARS: Bartlett, Red Bartlett, Stark Crimson, Red Anjou, Green Anjou, Red Comice, Green Comice, Bosc, Neil's, Flemish Beauty, The Ugly Pear, Asian. CHERRIES: Bing, Lambert, Van, Chinook, Lappan, Royal Ann, Rainier, Pie Cherries. APRICOTS: Tilton, More Park. PEACHES: Early Red Haven, Red Haven, Blushing Glory, Sun Crest, Rosa, Hail, Elberta. NECTARINES: Fantasia, Flavor Top. Blueberries, blackberries, marionberries, raspberries, cider, dried fruit, honey, jams, jellies, syrups, nuts, plums, gift packs, flowers.

7 EVE ATKINS DISTILLING CO./ MARICHELLE BRANDY TASTING ROOM & ORCHARD
4420 Summit Dr   541-354-2550
May 1-Oct 31; 11am-5pm daily.
Closed Sun & legal holidays.
Tasting room in 1868 historical post and bean building. See our European-type fruit brandy distillery in operation (one of a handful in America). Tours upon request. Free tasting of fruit eaux de vie: Pear, Cherry, Blueberry and Marionberry. Taste the only estate-bottled, four year old, barrel-aged Apple Brandy made in this country. We are an official state liquor agent, so purchases of our products are available here. Picnic area, public restrooms. Walk through our orchards of antique variety apples.

8 FLERCHINGER VINEYARDS, WINERY & TASTING ROOM
4200 Post Canyon   541-386-2828
Free wine tasting daily, 11am-5pm.
Enjoy great mountain views, covered patio and picnic area. Winery features Merlot, Chardonnay, Cabernet Sauvignon and Riesling.

9 THE FRUIT BARN AT WY'EAST ORCHARDS
Highway 35 & Glass Drive   541-386-1223
June-Nov
Seasonal fruit sold in a landmark barn. Tours welcome. FREE samples of fruit and food products. Limited U-pick available, pond, picnic tables, good views of Mt. Hood and the valley. Assorted farm animals including pot-bellied pigs, angora pygmy and "Pygora" goats, chicks and ducks. We ship our fruit gift packs, honey, jams and jellies.

10 HILL TOP RANCH
4425 Willow Flat Road   541-354-1854
Call ahead for times & availability. U-pick.
APPLES: Red Delicious, Gala, Fuji, Elstar, Empire. CHERRIES: Vans, Lamberts & Rainiers. PEARS: Stark Crimson. Nectarines.

11 HOOD RIVER VINEYARDS
4693 Westwood Drive   541-386-3772
Mar-Nov; daily 11am-5pm.
Family-run vineyard and winery featuring a broad selection of premium Oregon wines. Free wine tasting, picnic facilities, view.

12 KISS ORCHARD
2791 Glass Drive   541-386-3360
June 15 thru season; 7am-Sunset daily.
CHERRIES: Bing, Black Republican, Lambert, Rainier, Royal Ann, Van. U-pick also, picnic area with restroom.

13 KIYOKAWA ORCHARDS
8129 Clear Creek Road   541-352-7115
Sept 14-Nov 15; 10am-Sunset daily.
APPLES: Golden Delicious, Red Delicious, Jonagold, Pippin, Gravensteins, Gala, Mutsu, Fuji, McIntosh, Empire, Braeburn, Hanner, Red Rome, Elstar. PEARS: Asian (5 varieties), Bartlett (Red & Green), Bosc, Seckel, Stark Crimson, Cascade. VEGETABLES: Potatoes (Yukon Gold & Red), Cauliflower, Onions, Carrots, Broccoli and Garlic. Pumpkins and Squash (Danish, Butternut, Spaghetti), Cider, shipping available.

14 McCURDY FARMS
2080 Tucker Road   541-386-2628
Aug 15-Nov 15; daily.
APPLES: Golden Delicious, Granny Smith, Red Delicious, Gravenstein, Jonathan, McIntosh, Pippin, Red Rome, Rome Beauty, Winesap, Winter Banana, Criterion, Empire, Adane, Mutsu, Fuji, Gala, Jonagold, Spartan. PEARS: Anjou, Asian, Bartlett, Bosc, Flemish Beauty, Red Comice, Canal Red. Cider made from our own apples. Honey and beeswax candles. Harvest baskets.

15 MERZ ORCHARDS, INC.
8160 Clear Creek Road   541-352-6066
Sept 15-Nov 15; 9am-Dark, daily.
Cider, watch while being made daily. APPLES: Golden Delicious, Gravenstein, McIntosh, Red Delicious, Red Rome, Spitzenberg, Winter Banana. PEARS: Anjou, Bartlett, Bosc. Animals can be fed and petted.

16 MT. VIEW ORCHARDS FRUITSTAND
    541-352-6554
6670 Trout Creek Rd   800-529-6554
Sept 20-Nov 10; 9am-5pm daily.
APPLES: Golden Delicious, Red Delicious, Jonagold, Newtown-Pippin, Granny Smith, Gravensteins, Gala, Fuji, McIntosh, Braeburn, Jonathan, Spitzenburg, etc. PEARS: Red & Green Anjou, Bartlett, Bosc, Comice. PRUNES: Italian. Fresh cider, free samples of a well-blended juice.

17 PHOENIX PHARMS FISH & FLORA
4349 Baldwin Creek Rd   541-352-6090
Apr-Oct; 10am-5:30pm
U-Catch trout. Call about our private party facilities. Bring a picnic lunch and enjoy this tranquil setting with a majestic view of Mt. Hood. Great activity for kids of all ages. No license or equipment required. Wheelchair accessible. Natural Christmas trees.

18 RASMUSSEN FARMS
3020 Thomsen Rd.   541-386-4622
Follow blue state signs, turn east on Fir Mtn. Rd.--a scenic mile off Hwy 35.
Apr 1-Dec 23; 9am-6pm, open daily.
Valley's original in farm marketing since 1963. U-cut flowers. Ready & U-pick vegetables, herbs, pumpkins. Ready picked berries, cherries, pie cherries, apricots, peaches, pears, apples (over 20 kinds, sampling too!), cider. FLOWERS: annuals, hanging baskets, perennials, deck planters. Evergreen wreaths, holly and Oregon food products. We ship fruit gift packs. Trial flower & herb gardens mid-July to frost. Home of "Pumpkin Funland"™, Rasmussen's Pear Party.

19 RIVER BEND FARM & COUNTRY STORE
2363 Tucker Rd   541-386-8766
Mar 1-June 30; Tue-Sun 9am-5pm
July 1-Dec 24; daily 9am-5pm
Huckleberry milkshakes, homemade fruit pies and cobblers. Licensed canning kitchen. Free sampling of products made in our kitchen. U-cut flowers; 20 varieties of sunflowers, tulips, sweet peas and more. Honey, jams, jellies, syrups, dried fruits & nuts, cider, seasonal fruit and produce (organic and conventional). Baby animals, picnic tables and tent for groups. Free catalog.

20 SMILEY'S RED BARN
Hwy 35 & Ehrck Hill Rd   541-386-9121
June-Dec 23; 10am-6pm daily.
APPLES: Braeburn, Early Gold, Gala, Golden Delicious, Granny Smith, Gravenstein, Jonagold, Jonathan, McIntosh, Pippin, Red Delicious, Red Rome, Spartan Spitzenburg. PEARS: Anjou, Asian, Bartlett, Bosc, Cascade, Comice, Forelle, Red Bartlett, Stark Crimson. Apricots, berries, cherries, grapes, melons, nectarines, peaches, plums. Cider, dried fruit, nuts, gift packs, honey, jams, syrups, wreaths & Christmas trees.

Linn County

Linn County Mid Valley Growers Map

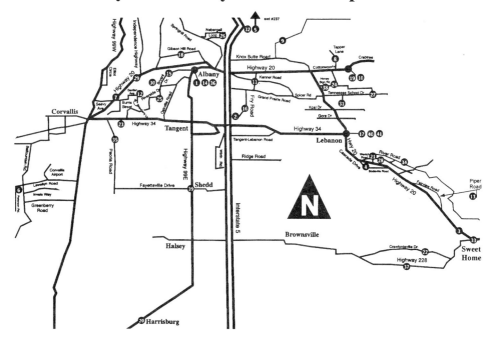

WHO HAS IT?

Apples: 3, 10, 12, 34, 40
Apple Cider: 3
Beans: 4, 12, 24, 28, 37, 40
Blackberries: 5, 6, 7, 10, 13, 15, 30
Blueberries: 23
Broccoli: 12, 28
Cabbage: 28, 37
Cauliflower: 12, 28
Chestnuts: 34
Corn: 4, 9, 11, 12, 28
Cornstalks: 19, 40
Cucumbers: 4, 11, 12, 17, 23, 37
Fresh Eggs: 38
Farm Equipment: 14, 36
Fertilizer/Manure: 2, 32, 36
Firewood: 26
Flowers (fresh, dried, edible): 1, 11, 16, 17, 20, 29, 31, 33, 36, 38, 39, 40, 41
Garlic: 39
Gifts: 20, 36, 38
Gourds: 38
Home Baked Goodies: 20, 31
Honey: 18
Horse Boarding: 32
Indian Corn: 19, 26
Jams & Jellies: 38
Marionberries: 24
Melons: 17, 24
Nectarines: 10
Onions: 12, 20
Peaches: 10, 40
Pears: 12, 40
Peas: 20, 28, 37
Peppers: 4, 17, 19, 20, 23, 28, 37, 40
Plants: 1, 11, 16, 17, 20, 29, 31, 33, 36, 37, 41
Plums/Prunes: 28, 40
Potatoes: 13
Pumpkins: 11, 13, 19, 23, 26, 37, 38, 40
Raspberries: 8, 20, 23, 27, 40
Squash: 12, 23, 24, 37, 40
Strawberries: 12, 13, 21, 22, 23, 25, 35, 40
Sunflowers: 19
Tomatoes: 4, 9, 11, 17, 19, 20, 23, 24, 29, 37, 40
Misc. Produce: 16, 20, 37, 38

WHEN CAN I GET IT?

Apples .... July thru Nov
Apple Cider .... Sept thru Nov
Beans .... July thru Aug
Beets .... mid-June thru Sept
Blueberries .... late June thru early Oct
Boysenberries .... July
Broccoli .... July thru Oct
Brussels sprouts .... Aug thru Dec
Cabbage .... July thru Oct
Carrots .... July thru early Nov
Cauliflower .... July thru Nov
Cherries (Sweet/Pie) .... late June thru July
Corn .... Aug thru early Oct
Crab Apples .... early Aug thru early Sept
Cucumbers .... late July thru late Sept
Currants .... late June thru late July
Dill .... mid-July thru early Sept
Evergreen Blackberries .. mid-Sept thru mid-Oct
Filberts .... late Sept thru Nov
Flowers .... June thru Nov
Gooseberries .... June
Gourds .... Oct thru Nov
Grapes .... Sept thru Oct
Honey .... Aug thru Nov
Lettuce .... June thru Aug
Loganberries .... late June thru mid-July

Credit: ©*Courtesy of Albany Democrat-Herald Growers Guide*

Marionberries	July thru mid-Aug
Melons	early Aug thru Sept
Nectarines	Aug
Onion/Garlic	Sept thru Oct
Peaches	mid-July thru early Sept
Pears	Aug thru early Oct
Peas	late June thru early Aug
Peppers	mid-Aug thru mid-Oct
Plums & Prunes	late July thru Sept
Potatoes	late July thru Nov
Pumpkins	Oct thru Nov
Raspberries	June thru July & Sept thru Oct
Rhubarb	early June
Squash	mid-July thru mid-Nov
Strawberries	June thru mid-July
Tomatoes	mid-July thru mid-Oct
Walnuts	mid-Oct thru Nov

CALL AHEAD--RIPENING OF PRODUCE CAN CHANGE DUE TO WEATHER!

FARM LISTINGS

1. Adair Floralscaping & Nursery
Wide variety of fuschias, exotic cactus, bedding plants, herbs, vegetables, perennials, houseplants, flower and shrub decoration and much more.
1240 First Ave, E. Albany **541-967-1200**

2. Altstock Poultry
Chicken manure fertilizer. Excellent for garden. Expect great results! $5/yard. We load, U-haul & some delivery available.
Three Lakes Rd & Seven Mile Ln **541-926-2880**

3. Antique Apple Orchard, Inc.
Over 150 varieties of apples available Aug-Mar. Cider pressing on 1913 Mt. Gilead Press (1st Sat in Oct, 9am, 11am & 1pm). Apple tasting & tours by appointment after Sept 15. From Albany, Hwy 20 E 24.9 m, 1st drive on left past mill.
28095 Santiam Hwy, Sweet Home **541-367-4840**

4. Bartman's Fresh U/We Pick Produce
Open daily until dusk. Containers provided. Blue Lake Pole Beans, hot & mild peppers, pickling cukes, sweet corn, tomatoes, etc.
1665 Cascade Dr, Lebanon **541-258-7347**

5. Bliesner's Berry Farm
Beautiful Benton & Totem Strawberries (June); U-pick/picked. Big & tasty Blueberries (July); picked only. Extra clean fields. Just off I-5 North. Dever-Conner exit #239. Follow signs. **541-926-1042**

6. Blueberry Bottom
U-pick or we-pick Blueberries, open daily late June thru Aug. Call to order. From Corvallis, go south on Hwy 99W, turn west on Llewellyn, turn left on Peterson Rd.
30699 Peterson Rd. **541-929-4625**

7. Blueberry Meadows
U-pick and picked. Our containers or yours. 9 varieties of Blueberries. Call for availability. Open 8am-7pm, 7 days a week from late June-late Aug. Ample parking and restroom.
3860 NE Hwy 20 (north of Conifer) **541-753-2614**

8. Childer's Berries
July. U-pick or picked Raspberries.
7 days a week, 7am-6pm.
36242 Tapper Lane **541-926-7478**

9. Clover Ridge Farms
Corn & Tomatoes. U/we-pick, orders. 8 delicious varieties of tomatoes & e awesome varieties of corn. Only a short mile from Timberlinn Park! Easy access to fields. Orders & info: **541-928-9386**

10. Couey's Summer Fruits
Blueberries, nectarines, peaches, summer apples. U-pick or orders beginning in July. Call for availability. 1/2 mile east of Hwy 20 at Cottonwoods,
36483 Hwy 226 SE, Albany **541-928-8778**

11. Cox Creek Garden & Nursery
Hanging plants ready now! Delicious corn, lemon cukes, tomatoes & pumpkins. U-pick or we-pick in season. Lean locker beef, $1.35/lb., includes kill, cut & wrap. East of I-5 off Grand Prairie Rd,
35500 Kennel Rd SE **541-926-7500**

12. Drahnacres Farm
U-pick strawberries, Asian pears, apples. Also available at our farm-produce stand: sweet corn, broccoli, cauliflower, cucumbers, squash, onions, green beans. Hwy 20 to Garden Av, 1.7 miles to:
2481 Strawberry Ln, Corvallis **541-754-6731**
or **541-758-9101**

13. Ewings U-pick Farms
Strawberries & Blueberries, Pumpkins & Red Potatoes in fall. Call for availability. Take Hwy 20 from Lebanon, 8 miles, left on Fairview, right on Piper Ln.
40494 Piper Lane   541-367-3942

14. Fisher Implement Co.
Mon-Sat, 8am-5pm. "Nothing runs like a Deere."
1920 Pacific Blvd   541-926-1534

15. Fitchett's Blueberries
U-pick & picked blueberries grown on the banks of the Willamette River. One mile west of Bryant Park, follow the signs.
31359 Bryant Way SW, Albany   541-928-8583

16. Fry Road Garden & Nursery
Bedding plants, hanging baskets, gallon shrubs, perennials. Also fresh garden produce July-Nov. Open Mon-Fri 10am-6pm; Sat 9am-6pm; Sun 2pm-6pm.
34989 Fry Rd SE, Albany   541-928-7038

17. Garrett Farms
Call for U-pick availability; 4 varieties of Peppers, 9 varieties of Tomatoes, 6 varieties of Melons, 4 varieties of Cucumbers. Vegetable and flower starts. Wholesale prices available. See me every Sat at Saturday Market, Elks parking lot.   541-259-2434

18. Gibson Hill Honey Farm
HONEY: Clover, Vetch & Mountain Flower. Extracted, pure raw honey. Bring your own containers. In business 25 years. Off Hwy 20, 1 mile up N. Albany Rd, to Gibson Hill Rd.
1033 Gibson Hill NW   541-928-7924

19. Grandpa's Pumpkin Patch
Different varieties of Sweetcorn, Tomatoes, Bell Peppers and a large variety of Salsa Peppers. All kinds and sizes of Pumpkins, Indian Corn, Sunflowers and Cornstalks.
36533 Hwy 226, Albany   541-928-2540

21. Heritage Farm
STRAWBERRIES: U-PICK. Sweet varieties for canning, desserts or fresh eating! Bring your own containers. Mon-Sat 8am-8pm. Take Hwy 20 1 mile south past Walmart. Left on Weirich, 1 mile to:
38355 Weirich Dr.   541-259-3971

22. J&S Strawberries
U-pick or we-pick. Beautiful new clean fields. Starts approximately June 1. Four miles south of Sweet Home on Hwy 228. Go 1 mile West to:
39834 Crawfordsville Dr   541-367-2353

23. Jim's Fruit Stand
Growers of strawberries, raspberries, tomatoes, cucumbers, peppers, squash and pumpkins. Most are organically grown.
29342 Hwy 34, Corvallis   541-757-1231

24. Joseph Heidt Farm
Boysens, Marions & Thornless Blackberries, Cantaloupe, spear melon, pole beans, tomatoes, summer squash, and other garden produce. Call first. Bring containers.
1 mile east of Honey Sign.   541-451-2770

25. Karsten's Old Farm
Sue's U-pick Strawberries. U-pick .50/lb., picked $1/lb. From Albany, west on Riverside Dr, right on Sellmacher, take the only gravel road to the right off Stellmacher.   541-928-5556

26. Kenagy's Family Farm
U-pick strawberries, firewood, all year, pumpkins & Indian corn in the fall. Hwy 20 west turn on Nebergall Loop, about 1 mile to farm.
1640 Nebergall Lp   541-926-8038

27. L & F Farms
Black Raspberries or Black Caps, U-pick. Corner of Honey Sign Drive:
35195 Tennessee Rd   541-451-5562

28. McAllister's
June: Sugar Pod Peas & early Broccoli, Cabbage & Cauliflower. July, Aug, Sept: Tomatoes, Corn, Broccoli, Green Beans, Peppers (Hot, Bell & Anaheim) and Brooks Prunes.
38635 Weirich Dr   541-258-8884

29. The Posey Peddler
Individualized service to every customer & top quality plants! Unique varieties of bedding plants, perennials & hanging baskets. Between Albany & Corvallis: 3087 NW Hwy 20.

30. Roman's Blueberries
BLUEBERRIES: PICKED OR U-PICK. Start app. July 1st, 8am-dusk Mon-Sat; Sun 1pm-dusk.
35923 Bryant Dr. SW, Albany   541-928-7379

31. Roth's Nursery
Spring bedding plants, hanging baskets. Home baked goods (in licensed kitchen): cinnamon rolls, pies, cookies, breads, bars. Call for orders or pick up at Albany's Saturday Farmers' Market. Open 9am-dusk, Mon-Sat. 37140 Tennessee School Rd, Lebanon
541-451-2689

32. The Roddy Ranch
Free horse manure at all times. We load, U-haul. Full-care horse boarding at a quality, clean facility. 80'x200' covered indoor arena, outdoor arena, paddocks, restroom, 8 hot water washer rack. Quality paint horses for sale.   541-926-9987

33. Santiam Feed & Garden
Garden & patio plants plus huge selection of hanging baskets, color spots, roses, rhodies and trees. Premium potting soil too! Lots of parking, OPEN 8am-5:30pm Mon-Sat. Across from Post Office:
1244 Long St, Sweet Home　　　**541-367-5134**

34. Santiam Orchards
APPLES: (Aug) Gravensteins; (Sept) Gala, Jonagold, Braeburn, Brock, Fuji. 14 varieties in all! Chestnuts (Oct). Closed Wed & Sun. Leave Hwy 20 at Russell Dr across from KFC, 2 miles on River Dr.
38102 River Dr., Lebanon　　　**541-258-7622**

35. Tami's Strawberries
U-pick, we-pick. Open 8am-6pm, Mon-Sat. Call for Sun availability. Phone orders taken.
31160 Peoria Rd.　　　**541-753-5676**

36. Tom's Garden Center
Tom's has it all: Fruit tree spray, flash tape, pea twine, soil thermometers, slug baits & more, plus all your favoite plants, trees and flowers.
410 SW Pacific Blvd, Albany　　　**541-928-2521**

37. Two Cylinder Acres
WE HAVE PRODUCE. Tomatoes, peas, beans, corn, squash, pumpkins, cabbage, cucumbers, peppers, herbs & many more vegetables! Bedding plants, flowers, all kinds. Between Holley & Crawfordsville,
39211 Hwy 228　　　**541-367-2549**

Marion County
Polk County
Yamhill County

Oregon Trail Farms

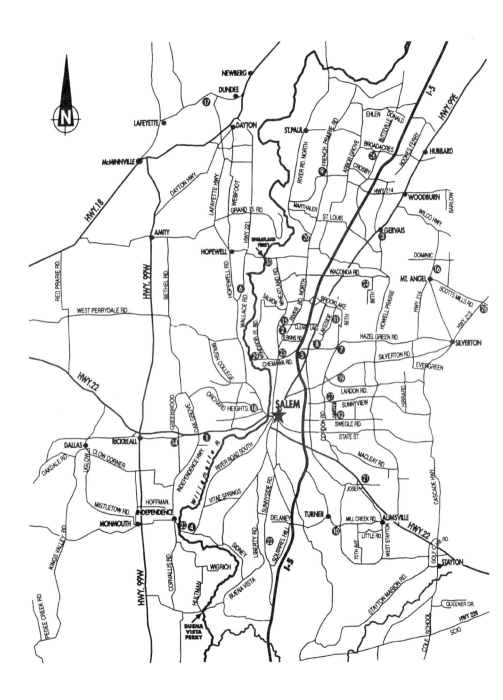

Oregon Trail Farms Direct Market Assn, 1417 Orchard Heights Rd. NW, Salem, 97304

PRODUCT REFERENCE GUIDE

Apple Cider: 3, 6, 7, 8, 17, 20
Apples: 1, 2, 3, 6, 7, 10, 11, 14, 15, 16, 17, 18, 20, 21, 27, 29
Apricots: 2, 3, 8, 17
Asparagus: 7, 8, 14, 17
Beans: 3, 6, 7, 8, 9, 10, 12, 16, 17, 20, 21, 26, 29, 30
Beets: 3, 6, 10, 17, 20, 26, 30
Black Caps (Black Raspberries): 3, 7
Black Eyed Peas: 29
Blueberries: 3, 4, 5, 6, 7, 8, 9, 10, 16, 18, 19, 21, 25, 26, 27, 29
Boysenberries: 3, 4, 7, 8, 18, 20, 26
Brandywines: 3
Broccoli: 1, 3, 7, 8, 9, 10, 16, 17, 20, 26, 30
Brussels sprouts: 8, 26
Cabbage: 1, 3, 6, 7, 8, 9, 10, 16, 17, 20, 26, 30
Carrots: 3, 20, 26, 30
Cauliflower: 1, 3, 8, 9, 10, 16, 17, 20, 26, 30
Cherries: 1, 2, 3, 8, 15, 16, 18, 20, 21
Christmas Green Trees: 1, 8, 21, 22
Corn: 3, 6, 7, 8, 15, 16, 18, 20, 21
Crab Apples: 18
Cukes: 1, 3, 6, 7, 8, 9, 10, 11, 14, 16, 17, 20, 26, 30
Currants (Red): 3, 7, 18
Dill: 3, 6, 8, 16, 20, 30
Dried Fruit: 7, 8
Eggplant: 3, 7, 26
Evergreen Blackberries: 3, 16
Figs: 1
Flowers & Plants: 1, 3, 6, 8, 9, 10, 14, 16, 21, 24
Garlic: 3, 8, 9, 14, 16, 21, 29, 30
Gooseberries: 3, 7, 8, 18
Gourds (Decorative & Indian corn): 3, 6, 8, 9, 17, 20, 30
Grapes: 1, 2, 6, 8, 15, 18
Hazelnuts (Filberts): 1, 3, 7, 8, 17, 20, 21, 30
Herbs: 1, 9, 20
Honey: 3, 8, 16, 20, 21, 27
Jams & Jelly: 3, 7, 8, 17, 21, 27
Kohlarabi: 3
Kotata Berries: 3, 4, 7, 8, 26
Lettuce: 1, 3, 7, 8, 9, 10
Loganberries: 3, 7, 8, 16, 20
Marionberries: 3, 4, 7, 8, 12, 16, 18, 19, 20, 21, 26, 28, 30
Melons: 1, 6, 7, 9, 14, 17, 20, 26
Nectarines: 1, 2, 3, 18, 21, 29
Onions: 3, 6, 7, 8, 9, 20, 21, 24, 30
Peaches: 1, 2, 3, 6, 7, 8, 10, 14, 15, 16, 17, 18, 20, 31, 23, 29
Asian Pears: 2
Peas: 9, 16, 20, 26, 29, 30
Peppers: 3, 6, 7, 8, 9, 10, 11, 14, 16, 17, 20, 21, 26, 29, 30
Plums/Prunes: 1, 3, 6, 7, 8, 10, 14, 15, 16, 17, 18, 20, 21, 24, 29
Popcorn: 8
Potatoes: 3, 7, 8, 9, 20, 26, 29, 30
Pumpkins: 3, 6, 8, 9, 14, 16, 17, 20, 26, 30
Quince: 18
Raspberries: 3, 4, 5, 6, 7, 8, 9, 10, 12, 16, 18, 19, 20, 22, 25, 26, 28
Rhubarb: 3, 7, 8, 16, 17, 26
Shallots: 3
Spinach: 3, 10
Squash: 1, 3, 6, 8, 9, 10, 11, 14, 16, 17, 20, 21, 26, 29, 30
Strawberries: 3, 4, 6, 7, 8, 9, 10, 12, 14, 16, 17, 19, 26
Sylvan Berries: 3
Tayberries: 3
Tomatillas: 3
Tomatoes: 1, 3, 7, 8, 9, 10, 11, 12, 14, 16, 17, 20, 21, 26, 29, 30
Waldo Blackberries: 3
Walnuts: 1, 2, 3, 7, 8, 17, 18, 20, 30
Misc. Vegetables: 1, 20, 26, 30

PRODUCE AVAILABILITY CHART

Apples .... July thru Nov
Apple Cider .... Sept thru Nov
Beans .... July thru Aug
Beets .... mid-June thru Sept
Blueberries .... late June thru early Oct
Boysenberries .... July
Broccoli .... July thru Oct
Brussels sprouts .... Sept thru Dec
Cabbage .... July thru Oct
Carrots .... July thru early Nov
Cauliflower .... July thru Nov
Cherries (Sweet/Pie) .... late June thru July
Corn .... Aug thru early Oct
Crab Apples ...... early Aug thru early Sept
Cucumbers .... late July thru late Sept
Currants .... late June thru late July
Dill .... mid-July thru early Sept
Evergreen Blackberries mid-Sept thru mid-Oct
Filberts .... late Sept thru Nov
Flowers .... June thru Nov
Gooseberries .... June
Gourds .... Oct thru Nov
Grapes .... Sept thru Oct
Honey .... Aug thru Nov
Lettuce .... June thru Aug
Loganberries .... late June thru mid-July
Marionberries .... July thru mid-Aug
Melons .... early Aug thru Sept
Nectarines .... Aug
Onion/Garlic .... Sept thru Oct
Peaches .... mid-July thru early Sept
Pears .... Aug thru early Oct
Peas .... late June thru early Aug
Peppers .... mid-Aug thru mid-Oct
Plums & Prunes .... late July thru Sept
Potatoes .... late July thru Nov
Pumpkins .... Oct thru Nov
Raspberries June thru July & Sept thru Oct
Rhubarb .... early June
Squash .... mid-July thru mid-Nov
Strawberries .... June thru mid-July
Tomatoes .... mid-July thru mid-Oct
Walnuts .... mid-Oct thru Nov

CALL AHEAD--RIPENING OF PRODUCE CAN CHANGE DUE TO WEATHER!

Farm Trail Members' Listings

1. **ANDY'S FRUIT STAND**
   5152 Salem Dallas Hwy, Salem
   362-1363 - Ready Pick
   Jan-Dec, Mon-Sun; Jun-Nov, 8am-7pm
   Head west on Hwy 22 (toward Dallas). We're app. 5 miles west of Salem.
   Peaches, berries, cherries, nectarines, plums, prunes, apples, squash (summer & winter), grapes, figs, tomatoes, melons, cucumbers, walnuts, hazelnuts, cabbage, broccoli, cauliflower, lettuce, herbs & other vegetables. Bedding plants, hanging baskets, Christmas greens.

2. **BAHNSEN'S ORCHARD**
   1620 Clear Lake Rd NE, Keizer
   393-3533 - U-pick, ready pick, pick to order
   Jun-Nov, Mon-Sat 9-6; Sun 1-5
   North on River Rd through Keizer, turn left on Clear Lake Rd, 1/2 mile to stand on left. Call ahead and bring containers. We have containers available for a deposit.
   Cherries, pie cherries, peaches, apricots, nectarines, apples, pears, asian pears, grapes, walnuts.

3. **BAUMAN FARMS**
   12989 Howell Prairie Rd NE, Gervais
   792-3524 - Ready pick, pick to order
   Jun-Feb 9-6.
   Take 99E (Portland Rd) 2 miles north of Gervais (1 mile south of Woodburn) to Howell Prairie Rd. Go 1/2 mile to the stand. We grow our own and it's picked fresh every day.
   Strawberries, rhubarb, gooseberries, cherries, Aurora's raspberries, black caps, loganberries, red currants, blueberries, sylvans, tayberries, brandywines, boysenberries, kotata berries, marionberries, waldo berries, evergreen blackberries, apples, peaches, pears, plums, prunes, apricots, nectarines, lettuce, green beans, sweet & super sweet corn, broccoli, cauliflower, spinach, kohlarabi, tomatoes, tomatillas, cucumbers, dill, beets, carrots, squash, shallots, garlic, onions, cabbage, peppers, eggplant, potatoes (red, white, yellow), pumpkins, ornamental corns, gourds, pumpkin patch w/ hayrides, fresh pressed cider, walnuts, filberts, our own berry jams & syrups, dried fruit, honey, hanging baskets, cut or u-cut fresh flowers, brown eggs, and holiday gift packs.

4. **BLUE HERON FARM**
   7496 River Rd S, Salem
   838-0495 - U-pick, ready pick, pick to order
   June-July, Mon-Sat 10-6; Sun 12-4
   2 miles east of Independence Bridge or 8 miles out from Commercial St (in Salem) on South River Rd. About 1/2 mile from the second railroad underpass.
   Picked only: strawberries, kotata berries, boysenberries, blueberries. Picked or u-pick: red raspberries, marionberries.

5. **CONRAD-BROWN'S BERRIES**
   5343 Portland Rd NE, Salem
   393-8838 - U-pick, pick to order
   June 15-Aug. Call ahead for picking times and placing orders.
   2nd house south (toward Salem) on Hwy 99E from Chemawa-Hazel-Green intersection on West side of Hwy 99E (Portland Rd) OR 1/4 mile north of Lancaster - Portland Rd intersection.
   Raspberries: June 15-July 15. Blueberries: July 10-Sept 1

6. **DAUM'S PRODUCE**
   8801 Wallace Rd NW, Salem
   362-7246 - U-pick, ready pick, pick to order
   June-Nov, Mon-Sat 9-6; Sun 12-6 until late fall, then 9-dark.
   9 miles from Marion St. Bridge going North on Wallace Rd (Hwy 221) towards Dayton-McMinnville. Pumpkin Patch for schools and families. Please call ahead to arrange time for group visits. Custom Cider made. Bring containers for U-pick.
   Marionberries, peaches, apples, plums, grapes, prunes/plums, beans (green, Romano, yellow, Shelly), beets, squash (summer & winter), dill, cucumbers (slicing & pickling), corn (Jubilee & Super Sweet), Peppers (sweet, green red, hot, very hot), apple cider, pumpkins, gourds, corn stalks, straw, decorative corn. Flowers (picked & U-pick) at stand only. Raspberries, blueberries, pears, cabbage, melons, onions.

7. **E.Z. ORCHARDS FARM MARKET**
5504 Hazel Green Rd NE, Salem
393-1506 - Ready pick
Jan-Dec, Mon-Fri 9-6; Sat 9-5; closed Sun
2 miles east of I-5 Chemawa Rd Interchange or 1 mile E of 99E, corner of Hazel Green and north end of Cordon Rd. Picnic area.
Strawberries, raspberries, black caps, logan, kotata, blue, marion, boysen, gooseberries, currants, peaches (7 varieties), pears (3 varieties), apples (21 varieties), fresh squeezed cider, brooks prunes, lettuce, sweet corn, green beans, broccoli, cabbage, rhubarb, asparagus, onions, potatoes, walnuts, hazelnuts, dried fruit, watermelon, cantaloupe, tomatoes, peppers, eggplants, pickling cukes, preserves, NW gourmet food, fresh baked bread & pies.

8. **FOSTER FARMS FRUIT STAND AND CIDER MILL**
4993 Hazel Green Rd NE, Salem
393-2932 - U-pick, ready pick, pick to order
Jun-Oct, Mon-Sat 9-6; Sun 1-5
Nov-Dec, Mon-Sat 9-5:30
1 mile E of Portland Rd (Hwy 99E) on Hazel Green Rd. School Tours welcome. Call ahead. Food stamps accepted.
Summer fun! Fresh fruit shortcakes, shakes, and drinks. Bedding plants & flower baskets. Asparagus, rhubarb, strawberries, raspberries, blueberries, boysen, logan, kotata, marionberries, gooseberries, sweet cherries, peaches, pears, apricots, grapes, prunes, broccoli, sweet corn, tomatoes, peppers, green beans, onions, garlic, pickling cukes, dill, Brussels sprouts, cabbage, cauliflower, lettuce, potatoes, squash, dried flowers, popcorn, pumpkins, gourds, Indian corn, fresh pressed apple cider (with cider viewing room), filberts, walnuts, honey, jams, syrups, dried fruit, gift packs, Christmas trees, wreaths, and holly. Gift items.

9. **FRENCH PRAIRIE GARDENS**
17673 French Prairie Rd, St. Paul
633-8445 - Ready pick, pick to order
Apr-May, Mon-Sat 10-6; Sun noon-5
June-Oct, Mon-Sat 9-7; Sun noon-5
From I-5, take Woodburn Exit, go W about 5 miles. Turn right on Hwy 219, go 1/4 mile & turn left on French Prairie Rd. Our market is on the left (white building with a red roof). Petting zoo, Pumpkin patch, tours by appointment. 121 year old historical home.
Bedding plants, hanging baskets, beans, blueberries, broccoli, cabbage, cauliflower, corn, cucumbers, garlic, herbs, lettuce, melons, onions, peas, peppers, potatoes, pumpkins, raspberries, strawberries, squash, tomatoes, zucchini, dried flowers, u-cut flowers, gourds, Indian corn & wreaths.

10. **GRANDPA'S GARDEN**
6100 block of Mill Creek Rd, Turner
Ready pick, pick to order.
June-Aug: Tue-Fri 10-6; Sat 10-4
Sept: Fri 10-6; Sat 10-4
1/2 mile E of Turner at the intersection of Mill Creek Rd and Marion Rd.
Flowers, lettuce, summer squash, tomatoes, cucumbers, bush beans, beets, corn, cabbage, peppers, broccoli, cauliflower, spinach, apples, plums, pears, strawberries, raspberries, blueberries, peaches.

11. **ED HARRIS FARM**
7816 Lakeside Dr NE, Brooks
393-6970 - U-pick, ready pick, pick to order
July-Sept: Mon-Sat, call before coming out
From Hwy 99E in Brooks, go E .8 miles to Lakeside Dr NE. Take a right on Lakeside. Go .7 miles to Ed Harris farm.
At stand: tomatoes, bell peppers, hot peppers, cukes, corn, apples, pears, zucchini, winter squash. U-pick: tomatoes, cukes, bell and hot peppers.

12. **BRET HAURY FARMS**
1660 Hampton Ln NE, Salem
364-2388 - U-pick, ready pick, pick to order
June-Oct, Mon-Sat 7-7
From Center St, go N on Cordon Rd 1/2 mile to Swegle Rd. Turn E, go 1/2 mile to Hampton Lane. Bring containers.
Strawberries, raspberries, marionberries. U-pick only: pole beans, sweet corn, tomatoes.

14. **HEWITT'S GREENWOOD GARDENS**
525 Greenwood Rd S, Independence
838-0276 - U-pick, ready pick, pick to order
Mar-Nov: Mon-Sat 9-7
7 1/2 miles W of Salem, off Hwy 22 on Greenwood Rd. between Oak Knoll Golf Course and Rickreall Dairy. Watch for the signs. Not all items are U-pick. Please bring containers and call ahead for day to day specialties and availability. Families & children are welcome. Please, no pets. Picnic area and small petting zoo (parental supervision required).
Asparagus, strawberries, tomatoes, peppers, cucumbers, corn, melons (all types), garlic, apples, peaches, prunes, pumpkins, squash, etc. Bedding plants/vegetables starts also available. All natural face & body soaps (made here on our farm). Various herbal blends, scented or not.

15. RICK JOHNSON FARM
1585 Clear Lake Rd, Keizer
393-0859 - U-pick, ready pick, pick to order
Jun-Jan: Mon-Sat 8-7; Sun 1-5
Out Wheatland Rd (2 1/2 miles north of McNary Golf Course), turn right on Clear Lake Rd. Go 1/2 mile, farm on North side of road.
At stand: cherries, peaches, and apples. U-pick: cherries (black & Royal Ann), peaches, apples, grapes, plums.

16. KRAEMER'S CORNER CROPS & GARDEN CENTER
13318 Dominic Rd NE, Mt. Angel
845-2860 - Ready pick, pick to order
June 1-Oct 1: Mon-Sun 10-5
1 mile north of Mt. Angel on the corner of Hwy 214 and Dominic Rd. Used grocery bags welcome.
Strawberries, blueberries, marionberries, evergreen blackberries, peaches, pears, apples, raspberries, cherries, rhubarb, loganberries, corn, broccoli, cabbage, squash, prunes, tomatoes, beans, cucumber, dill, peppers, pumpkins, cauliflower, honey, onions, garlic, peas, zucchini, dried flowers, pies. Garden center now open. Nursery stock, perennials, herbs, bedding plants, hanging baskets, etc.

17. LAUBE ORCHARDS
18400 N. Hwy 99W, Dayton
864-2672 - Ready pick, pick to order
Jan-Dec: Mon-Sun 9-7
On Hwy 99W between Lafayette & Dundee (Big Red Barn). Look for blue signs.
Rhubarb, asparagus, strawberries, peaches, pears, apples, melons, tomatoes, cucumbers, peppers, squash, broccoli, cauliflower, beans, corn, apricots, beets, pumpkins, decorative gourds, plums, prunes, walnuts, hazelnuts, apple cider. We also do jam & syrups plus gift baskets. made to order (UPS available) are fruit baskets and corporate gift baskets.

18. LINDBECKS FRUIT FARM
1417 Orchard Heights Rd NW, Salem
581-1855 - U-pick, ready pick, pick to order
June 15-Oct: Tue-Sat 9-5:30
West Salem, 3/4 mile from Wallace Rd on Orchard Hts Rd. First house on right past Orchard Hts Park. Food stamps accepted.
Gooseberries, red currants, raspberries, blueberries, marionberries, boysenberries, cherries, peaches, nectarines, apples, crabapples, pears, prunes, quince, grapes, u-pick walnuts.

19. NANNEMAN FARMS
5682 Silverton Rd NE, Salem
362-6070 - Ready pick, pick to order
June-July: Mon-Sat 7:30-6
1 mile East of Cordon Rd on Silverton Rd. Please bring containers.
Strawberries, raspberries, blackberries, blueberries.

20. D.A. NUSOM ORCHARDS
13501 River Rd NE, Gervais
393-6980 / Toll free 800-728-6980
U-pick, ready pick, pick to order
June 17-Sept 15: Mon-Sun 9-6
Sept 16-Nov 23: Tue-Sun 11-5
8 miles North of Keizer on River Rd, North. Call ahead. Please bring containers. Food stamps accepted.
Cherries (Royal Anne, Bing, Lambert, pie), peaches, pears (Barletts, Bosc, Comice), apples (summer & winter), prunes, walnuts, hazelnuts, dried prunes, blueberries, raspberries, loganberries, marionberries, boysenberries, corn, tomatoes, beans, cucumbers, cauliflower, broccoli, peppers, onions, squash, pumpkins, potatoes, misc. vegetables, honey, apple cider, beets, carrots, dill herbs, gourds, lettuce, melons, peas.

21. OLSON PEACHES
6925 Joseph St SE, Salem
362-5942 - U-pick, ready pick, pick to order
July 15-Sept 15: Mon-Fri 9-7; Sat 9-6; Sun 11-7
Please bring containers. Call ahead for U-picking dates. Not all items available for U-pick. 4 miles E of I-5 on Hwy 22 at the Joseph St. Exit.
Peaches, nectarines, pears, apples, prunes (fresh & dried), plums, blueberries, caneberries, cherries, tomatoes, corn, onions, garlic, squash, beans, flowers (fresh & dried), peppers, jams, jellies, honey, filberts, Christmas items, holly, garlands, door swags, centerpieces, wreaths (holly & Noble fir), candy canes, & misc. Shipping available.

22. RASPBERRIES BY "LUCI"
7986 Sunnyside Rd SE, Salem
364-6360 - U-pick, pick to order
June 22-July 15/Aug 25-Oct 5:
Mon-Sun 7-dusk.
I-5 to Sunnyside-Turner Rd (exit 248). Go West on Delaney Rd. to Sunnyside Rd. Turn left 1/3 mile. See sign. OR take South Commercial to Sunnyside Rd, then 4 miles South on Sunnyside to Farm. See sign. No chemical sprays used.
Raspberries (summer & fall varieties). Christmas trees, U-cut in Dec.

23. **SCHINDLER FARMS**
    South River Rd, Salem
    No Phone - U-pick only
    Mid-July-Sept 10: Mon-Sun 8-5
Take South River Rd from Salem 1 1/4 mile before Independence Bridge. On right side of road. Big sign. Check current ads in Statesman Journal newpaper. Please bring containers.
Peaches: Sun Haven, Sun Hi, Red Haven, Sun Crest, and improved Elberta. Nectarines.

24. **SCHLETCHTER FARMS, INC.**
    10143 86th Av NE, Salem
    792-3328 - Ready pick, pick to order
    Aug-Sept: Mon-Sun 7-7.
Northeast of Brooks. From Salem take I-5 to exit 263. Right on Brooklake Rd to 99E. North on Hwy 99 to Waconda Rd. East on Waconda to 86th Av. Right on 86th to second house on right. Follow signs. Please call for availability.
Super sweet corn (yellow, white), Brooks plums, onions, flowers (fresh & dried).

25. **SCHMERBER FARM & NURSERY**
    3310 Perkins St NE, Salem
    393-8911 - U-pick, ready pick, pick to order
    Late June-Aug: Mon-Sat 8-7; Sun 12-6
2 miles north of Keizer on River Rd. Turn east on Perkins 1 mile. On south side of road. if large quantity is needed, please call ahead for availability.
Blueberries, raspberries.

26. **SONNEN FARM**
    8644 Broadacres Rd NE, Aurora
    982-0351 / 678-2031
    U-pick, ready pick, pick to order.
    June-Oct: Mon-Fri 9-6; Sat 10-5;
    closed Sun
Take I-5 south to Woodburn exit. Turn left on Hwy 219. Go 1 mile to Bradacres-Donald turnoff & follwo signs to Broadacres. Used paper grocery bags welcome. Food stamps ok. Free hay maze in Oct. School, church & club groups welcome in Oct by appt.
Strawberries, rhubarb, peas, kotata blackberries, marionberries, boysenberries, blueberries, fall raspberries, beans, carrots, cauliflower, peppers, eggplant, melons, pickling cukes, tomatoes, sweet corn, zucchini, beets, cabbage, broccoli, Brussels sprouts, winter squash, pumpkins (mini to giant), potatoes, turnips, parsnips.

27. **SUNNYVIEW BLUEBERRIES & GOURMET FOODS**
    5233 Sunnyview NE, Salem
    364-3881 - U-pick, ready pick, pick to order
    July-Sept: Mon-Sat 6-7pm
From Lancaster Dr, turn East on Sunnyview to 1000 ft. beyond Cordon Rd. North side of road, watch for our signs. Bring your own containers or we have buckets, plastic liners for picking.
Blueberries, apples, honey, jams & jellies. Our "Gourmet Kitchen" opens June 1. Please try our: blueberry desserts, ice cream, cake, breads, sandwiches, soups & fruit juices all made in our new Agriculture Kitchen.

28. **TEENEY'S BERRY FARM**
    17458 Mt. Angel-Scotts Mills Rd, Silverton
    873-5187 - U-pick, ready pick, pick to order
    Please call for availability and hours.
4 miles north of Silverton (from Salem, take Silverton Rd through Silverton. Follow signs to Hwy213, 5 miles north of Silverton take right at 3rd yellow blinking light towards Scotts Mills. We are 1 mile on the right. Signs at the intersection.
Raspberries, marionberries.

29. **VEAL'S**
    5500 Windsor Islan NE, Keizer
    No phone - U-pick, ready pick, pick to order
    Early July-Nov: Mon-Sun 8-7
From River Rd, West on Lockhaven to Windsor Island Rd. Go north 150 feet to our stand.
At stand: apples, peaches, pears, plums, nectarines, blueberries, garlic, corn, tomatoes, potatoes, squash (summer & winter), peppers (sweet & hot), green beans. U-pick: beans, blackeyed peas, tomatoes, peppers (sweet & hot), cukes, pears.

30. **WHITE'S PRODUCE**
    11392 Wheatland Rd N, Gervais
    393-0753 - U-pick, ready pick, pick to order
    June 1-Dec 1: Mon-Sat 8-6; Sun 10-5.
1 1/2 mile north of intersection of Keizer Rd & Chemawa. Turn left on Wheatland Rd. Go 4 miles to White's sign. Angle left onto Mission Bottom 2 1/2 miles. Stand is on right. Bring containers. Not all U-picks. Call ahead.
Peas, berries, beets, corn, beans, cukes, dill, peppers (Bell & hot), tomatoes, squash, pumpkins, Indian corn, gourds, carrots, potatoes, onions, garlic, cabbage, broccoli, cauliflower, filberts, walnuts, & more. Most all fruits picked and ready at stand.

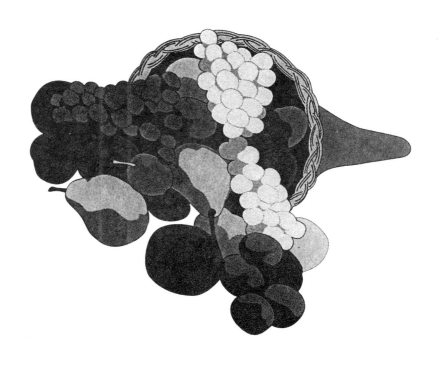

8775 NE. SILVERTON ROAD, SILVERTON (at Central Howell) 873-3421

COME SEE US! MARLI, KOREY & DARREL BROWN
OPEN 9:00 AM - 6:30 PM • 7 DAYS A WEEK

Areas for Oregon Farmers' Markets

Please use in conjunction with a commercial map.

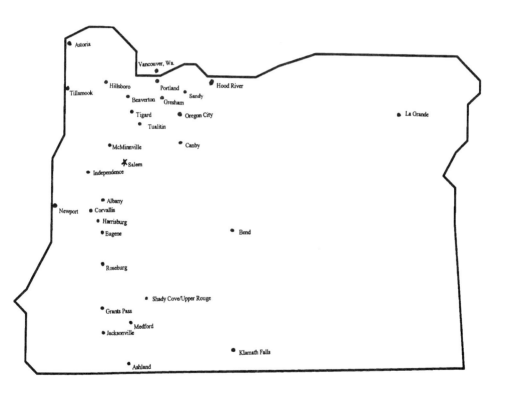

Oregon Farmers' Markets

ALBANY-CORVALLIS

Corvallis Farmers' Market
Riverfront Park "Blue Lot"
First Street between Jackson & Monroe
Sat 9am-1pm, thru Nov 22

ASHLAND-MEDFORD AREA

Rogue Valley Growers & Crafters Market
Ashland: Water St under Lithia/Siskiyou overpass, half-block north of plaza.
Tue 8:30am-1:30pm, thru Nov 4.
Medford: Medford Center parking lot outside Emporium, Stevens & Biddle Rd.
Thur 8:30am-1:30pm, thru July 10.
Jacksonville: Fourth & California Sts.
Sat 9am-2pm, thru Oct 25.

Upper Rogue Farmers Market
Hwy 62 & Mallory Rd. in Shady Cove
Fri 4pm-7:30pm, thru Sept 5.

ASTORIA

Astoria Farmers' Market
20th St and Marine Dr (next to museum)
Sat 9am-2pm, thru Oct 25.

BEAVERTON

Beaverton Farmers' Market
SW 5th St & Hall Blvd, behind fire station
Sat 8am-1:30pm thru Oct 25;
Wed 3pm-7pm, July 2-Sept 24.

Weekend Garden Market
Tri-Met Park & Ride,
NW Cornell & Bethany Rd at Hwy 26
(158th Av & Cornell, exit 65)
Sat 9am-3pm, thru Oct 25.

BEND

Bend Farmers' Market
Brooks St Riverfront Plaza at Mirror Pond, downtown Bend
Wed 5pm-8pm, July 2-Sept 24.

CANBY

Canby Growers' Market
First Av Carpark, corner of Holly & First
Sat 9am-1pm, thru Oct

EUGENE

Lane County Farmers' market
E Eighth & Oak St
Sat 9am-5pm thru Nov 22;
Tue 10am-4pm, July 1-mid Oct.

GRANTS PASS

Grants Pass Growers' Market
Corner of F & Fourth Sts
Sat 9am-1pm, thru Nov 15.

GRESHAM

Gresham Farmers' Market
Roberts Av between Thrid & Fifth Sts in downtown Gresham
Sat 8:30am-2pm, May 10-Oct 25.

HARRISBURG

Harrisburg Farmers' Market
255 Smith St, half block W of Hwy 99E
Wed 10am-2pm, May 14-Sept 10

HILLSBORO

Hillsboro Farmers' Market
NE First Av & Lincoln St
Sat 8am-1pm, thru Oct 25.

HOOD RIVER

Farmers in the Park
Corner of 13th & May Sts,
in front of Jackson Park
Sat 9am-2pm, thru Oct 25.

INDEPENDENCE

Independence Farmers' Market
Monmouth/Independence Chamber of
Commerce; Hwy 51 to downtown
Independence in Riverview Park
on the waterfornt, N of the boat ramp.
Sat 9am-1pm, thru Oct 11.

KLAMATH FALLS

Klamath Falls Saturday Market
No market this year.

LA GRANDE

Blue Mountain Producers Market
Front lawn of Sunflower Book Store,
1114 Washington Av
Sat 9am-noon, June-Sept
(may go later, depending on supply/weather)

McMINNVILLE

Farmers' Market at Wilco
Wilco parking lot, 2741 N. Hwy 99W
Sat 9am-Noon (or until sellout),
July 5-Sept 27.

MEDFORD

Rogue Valley Growers & Crafters Market
Medford Shopping Center parking lot
outside Sears
Thur 8:30am-1:30pm, thru end of Nov.

NEWPORT

Lincoln County Saturday Farmers' Market
Lincoln County Farigrounds in Newport,
next to high school
Sat 9am-noon, thru Oct 25.

PORTLAND

Hollywood Farmers' Market
Washington Mutual Parking Lot,
4333 NE Sandy Blvd
Sat 8am-1pm, May 31-Oct 11.

People's All Organic Farmers' Market
3029 SE 21st Av
Wed 2pm-7pm, until first hard frost.

Portland Farmers' Market
Albers Mill parking lot,
1200 NW Naito Pkwy
Sat 8am-1pm, thru Oct 25.

Portland Farmers' Market in Pioneer Courthouse Square
Wed 11am-3pm, July 2-Sept 24.

SANDY

Sandy Farmers' Market
Downtown Sandy on Hoffman Av, between
eastbound & westbound lanes of Hwy 26,
across from City Hall.
Sun 10am-3pm, June 1-Oct 26.

ROSEBURG

Douglas County Farmers' Market
Roseburg Valley Mall Bon Marche pkg lot,
Stewart Pkwy & Garden Valley Blvd
Sat 9am-1pm, May 17-Nov 1.

TIGARD

Tigard Farmers' Market
HealthFirst Med Clinic, Hall & Greenburg
Sat 8:30am-1:30pm, June 7-Oct 25.

TILLAMOOK

Beaver Farmers' Market
15 miles S of Tillamook on Hwy 101
by Beaver Mercantile
Daily 9am-6pm, thru Oct.

TUALATIN

Tualatin Lakeside Market
Tualatin Commons on the Lake fountains,
SW Nyberg & Seneca
Sat 9am-1pm, June 14-Oct 4.

VANCOUVER, WASHINGTON

Vancouver Farmers' Market
Fifth St. & Broadway
Sat 9am-3pm, thru Oct 25.

Travel Notes
OREGON

Date   **Place**   **Comments**

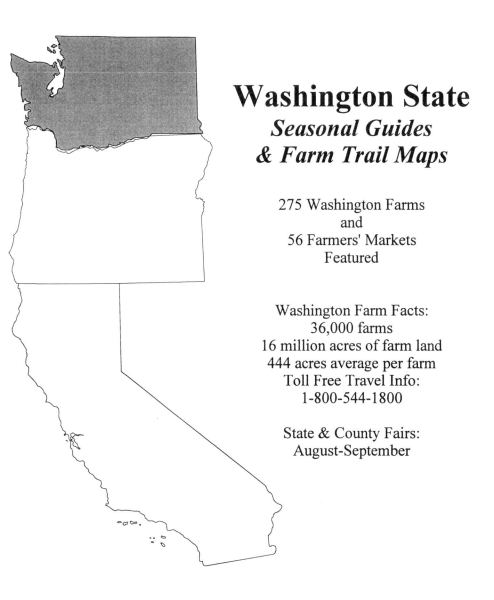

Washington State
Seasonal Guides & Farm Trail Maps

275 Washington Farms
and
56 Farmers' Markets
Featured

Washington Farm Facts:
36,000 farms
16 million acres of farm land
444 acres average per farm
Toll Free Travel Info:
1-800-544-1800

State & County Fairs:
August-September

Washington State has an agricultural industry which includes delicious varieties of apples, potatoes, pears and sweet cherries, as well as other numerous farm grown products. From Puget Sound near Seattle, to the beautiful Yakima Valley with its rich volcanic soil, to the other lush farm counties, Washington State has an abundant, productive agricultural base.

Source: 1995 World Almanac and Book of Facts, *Funk & Waganalls*

Bainbridge Island
Skagit County
Snohomish County

Vashon Island
Whatcom County
Whidbey Island

Northwest Washington Farms

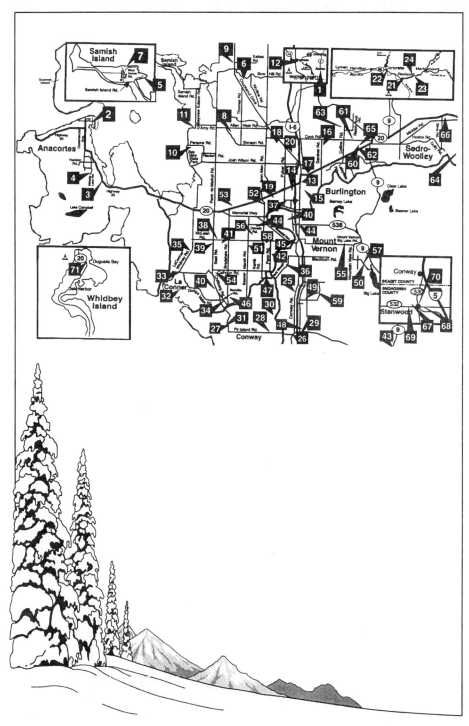

Credit: Skagit Valley Herald

Farm Listings

ACME

OLIVE'S HEARTH & HAVEN
Olive Curtis   360-595-2485
INFORMATION: For a $25 monthly fee, a delivery of fresh vegetables, herbs, flowers and plants is made to your home. Seasonal preserves and vinegars are also available and oucld substitute for unwanted fresh items. The delivery service is available until Oct 31.

1 TWIN SISTERS MUSHROOM FARM
Roger & Lynn Mairs   595-2979
5410 Saxon Rd, PO Box 173, Acme 98220
15 miles north of Sedro-Woolley on Hwy 9.
INFORMATION: Fresh mushrooms, growing kits, compost, marinated mushrooms, Shiitake, oyster and Portabella mushrooms. Open 8am-5pm, daily, year round. Free tours Sunday afternoons.

ANACORTES

2 DEPOT FARMERS' MARKET
Anacortes Arts Foundation   293-4803
Seventh St & R Av, Anacortes
Take exit 230 from I-5, travel west on SR20, 13 miles to Anacortes. Go Commercial Av north, turn right on Seventh St two blocks to R Av, at Burlington-Northern Train Depot.
INFORMATION: Organically grown produce from Mother Flight Farm; Skagit Rose Farm unique herbs, fresh flowers; Happy Valley Farms dried flowers; Cedar Spring jams, jellies, chutney, relishes; La Vie en Rose French bread; Christies baked goods, pastries, desserts, handcrafted clothes, toys, gifts. May 18-Oct 12, 10am-3pm Saturdays.

3 FOXGLOVE FARM
Sheryl Jones   293-8817
212 Ginnett Rd, Anacortes
I-5 to exit 230, west on Hwy 20 to Oak Harbor Junction, left 5 miles to Rosario Rd, right to Sharps Rd, right to Ginnett Rd, nursery on right.
INFORMATION: Herbs; Antique perennial flowers; native, woodland, "cottage garden" and shade plants; dried flowers; gift shop; display garden; picnic area. Open 10am-4pm Tus-Sun, April 1-Aug.

4 WHISTLE LAKE U-PICK
Sue Farnsworth   293-0146
1129 Whistle Lake Rd, Anacortes
INFORMATION: Carrots, green beans, beets, corn, squash, pumpkin, zucchini. All produce is grown organically, no chemicals used. U-pick, we pick. Bring container. Open 7-10am Sun-Fri, July-Oct. Call for availability and picking times.

BOW--BAY VIEW

5 ALICE'S GARDEN
Rousseau Family   766-6396
982 Scott Rd, Samish Island, Bow
Turn right on Scott Rd before billboard map.
INFORMATION: Rhubard (May-June), Herbs, oregano, rosemary, sage, tarragon, thyme, mint, chervil and parsley (June-Oct), yellow lily (June), yellow and purple plums (July-Aug), Asian pears (Aug-Sept), hops (Sept), French pumpkins (Oct). Organic garden at Alice Bay Bed and Breakfast harvested by Rousseau children. Roadside stand open 10am-4pm Thur-Sun, June-Oct.

6 ANDERSON BLUEBERRY FARM
Gus & Dorothy Anderson   766-6173
1360 Bow Hill Rd, Bow
From I-5, take exit 236, go west on Bow Hill Rd for 3 miles. Farm stand is on the left.
INFORMATION: Fresh blueberries July20-Aug. Blueberry jam, jelly, chutney, vinegars, gift items. We pick. Open 9am-5pm Mon-Fri; 9am-3pm Sat; closed Sun; mid-July-Aug.

7 BLAU OYSTER CO.
E.E. Blau & Sons   766-6171
919 Blue Heron Rd, Bow
On Samish Island, seven miles west of Edison via Bay View-Edison Rd & Samish Island Rd.
INFORMATION: Pacific oysters alive in the shell and freshly shucked and live Manila steamer clams, year round. Live Dungeness crab, Oct-Apr. Fresh whole-cooked northern shrimp (Apr-Oct). A selection of fresh and frozen seafoods including smoked salmon, butter clams, prawns, scallops and more--availability varies. Free ice with purchase; fresh products can be packed to travel or ship via UPS. Orders placed 24 hours in advance receive 10% discount off regular prices. We pick. 8am-5pm Mon-Sat; closed Sun & holidays. Open all year.

8   CONFORTI'S PRODUCE
Dan & Debbie Conforti   757-6310
943 Benson Rd, Bow
Chuckanut Dr north to Allen West Rd, turn left, app. 3 miles to Benson Rd, left at Benson.
INFORMATION: Apples: Gravenstein (late Aug); Chehalis & Sumered (Aug); Gala (Sept); Jonagold & Melrose (late Sept); sweet corn (mid-Aug); greenhouse tomatoes and peppers, misc. produce (July); U-cut sunflowers and misc. flowers (July); pumpkins, ornamental corn and gourds (late Sept-Oct). We pick. Open noon-6pm Wed-Sun, July 1-Oct 31.

8   DOC'S PRODUCE
Linora Dockter   766-6486
528 Chuckanut Dr, PO 134, Bow 98232
1,200 feet north of Bow Post Office; across from Estes Rd on left.
INFORMATION: Raspberries, beans, beets, carrots, corn, cucumbers, pumpkins, squash, pigs. All certified organic. We-pick. Bring container. Open 10am-6pm, 7 days a week from June 15 to Nov.

10   HIGHLANDS NORTHWEST
Roger & Marsha Pederson   757-4906
1032 Bay View Cem. Rd,
PO 245, Mt. Vernon 98273
Approximately 5 miles north of Farmhouse Restaurant on Hwy 20, just off Bayview-Edison Rd.
INFORMATION: Farm direct freezer beef. No hormones or antibiotics. Lean/flavorful grass-fed ranch beef (can grain on custom basis) from Highland cattle. Available by package, variety pack or beef halves, USDA inspected. Food stamps accepted. 10am-6pm Fri-Sun. By appointment year round.

11   MERRITT'S APPLES
Alan Merritt   766-6224
896 Bayveiw-Edison Rd, Mt. Vernon
2 miles north of Bayview State Park, exit 231 from I-5, west side of overpass take Wilson Rd to Bayview.
INFORMATION: Gravenstein (Aug-Sept); Jonagold (Sept-Christmas). Several other varieties, seasonal, call for information. Gift items, juice, jam, honey. We pick. Hours 9am-5pm. Tue-Sat, mid-Aug to Christmas.

BELLINGHAM

12   FARMERS' MARKET
Christine Porter   647-2060/800-487-2032
304 36th St #146, Bellingham, 98225
Corner of Railroad and Chestnut St, Bellingham
INFORMATION: Fresh flowers, corn and tomatoes in season, lettuce, spinach, herbs, berries, fresh fish, shell fish. Crafts. Specialty meats. Outdoor restaurants, music, entertainers, spinners, weavers, jewelers. Bakery goods. 3rd largest farmers' market in Washington. Festivals: Strawberry, June 15; Raspberry, July 27; Salmon & corn, Sept 14. Open 3-6:30pm Wed; 10am-3pm Sat thru Oct.

BURLINGTON

13   COUNTRY FARMS
Jay Waters Inc   755-0488
480 S. Burlington Blvd, Burlington
I-5 north, Burlington Exit, right at bottom of ramp, left on Burlington Blvd to Rio Vista.
INFORMATION: Full selection of freshest produce direct from farm to you. Vine ripe tomatoes, cantaloupes, watermelon, local grown asparagus in season through Nov. Local strawberries, Washington cherries (July 1), Walla Walla onions (mid-July), green beans, blueberries, corn, apricots, peaches, pickles, hot and mild peppers, nectarines, Gravensteins, apples, pears, carrots, hard squash, pumpkins, winter keeper potatoes, and onions. Christmas trees and wreaths, custom flocking. We pick. 7 days a week, Mar 28-Nov 4.

14   DELLINGER BERRY STAND
J.C. Dellinger   424-7583
AM/PM Holiday Mkt, Hwy 20, Burlington
INFORMATION: Strawberries. 9am-6pm.

15   DYNES BROADVIEW FARMS INC.
Bill & Chuck Dynes   757-4025
1146 S. Anacortes St., Burlington
INFORMATION: Farm fresh eggs, 15 dozen minimum, all sizes, double yolk, other specialties. Year round, 9am-3pm Mon-Fri.

16 GALBREATH MEAT PACKING
Jess & Martin Galbreath   757-0211
982 Gardner Rd, Burlington

Take I-5 Cook Rd exit 232, go east on Cook Rd 1 3/10 miles to Gardner Rd. Turn south on Gardner Rd, go 4/10 mile and down the lane.
INFORMATION: Gourmet steaks & roasts, extra lean hamburger, family packs, custom butchering, special orders cut as requested. FDA inspected for your family safety, quality grain fed beef. 8am-5pm weekdays; 8am-noon Sat; year round.

17 POTATO SHED
Norm Nelson   755-9319
605 Avon Av, PO 444, Burlington 98233

On Hwy 20 East.
INFORMATION: Reds, white rose, Yukon golds, purples. 9am-5pm Mon-Sat; after Thanksgiving 9am-1pm; mid-Sept through end of Feb.

18 SAKUMA BROS. FARMS
PO Box 427   757-1141
969 Chuckanut Dr, Burlington 98233

Corner of Chuckanut Dr & Cook Rd.
INFORMATION: Strawberries (June), Raspberries (July), Blueberries (mid-July thru Aug). Place orders at the stand. We pick. 9am-5pm Mon-Sat, June-Aug.

19 TLC SEAFOOD/RIEDEL FARMS
Wes & Lana Riedel   757-1757
1552 Hwy 20W, Burlington 98233

I-5 Exit 230 to San Juan Islands west on Hwy 20 one mile, bright blue building.
INFORMATION: Strawberries, raspberries, cherries (Jun-Jul); Blueberries, apricots, peaches, nectarines (Jul-Aug); Apples & pears (Sept). 10am-6pm 7 days a week, Mar-Oct.

20 WALLACE FARMS, INC.
George & Dick Wallace   757-0981
1/2 mile off I-5, Chuckanut Dr, Burlington

INFORMATION: Red, white, yellow and blue potatoes. Also red and yellow organic potatoes. We pick. 8am-5pm Mon-Fri, Aug-Apr.

CONCRETE-ROCKPORT

21 CASCADIAN FARM ROADSIDE STAND
Jim & Davida Meyer   853-8173
5375 Hwy 20, Rockport

Hwy 20, 3 miles east of Rockport milepost 100.
INFORMATION: Strawberries (3rd, 4th weeks June), Raspberries (Jul), Blueberries (mid-Jul to mid-Sept). All organically grown here on the farm. Homemade ice cream, berry shortcake, organic espresso, organic jams and pickles. Sweet corn (Aug-Sept), pumpkins and autumn decoration (Oct). Flowers, picnic tables, restrooms. U-pick, we pick. Bring contatiners. Call for availability. Open 8am-7pm daily, May 1-Oct 31.

22 CONCRETE SATURDAY MARKET
Skagit Cty Mkt Assn   853-8261
PO Box 174, Concrete 98237

Old train depot just off Hwy 20, signs posted.
INFORMATION: Produce in season, arts and crafts market (call to reserve table space, ask for Mary Killman). 9am-5pm Sat, May 18-Aug 31.

23 HIGHTOWER FARM
Lance & Ingeborg Hightower   873-2571
5570 Hwy 20, Rockport 98283

On Hwy 20, 4 miles east of Rockport, milepost 103.
INFORMATION: Piglets, grain fed, we raise or you raise (halves available); the parents are purebred Berkshire, Landrace, Duroc, and Hampshire pigs, selected for fast growth and lean meat. We have piglets off and on year round. Telephone calls encouraged for appointment and/or information.

24 THE OLD JOHNSON FARM
Russ & Tammy Johnson   853-8067
5341 Hwy 20, Rockport

Milepost 100, 3 miles east of Rockport.
INFORMATION: Organic raspberries and blueberries. We pick. 9am-5:30pm, every day, Jul-Aug.

CONWAY

25 CEDARDALE ORCHARDS
Larry & Sharon Johnson   445-5483
2099 Dike Rd, PO 594, Conway 98238
3 miles south of Mt. Vernon. Take Exit 221 from I-5, go north 3 miles on Conway Rd (west frontage rd)
INFORMATION: Apples: Gravenstein, Summer Rd, Jonamac, Akane, Spartan, Jonagold, Melrose, Gala (late Aug-Oct). Asian pears (mid-Sept-Oct). Cider. We pick. Open 10am-5:30pm daily, mid-Aug to late Oct.

26 CONWAY COUNTRY CORNER
Larry & Jessica Sande
Wayne & Pam Lindall   445-5508
1677 Fir Isl. Rd., PO 757, Conway 98238
From I-5, take exit 221. Drive W to Conway.
INFORMATION: Fresh fruit, vegetables, flowers, and seafood in season. Quality local crafts. Deli, espresso and ice cream cones. 9am-6pm daily, Mar-Oct.

27 FROG'S SONG FARM
Nate O'Neil & Michaelyn Bachhuber
2098 Dry Slough Rd, Mt. Vernon   445-3054
I-5 exit 221, through Conway and over South Fork Bridge, right on Dry Slough Rd to corner Fir Island.
INFORMATION: Spinach, lettuce, salad mix, arugula, radishes, sweet onions, Walla Walla onions, peas cabbage, cauliflower, broccoli, nursery stock, hanging fuschia baskets (May-Jun); artichokes, carrots, beets, cukes, early corn, basil, herbs, cut flowers, beans, onions, Kohlrabi, elephant garlic, bunching onions, cilantro, oriental greens; storage potatoes, onions, winter squash, dry beans, raspberries, bulk basil, late corn, cukes on farm, pumpkin sales (pie, canners, Atlantic giants 250lb.) (Sept-Oct). Many available throughout the season. We encourage home canners and others wanting winter storage goods to place orders early. Open 7 days, Apr-Oct. Snowgoose Produce, Sat at Mt. Vernon Farmers' Market.

28 HUGHES FARM, INC.
Hughes Family   445-4232
1517 Fir Island Rd, Mt. Vernon
One mile west of Conway on Fir Island Rd, exit 221 on I-5.
INFORMATION: Broccoli (Aug-Sept); five cukes, zucchini (in season); Brussels sprouts, winter cabbage, acorn squash, others, miniature pumpkins (Oct). We pick. Orders will be taken for freezing or canning. Hours are 9am-5:30pm 7 days a week, Aug-Dec, weather permitting.

29 KING CORN
Vic & Linda Benson   428-1990
1957 Kanako Ln, Mt. Venon 98273
East side of I-5 at Conway exit; near Texaco.
INFORMATION: Super-sweet jubilee sweet corn, fresh picked (early Aug-mid-Oct). We pick. Bring containers if convenient; 8 ears for $1. 9am-dusk daily mid-Aug to mid-Oct.

30 LARKSPUR FARM
Jan Johnson   445-2292
2076 Skagit City Rd, Mt. Vernon
I-5 exit 221, west through Conway to Fir Island, first right after bridge.
INFORMATION: Fresh cut flowers (mid-June-frost), dried flowers (mid-Jul-season). Flowers for special occasions, parties, reunions, weddings, etc., full service or your puchase by the bucket. We pick. Bring containers. Open 11am-5pm Thur-Sun or by appointment, June-frost.

31 SNOW GOOSE PRODUCE
Mike & Mary Louise Rust   445-6908
2010 Fir Island Rd, Mt. Vernon
Exit 221 west of Fir Island Rd, towards LaConner.
INFORMATION: Plants, asparagus, salad mix, lettuce, radishes (May); all the above plus strawberries (June); all above plus raspberries (July); peaches, pears, etc. (Aug); fresh seafood, great ice cream cones, new soup n' sandwich all season. We pick. 8am-sundown every day through Oct.

LA CONNER

32 BONSAI GROVE
Carolyn Higgins & Cindy Genther
6th & Morris, LaConner   466-2955
INFORMATION: Bonsai trees available Apr-Sept, part of Dec. Open 11am-5pm Fri-Sat; 1:30-5:30pm Sun.

33 **HEDLIN FARMS**
David Hedlin & Serena Campbell
1027 Valley Rd, Mt. Vernon   466-3977
Pioneer Memorial at entrance to La Conner.
INFORMATION: Strawberries (June 1), tomatoes (May 15), dahlias (Aug 1). We pick. 10am-6pm 7 days, May 15-Oct 1.

34 **PLEASANT RIDGE FARM**
David & Gayle Tjersland   466-3228
1920 Rexville Rd, Mt. Vernon
4 miles east of La Conner, off Chilberg Rd.
INFORMATION: Apples: Spartan, Akane & Jonagold. Flemish beauty pears. We pick. 9am-6pm 7 days, mid-Aug-Oct.

35 **SWANSON'S**
Dean & Jeff Swanson   424-6338
1350 Flats Rd, Mt. Vernon 98173
One mile north of La Connor off La Conner-Whitney Rd, turn west onto Flats Rd.
INFORMATION: Strawberries (Jun 15-Jul 15); raspberries (Jul 1-Jul 25); tayberries (Jul 1-Jul 25); loganberries (Jul 5-Jul 25); marion blackberries (Jul 15-Aug 10); Waldo & Katata blackberries (Jul 15-Aug 15); apples (Sept 5-Oct 31); cucumbers, carrots, green beans, potatoes, Patty Pan squash (Aug 1-30); corn (Aug 20-Oct 3). Visit our strawberry sampling garden! U-pick, we pick. Bring containers or use ours. Open 9am-6pm daily, June 15-Oct 31.

MOUNT VERNON

36 **BRITT SLOUGH ORCHARDS**
Matt & Gladys Hayden   336-5931
1720 Britt Slough Rd, Mt. Vernon 98273
1 mile south on Britt Slough Rd from end of Blackburn Rd.
INFORMATION: Asian pears (Sept-Oct) delivered in Mt. Vernon area with $20 minimum order, $1 lb. Some apples available. We pick. Open most days, call first, Sept-Oct.

37 **CARSTENS U-PICK**
Jim & Frances Carstens   428-5620
1342 Pulver Rd, Mt. Vernon 98257
From I-5 take George Hopper or McCorquedale Rd, 1 mile west from I-5 Auto World to Pulver Rd.
INFORMATION: Strawberries (Jun-Jul). U-pick, we pick. Bring containers. 8am-5pm daily, Jun-Jul 12.

38 **CHRISTENSEN BERRY FARMS**
Scott & Christine Christensen   424-3118
1251 McLean Rd, Mt. Vernon
McLean Rd between Bradshaw & Best, 4 miles west of Mt. Vernon.
INFORMATION: Raspberries, full/half flats and freezer containers (Jun 26), blueberries, full/half flats & freezer containers (Jul 10), wildlife farm, wild turkey, chukar partridge, pheasant exhibits. We pick. Open 10am-6pm 7 days, June 26-July 31.

39 **CHRISTIANSON'S NURSERY**
John & Toni Christianson   466-3821
1578 Best Road, Mt. Vernon
From Hwy 20 south on Best Rd, 2 miles.
INFORMATION: Flowers in season, fruit trees & berry shrubs, herbs & herbal topiaries, vegetable starts and tomatoes (Jun-Jul), roses & ornamental flowering trees & shrubs available all year, daffodil and tulip bulbs (Sept). Greenhouse open year round 9am-6pm daily.

40 **DELTA FARMS, INC.**
803 Bradshaw Rd, Mt. Vernon   424-3105
4 blocks north of Eagle Harward on Chilberg Rd.
INFORMATION: Strawberries (Jun 6-Jul 10), raspberries (Jul 10-Aug 15). Open 10am-6pm daily. We pick.

41 **GORDON BROTHERS PUMPKINS**
Todd & Eddie Gordon   424-7262
1360 McLean Rd, Mt. Vernon
INFORMATION: Pumpkins, all shapes, sizes & colors (Oct 1-31). Acorn, Hubbard, delicata squash, gourds, ornamental corn and stalks, apples. School and tour groups welcome. Wholesale and retail, large U-pick field, festive retail display area, also we pick. 9am-6pm 7 days a week, Oct 1-31.

42 **HARMONY HERBS**
James & Janet Pierce   424-3574
1434 Jungquist Rd, Mt. Vernon
West on McClean Rd to Kamb Rd, left to Jungquist, turn right.
INFORMATION: Sages, Greek oregano, thymes plants, various fresh cut basils. We will be open most days and weekends. We pick. Open noon-6pm Apr-Oct.

43 HOLLYBROOK FARM & LLAMA RANCH
Cliff & Patricia Skelton 445-5262
2302 Legge Rd, Mt. Vernon
Exit 221 from I-5, east on Conway Rd 5 miles to Hwy 9, south 1.5 miles to Legge Rd.
INFORMATION: Llamas, all ages & states of reproduction, pets, packers, guards, breeder. Fiber: raw, roving for spinning, batts for felting, yarn to knit or weave. Please call first for appointment. Open year round.

44 JARMIN'S ORCHARD
Marvin & Miriam Jarmin 424-6574
1486 Donnelly Rd, Mt. Vernon
West on Memorial Hwy to Avon Allen, left one block, right on Donnelly.
INFORMATION: Apples: Gala (Sept 5); Jonagold (Sept 15); fresh apple cider (Sept). We pick 9am-4pm. Mon-Sat through Dec.

45 KAPS COUNTRY MARKET
Mark Iverson 336-2722
619 S. Second St, Mt. Vernon
Pine Square
INFORMATION: All crops as they come into season. Arts & crafts, fresh seafood, landscaping materials. Open 9am-1:30pm Sat, Jun 1-Sept. Thursday night market: 4:30-7:30pm beginning in July.

46 LENNING FARMS
Todd & Bev Lenning 466-3675
1347 Summers Dr, Mt. Vernon
West on McLean Rd, left on Bradshaw to end, left 1/2 mile on left side.
INFORMATION: Pickling cucumbers (Aug 1-Sept 1), blueberries (Jul 22-Sept 1), sweet corn (Aug 26-Sept 13). Depending on weather. Call for special orders. We pick. Bring containers for cucumbers. Stand open noon-5pm, July 22-mid-Sept.

47 McMORAN FARMS POTATO WAREHOUSE
Mary & Don McMoran 424-1341
1270 McLean Rd, Mt. Vernon
Go west from Mt. Vernon to McLean Rd, left at Penn Road to Calhoun, left to road end.
INFORMATION: Red potatoes (Aug 1); Norkota potatoes (Sept 1). Packaged in 5-, 10-, 15-, 50-, and 100-pound packages. 8am-4:30pm Mon-Sat, Aug 1-Jul 4.

48 MIKE & JEAN'S BERRY FARM
Michael & Jean Youngquist 424-7220
1442 Jungquist Rd, Mt. Vernon 98273
Stands at: Shakey's parking lot, Riverside,; College Servu on E. College Way; BP station on Section St; farm at Jungquist & Kamb Rds.
INFORMATION: Strawberries (Jun 15-Jul 6), raspberries (June 1-Aug 1), blueberries (Jul), cucumbers (late Jul-Sept), cauliflower (mid Jul-mid Oct). We pick. 10am-5:30pm seven days during berry season. Farm open mid-June thru mid-Oct.

49 OLSON FARMS
Brian & Joanne Olson 428-3058
1739 Stackpole Rd, Mt. Vernon
South of Mt. Vernon to Stackpole Rd, east 1/2 mile to farm.
INFORMATION: Green beans (mid-Jun-summer), beets (2nd half Jul), carrots (mid-Jul-mid-Aug), dill (mid-Aug-mid-Sept), kiwi (Sept). Call ahead for we-pick orders. U-pick, we pick. Bring containers. Call before coming out. 9am-5pm Mon-Sat, mid-June through late Aug.

50 PERENNIAL PLACE
Virginia Beck 422-5003
2092 Mtn View Rd, Mt. Vernon 98273
South on Hwy 9 to Big Lake School, right on W. Big Lake Blvd, right on Mountain View Rd.
INFORMATION: Home-grown Perennials: iris, shasta daisy, Scabiosa, lychnis, day lily, many others. Cut flowers. You dig. 10am-6pm Thur-Sat, Jun-Sept.

51 ROOZENGAARDE
Roozen Family 424-3113
1587 Beaver Marsh Rd, Mt. Vernon
Go west of Mt. Vernon on McLean Rd to Beaver Marsh Rd. Take a left at Evergreen Grocery store and go 1/4 mile.
INFORMATION: Fresh flowers year round (will ship). Order bulbs through Aug 31 for fall delivery or fall pick-up in Oct. Buy bulbs at the store Sept-Nov (while supply lasts). Potted plants available most of the time (year round). We pick. Open Mon-Sat, June-Feb, 7 days a week Mar-May.

52 SCHREUDER'S SECRET GARDEN
Jerry & Doreen Schreuder 428-6788
1343 Avon Allen Rd, Mt. Vernon
4/10 mile south of Hwy 20 on Avon Allen Rd.
INFORMATION: Lettuce, broccoli, gourmet greens, beets, carrots, sugar snap peas, shelling peas, green beans, yellow beans, kohlrabi, sweet corn, Walla Walla onions, yellow onions, squash, potatoes, garlic, basil and flowers all in season. We pick. Open 9am-6pm daily except Thur afternoons & Sat, Jun-Aug.

53 SCHUH FARMS
Steve & Susan Schuh   424-6982
1353 Memorial Hwy, Mt. Vernon 98273
Go 3 miles west of Mt. Vernon on Memorial Hwy.
INFORMATION: Strawberries, raspberries, marionberries, blueberries, loganberries, tayberries. Rhubarb, cabbage, broccoli, cauliflower, summer & winter squash, green & yellow beans, corn, yellow and white carrots, herbs, cut flowers, cherries, sugar snap peas, honey, cucumbers, dill, pumpkins, kraut cabbage. Noble Christmas trees: Thanksgiving until sold out. We pick. Open 9am-7pm daily, Jun-Oct 31.

54 SKAGIT ROSE FARMS
Bob & Mary Rose   466-2564
1703 Best Rd, Mt. Vernon
INFORMATION: Fresh and dried flowers all summer. Basil (Jul 15-Oct 1), summer squash (Jul 15-Sept 1), winter squash (Oct 1), shallots, garlic (Aug 15). Northwest native bulbs as available. U-pick, we pick. 10am-6pm weekends or by appointment Jul 1-Oct 30.

55 SUMMERSUN GREENHOUSE CO.
Carl & Cheryl Loeb   424-1663
4100 E. College Way, Mt. Vernon
2 1/2 mile east off I-5 on E. College Way.
INFORMATION: Three-acre nursery & greenhouse, bedding plants, perennials, vegetable & herb starts, indoor foliage & supplies, containers & garden related gift items, annual poinsettia, gift certificates, festival and tours (Thanksgiving weekend). Perennial festival and tour in Sept at Fir Island location. Frequent seminars Mar-Jun, call for specifics. Fast gardening facts on Skagit Valley Herald InfoLine. Open 8:30am-5:00pm 7 days, spring & summer, all season.

56 TAYLOR'S
Bob & Mary Taylor   424-9192
1472 Dunbar Rd, Mt. Vernon
West of Avon Allen between Memorial Hwy & McLean Rd.
INFORMATION: Blueberries (Jul 24-Aug 31). Bushes available. U-pick, we pick. Call before coming.

57 TINGLEY FISH FARM
Marie Tingley   422-5492
2075 Mountain View Rd, Mt. Vernon
East on College Way to Hwy 9, right at Big Lake School, past Big Lake Fire Department, turn right on Mt. View Rd.
INFORMATION: Trout, you catch. Pay 25 cents an inch. No license required. Bring worms for bait. Open 8am-8pm 7 days, until July 5.

58 VAN DER VEEN DAIRY
Van der Veen Family   424-7892
1524 McLean Rd, Mt. Vernon 98273
1.5 miles west of Mt. Vernon, between Penn & Kamb Rds on McLean Rd.
INFORMATION: Yellow, white, super-sweet, and jubilee sweet corn grown under sustainable agriculture program using approved conservation plan. We-pick. Bring containers. Open 10am-7pm daily mid-Aug through late-Sept.

59 WALSER'S BLUEBERRY FARM
Herbert Walser   424-7856
1868 Stackpole Rd, Mt. Vernon
From I-5 take Anderson Rd exit, then south on Cedardale to Hickox. Go east of Hickox Rd. to Stackpole, south on Stackpole to farm.
INFORMATION: Blueberries (July 15-Sept 1). Gourmet blueberry & marionberry jams & syrups, chocolate covered blueberries, blueberry recipe cookbooks (call all year 757-0414) sold at stand. We pick. Call 424-0108 to pick up berries. Open 8am-4pm Mon-Fri, Jul 15-Sept 1.

SEDRO-WOOLLEY & UPPER RIVER

60 ANDERSON KIDS BERRIES
Jade & Skyler Anderson   856-0705
2079 Hwy 20, Sedro-Wooley
West at Trail Rd & State St intersection.
INFORMATION: Strawberries (June 10). Open 9:30 am until sold out through strawberry season. Stand is managed and owned by kids.

61 BORROWED EARTH
Dallas & LeAnne Trople   856-2922
1951A Cook Rd, Sedro-Woolley
Northeast corner of Cook & Collins Rds.
INFORMATION: Seasonal vegetables & fruits, including beans, peas, carrots, corn, multiple varieties of lettuce greens, and much more (Jun-Sept). Cut flowers and herbs. Organically grown. We pick. Open daily as crops allow Jun-Sept. Watch for signs.

62 DELLINGER BERRY STAND
J.C. Dellinger   424-7583
Hy-Stop Gas Station, Hwy 20, Sedro-Woolley.
INFORMATION: Strawberries now through end of season. 9am-6pm.

63 DUNWHEELIN FARM
Grace Haynes 856-6269
987 Collins Rd, Sedro-Woolley
Exit 232 off I-5, Cook Rd, right to Collins Rd, left on Collins, first driveway on left.
INFORMATION: Lettuce, onions, rhubarb, radishes, spinach. Carrots, beets, beans, corn, broccoli, cauliflower, cabbage, potatoes, tomatoes, peppers (seasonal). Fruit: apples, pears, etc. (in season). Peas (Jun 1). We pick. Open 8am-5pm Tue-Sun, until mid-Oct.

64 FINNEY CREEK FARM
Salmonberry Com. Land Trust 826-4004
4004 S. Skagit Hwy, Sedro-Woolley
App. five miles southwest of Concrete.
INFORMATION: Blueberries, no spray (Jul-Sept). Vegetables & flowers (June-Sept). Eggs & goat cheese available. U-pick, we pick. Bring containers. All day, 7 days weekly Jun-Sept.

65 KOOZER'S POULTRY FARM
HI Q COMPOST
Howard & Barbara Koozer 856-4770
2061 Hwy 20, Sedro-Woolley
1 mile east of United General Hospital on Hwy 20 directly opposite Rhodes Rd.
INFORMATION: Brown & white eggs, cured compost (year round). 9am-5pm Mon-Sat, except holidays.

66 PERKINS VARIETY APPLES
Tom, Sue & Jim Perkins 856-6986
816 Sims Rd, Sedro-Woolley
3 miles east of Sedro-Woolley off hwy 20.
INFORMATION: Apples: Gravenstein, Paulared, Sunrise (Aug); Okane, Jonamac, Gala, Elstar, pears (Sept); Jonagold, Melrose, Hawaii, Spartan, Bramley (Oct); Mutsu, Braeburn (Nov); Gift packs & winter keepers (Dec). Dozens of other varieties plus orchard honey & fresh apple cider. We pick. 1pm-6pm Wed-Fri; 8am-6pm Sat-Sun. Season Aug 10-Dec 31.

STANWOOD

67 ALBERT'S U-PICK/WE-PICK
Albert Partnership 629-4534
28627 Old Pacific Hwy, Stanwood 98292
Take Conway exit, south on 530 to Stanwood, right on Old Pacific Hwy 1 1/2 miles on left.
INFORMATION: Raspberries (Jun 24-Jul 31). U-pick, we pick. 8am-6pm, 7 days June 24-Aug 15.

68 BECKMANN FARM
Eric & Annie Beckmann 629-9369
26316 64th Av. NW, Stanwood 98292
Exit 212 off I-5, stand at southwest corner of 64th NW & SR 532.
INFORMATION: Flowers (Jul 2), snap peas (Jul 1), green beans, squash, cucumber (mid-July), corn (late Aug), garlic braids, shallot, sweet basil, carrots, beets. We pick. 9am-dusk Sun-Fri, Jul 1-Oct 31.

69 SCHUH FARMS
Steve & Susan Schuh 629-6455
State Hwy 532, Stanwood
West of the Cookies Mill on State Hwy 532.
INFORMATION: Strawberries, raspberries, marionberries, blueberries, loganberries, tayberries. Rhubarb, cabbage, broccoli, cauliflower, summer & winter squash, green & yellow beans, corn, yellow & white carrots, herbs, cut flowers, cherries, sugar snap peas, honey, cucumbers, dill, pumpkins, kraut cabbage. Noble Christmas trees (Thanksgiving until sold out). We pick. Open 9am-7pm daily, Jun-Oct 31.

70 STANWOOD FARMERS MARKET
PO Box 935, Stanwood 98292 652-6527
American Legion parking lot on 88th Av, across from Viking Village.
INFORMATION: Fresh produce, herbs, plants, native shrubs, flowers. Open 9am-2pm Saturdays, thru Oct 14.

WHIDBEY ISLAND

71 DUGUALLA BAY FARMS
Bob & Carolyn Hulbert Jr. 679-2192
5 E. Frostad, Oak Harbor
3 miles south of Deception Pass Bridge.
INFORMATION: U-pick strawberries (Jun-Jul), u-pick raspberries (Jul-Sept), blueberries (Jul-Aug), corn (Sept), U-pick pumpkins (Oct(, fresh cider (Aug-Oct). Also featuring fresh jams & local honey, ice cream cones, dried/fresh-cut flowers, Northwest gift items. Open 9am-7pm 7 days a week, Jun 1-Oct 31.

King County North
King County South
Skagit County

Snohomish County
Pierce County
Vashon Island

Puget Sound Farm Fresh Map

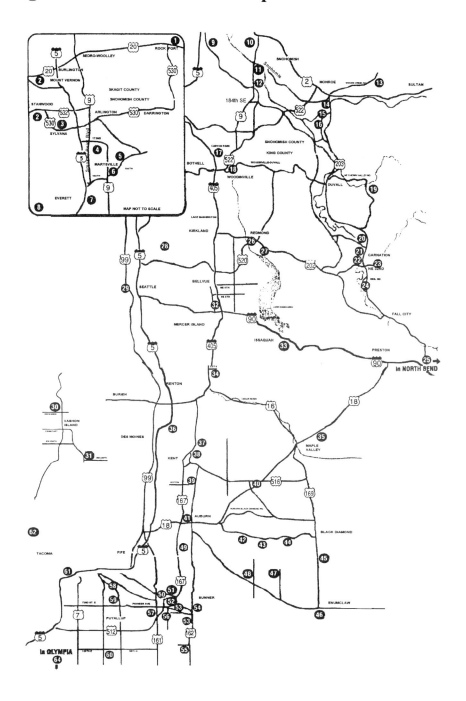

Products Reference Guide

Apples: 2, 17, 24, 31, 42, 45, 48, 50, 52, 58, 59
Apricots: 31
Beans Green: 1, 2, 5, 14, 16, 23, 31, 36, 37, 42, 45, 48, 50, 51, 55, 58, 59
Beans Shell: 36
Beans Yellow Wax: 2, 36, 45
Bedding Plants (Annuals): 2, 5, 23, 31, 37, 40, 42, 45, 48, 51, 55
Bedding Plants (Baskets): 2, 5, 23, 31, 37, 40, 42, 45, 48, 51, 55
Bedding Plants (Perennials): 2, 5, 6, 23, 31, 37, 40, 45, 48, 51, 55
Beef: 20, 60
Beets: 1, 2, 5, 12, 23, 31, 36, 37, 42, 45, 48, 51
Blackberries: 14, 37, 42, 45, 48, 50, 53, 54, 58, 59
Blueberries: 1, 2, 5, 6, 9, 10, 13, 14, 23, 32, 34, 37, 42, 45, 48, 50, 55, 56, 59
Boysenberries: 2, 23, 36, 45, 48, 50, 53, 59
Broccoli: 1, 2, 5, 16, 23, 31, 36, 37, 42, 45, 48, 50, 51, 58
Brussels sprouts: 2, 23, 37, 48
Bulbs/Tubers: 23, 37
Cabbage: 2, 5, 23, 31, 36, 37, 42, 45, 48, 50
Canning Supplies: 2
Carrots: 1, 2, 5, 14, 16, 23, 24, 31, 36, 37, 42, 45, 48, 50, 51, 58
Cauliflower: 2, 5, 16, 23, 24, 31, 36, 37, 42, 45, 48, 50
Celery: 23, 37, 45, 48, 50
Cherries (pie): 31, 42, 54
Cherries (sweet): 23, 31, 42
Chinese Vegetables: 1, 2, 31, 37, 42, 51
Cider: 23, 24, 58
Corn: 1, 2, 5, 12, 14, 16, 23, 24, 31, 36, 37, 42, 45, 48, 50, 51, 55, 58, 59
Christmas Trees: 2, 7, 23, 27, 37, 40, 50
Wreaths: 2, 7, 23, 27, 37, 50
Cucumbers: 1, 2, 5, 14, 23, 31, 37, 42, 45, 48, 50, 51, 59
Currants (Black): 59
Currants (Red): 6, 48, 59
Dairy Products: 23, 50
Dill: 2, 5, 12, 14, 23, 24, 31, 36, 37, 40, 45, 48, 50
Eastern WA Fruit: 2, 5, 23, 37, 42, 45, 48, 50, 55, 59
Eastern WA Vegetables: 5, 23, 37, 45, 48, 50, 55, 59
Eggs: 16, 23, 24, 37, 45, 48, 50, 54, 58, 60
Farmer's Markets: 3, 8, 11, 18, 26, 28, 29, 30, 33, 38, 41, 46, 57, 61, 62
Figs: 31
Flowers (Fresh): 1, 2, 5, 12, 14, 24, 31, 36, 37, 55
Flowers (Dried): 1, 2, 14, 23, 24, 37, 40, 45
Garlic: 2, 5, 17, 23, 24, 31, 37, 40, 45, 48, 50, 51, 59
Elephant Garlic: 2, 24, 37, 45, 48, 50
Gifts, Handcraft: 1, 2, 6, 7, 12, 23, 40, 44
Goat: 22
Greens: 1, 2, 5, 16, 20, 23, 31, 37, 48, 51, 58
Gooseberries: 23, 59
Herbs: 1, 2, 5, 16, 23, 24, 37, 40, 45, 48, 51

Holly: 2, 13, 23, 24, 37
Honey: 2, 5, 7, 13, 14, 23, 24, 36, 37, 45, 48, 50
Houseplants: 23, 50
Jams, Jellies, Vinegars, Syrups: 1, 2, 5, 6, 7, 13, 14, 23, 24, 40, 45, 50
Kiwi: 31, 42, 48
Kohlrabi: 2, 5, 23, 37, 45, 48
Lambs/Sheep: 5, 22, 60
Leeks: 23, 31, 37, 42, 48, 51
Lettuce: 1, 2, 16, 23, 31, 37, 42, 45, 48, 50, 51, 58
Loganberries: 2, 23, 45, 50
Mail Order: 1
Marionberries: 2, 23, 36, 42, 45, 48, 50, 53, 58, 59
Melons: 42, 48, 59
Nursery Stock: 5, 6, 7, 20, 23, 31, 37, 48
Nuts: 2, 23, 31, 37, 50
Onions: 2, 5, 14, 16, 23, 31, 37, 42, 45, 48, 50, 51, 59
Organically Grown: 1, 16, 31, 34, 40, 48, 51, 56, 58, 60
Ornamental Corn: 7, 23, 24, 36, 37, 42, 45, 48, 50, 55
Ornamental Gourds: 2, 5, 7, 23, 24, 36, 37, 42, 45, 48, 50, 55
Parsnips: 23, 31, 37
Peaches: see Eastern WA fruit
Pears Local: 42
Pears Asian: 2, 31, 45, 47, 48, 50
Peas (Chinese): 23, 31, 37, 42, 50
Peas (Sugar Snaps and/or Shell): 2, 16, 23, 31, 37, 42, 45, 48, 50, 51, 58
Peppers (Sweet): 1, 2, 14, 24, 31, 42, 48
Peppers (Hot): 2, 24, 31, 42, 48, 50
Picnic Area: 1, 7, 13, 23, 24, 31, 40, 48, 50, 55, 59
Plums: 2, 23, 31, 37, 42, 45, 48, 50, 59
Pork: 60
Potatoes: 1, 2, 5, 12, 14, 23, 24, 31, 37, 42, 45, 48, 50, 51, 55, 59
Poultry: 16, 22, 51, 60
Prunes: 2, 23, 31, 37, 45, 48, 50
Pumpkins: 1, 2, 5, 7, 12, 14, 16, 20, 23, 24, 31, 36, 37, 42, 45, 48, 50, 51, 55, 58
Rabbit: 60
Radishes: 1, 2, 23, 31, 37, 42, 45, 48, 51
Raspberries: 1, 2, 5, 7, 14, 15, 23, 31, 32, 36, 37, 42, 45, 48, 49, 50, 52, 53, 54, 55, 58, 59
Fall Raspberries: 1, 31, 58
Rhubarb: 2, 23, 36, 48, 54
Shallots: 24, 37, 48, 50
Sheep (Skins, fleece or yarn): 22, 44
Spinach: 1, 2, 16, 23, 31, 37, 42, 45, 51
Squash: 1, 2, 5, 14, 16, 23, 24, 31, 36, 37, 42, 48, 50, 51, 58, 59
Strawberries: 1, 2, 4, 5, 7, 14, 23, 31, 35, 37, 42, 45, 48, 50, 53, 55, 58, 59
Everbearing Strawberries: 31, 48, 58
Tayberries: 7
Tomatoes: 1, 2, 31, 42, 45, 48, 51, 59
Tours: 2, 7, 13, 23, 24, 31, 40, 42, 48
Turnips: 23, 31
Vegetable Starts: 5, 20, 23, 31, 37, 40, 45, 48, 51
Zucchini: 1, 2, 5, 14, 16, 23, 31, 36, 37, 42, 45, 48, 50, 51, 58, 59

Seasonal Guide

Animal Products .... Year Rd
Apple Cider .... Year Rd
Apples .... Aug-Nov
Asparagus .... Apr-May
Beans .... Jul-Sept
Beets .... Jun-Oct
Blackberries .... Aug-Sept
Blueberries .... Jul-Sept
Boysenberries .... Jul-Aug
Broccoli .... Jun-Sept
Brussels Sprouts ...... Sept-Nov
Cabbage .... Jun-Oct
Carrots .... Jul-Nov
Cauliflower .... Jul-Sept
Celery .... Aug-Nov
Cherries (pie) .... Jul-Aug
Cherries (sweet) .... Jun-Jul
Christmas trees .... Oct-Dec
Corn .... Aug-Oct
Cucumbers .... Jul-Sept
Currants .... Jun-Aug
Dill .... Jul-Sept
Eggs .... Year Round
Fruit (Yakima) .... Jul-Nov
Garlic .... Aug-Oct
Gooseberries .... Jul-Aug
Herbs .... Apr-Oct
Honey .... Year Round
Lamb .... Year Round
Lettuce .... May-Nov
Loganberries .... Jul-Aug
Marionberries .... Jul-Aug
Melons .... Aug-Oct
Nursery Stock ..... Year Round
Nuts .... Sept-Oct
Onions .... Jun-Oct
Peas .... Jun-Jul
Peppers .... Aug-Oct
Plants (bedding) .... Apr-Jun
Potatoes .... Year Round
Pumpkins .... Oct
Quince .... Oct
Raspberries .... Jun-Aug
Fall Raspberries .... Aug-Oct
Rhubarb .... Apr-Jun
Spinach .... Apr-Oct
Squash .... Jul-Oct
Strawberries (June) ..... Jun-Jul
Strawberries (Ever) ...Jun-Sept
Tomatoes .... Jul-Oct
Zucchini .... Jul-Oct

Farm Listings

SKAGIT COUNTY

1 Cascadian Farm   360-853-8173
Certified Organic U-pick or freshly picked: raspberries, blueberries, sweet corn and pumpkins. Also, organic conserves, pickles & sauerkraut. Come enjoy our berries in homemade ice cream, milkshakes and baked goodies, and on sundaes and shortcake. Full organic espresso bar. Picnic in the scenic beauty of the Upper Skagit River Valley. Open 8am-8pm daily, Jun-Aug. Shorter hours May, Sept & Oct. Please call ahead to order flats of berries and to ensure availability of U-pick. *5375 Hwy 20, Rockport 98283: 3 miles east of Rockport at milepost 100 1/2.*

2 Schuh Farms Mt. Vernon 360-424-6982
                    Stanwood 360-629-6455
Strawberries, raspberries, marionberries, tayberries, boysenberries, loganberries and blueberries, fresh and in jams, syrups and vinegars. Broccoli, cauli, cukes, beans, carrots, squash, cabbage, sweet corn, pumpkins, and cutflowers. Eastern WA asparagus, melons, tomatoes, stone fruit and peppers. Christmas trees, wreaths, holly, ornaments and nuts. U-pick: raspberries, tayberries, and pumpkins at Mt. Vernon. *Location of stands: Mt Vernon, 1353 Memorial Hwy; daily Jun-Dec oam-6pm. Stanwood, 9828 SR532; daily May-Dec 9am-6pm.*

SNOHOMISH COUNTY

3 Silvana Farmers' Market 360-652-5708
Produce & berries: fresh picked, locally grown (mostly organic). Nursery stock: Woodland shade plants & natives, unusual perennials, medicinal & culinary herbs. In spring, tomatoes, vegetables, flower starts. Unique handcrafts, homebaked goods & cookie lady. Special events, classes, master gardners thru June. *Rain or shine, Sat 10-4, Apr 26 into Oct. Discover us in the park between Faye's Country Cafe & the colorful mural on Apple Barrel Antiques. I-5 exit 208, west 2 miles to Friendly Historic Silvana.*

4 Due's Berry Farm   360-659-3875
Strawberries (Shuksan, Rainier) U-pick, mid-Jun to mid-Jul. Weekdays 8am-6pm; Sat-Sun 9am-5pm. Commercial quality, clean fields. Plants on mounded rows. Senior citizen discount. Call first to ensure availability and time changes due to weather. *14003 Smokey Point Blvd, Marysville 98271. Take exit 116th St off I-5N and follow signs north.*

**5 Bakko's Farm market & Nursery Inc.
                          425-334-3581**
Locate 5 1/2 miles from Hwy 9 on Hwy 92 (Granite Falls Hwy). Nursery hours before, strawberry season will be, 9am-5pm Wed-Sun. Beginning with Strawberry season we will be open 7 days a week from 9am-5pm. We stock trees, shrubs, bedding plants and related supplies. We also have the new "GIESLA" dwarf cherry trees. Shukan & Rainier strawberries, vegetables, Meeker raspberries, blueberries, Bodacious & Golden Jubilee corn and a pumpkin patch. Please see Product Guide for complete listing. *7808 State Road 92, Lake Stevens, 98258.*

6 The Blueberry Patch   425-334-5524
No sprays used, well tended blueberries. U-pick or fresh picked. Available late July through mid-Sept. Call ahead for pre-picked orders. Gift shop features our own jam, sauce and crafts. We have Blueberry plants, varieties of Hosta anada lilies. Open Mon-Sat 8am-7pm; Sun 10am-5pm. A great family outing. Children welcome to accompany adults. From I-5, Marysville exit 199, go east on Hwy 528 to Hwy 9. South to Lk. Cassity Rd (160th St). Go past the lake to 54th Pl NE, turn left to farm. *10410 54th Pl NE, Everett, 98205.*

7 Biringer Farm   425-259-0255
Seasonal U-pick & Farm Market: Strawberries (mid-Jun-Jul); raspberries, tayberries (Jul); pumpkins (Oct); Christmas trees (Dec). Trolley to fields, special events, farm tours, farm kitchen, picnic area. Country fun! Hours vary with crops. Call before you come. *Location: I-5, Marysville exit 199, right to State St light, right Hwy 529 S, right 50 ft. past 2nd bridge to Farm Gate. Marysville, 98271.*

8   Everett Farmers' Market 425-347-2790
This open air Market features the best homegrown & handmade goods including fruits & vegetables, organic produce, herbs, flowers, honey, baked goods and crafts by local artists. *Everett Market operates every Sat, Jun 1-Sept 28, 11am-5pm. Located on West Marine View Dr, just north of Marina Village on the waterfront.*

9   Mountain View Berry Farm   360-668-3391
Blueberries, U-pick or boxed at farm. Jul & Aug. Sometimes U-pick extends into Sept. Hours: 9am-7pm Mon-Fri, 9am-4pm Sat-Sun. May be closed occasionally due to weather. Call before coming. Orders taken. *7617 E. Lowell-Larimer Rd (131st SE), Snohomish, 98290.*

10   Blue Heron Blueberries   360-568-0192
Blueberries: large, sweet, hybrid varieties, early season fruit. July10-Aug. U-pick & we-pick. Open 9am-dusk. Closed if it rains. Picking buckets and boxes available. Call to place orders for same day pick-up. *Located 1 mile north of City of Snohomish just 600 ft. W of Bickford Av on Fobes Rd, or turn W on 56th St SE off Hwy 9 north of Snohomish. Follow signs. Honey available. 8628 Fobes Rd, Snohomish.*

11   Snohomish Farmers' Mkt 206-347-2790
This lively market now in its 6th season is located by the river, in our quaint downtown area on 1st Av, 2 blocks west of the bridge. We feature fruits & vegetables, plants & flowers, herbs, honey, baked goods & arts & crafts. *This evening market operates every Thur 5-9pm, May 8-Sept 25.*

12   Bailey Vegetables   360-568-8826
U-pick fresh vegetables in season. Beans, pickling cucumbers, beets, new potatoes, corn, pumpkins, and flowers. Compost for sale at farm. Open daily 8am-8pm in season. *12711 Springhetti Rd, Snohomish 98296: 3 miles S of Snohomish on Springhetti Rd parallel to Hwy 9.*

13   Blueberry Farm   360-794-6995
U-pick & fresh picked blueberries available from mid-Jul-Aug. Please call ahead for 10# fresh flats. Our gift shop features our own jam and syrup, flowers and crafts. Wheelchair accessible. Kids play area, picnic area. Families welcome! Open 9am-6pm Tue-Sat; noon-6pm Sun; closed Mon. *12109 Woods Creek Rd, Monroe 98272: 4 miles north of Hwy 2. Turn north at Red Barn Bakery onto Woods Creek Rd. Stay right at Y onto Yeager Rd. Go 1/2 mile past stop sign at Bollenbaugh Hill Rd. Farm is on right.*

14   Sunny Acres Berry Farm 360-794-8855
At roadside stand: direct from the farm, seasonal fruits and vegetables. Green beans, cucumbers, sweet corn, potatoes and honey. Strawberries, in June. Raspberries in July with special U-pick days. Blueberries Jul-Aug. Please call before coming. *17516 SR 203, Monroe 98272: 1/2 mile S of Monroe on Duvall Hwy 203.*

15   Snow's Berry Farm   360-794-6312
Raspberries: U-pick, fresh picked, or pre-ordered when in season. Daily 7am-7pm. *18401 Tualco Rd, Monroe 98272: 1/2 mile past bridge, turn right on Tualco Rd. A Centennial Farm.*

16   Alden Farms   360-805-0911
Alden Farms will be open on weekends 10am-5pm Jun-Halloween. Located in Tualco Valley, Alden Farms is a WA state certified organic farm. Vegetables, eggs and poultry are available. U-pick pumpkins and hay rides for Halloween. *19604 Tualco Rd, Monroe, 98272.*

17   Canyon Park Orchard   425-483-8654
Specialty apples: "Rediscover Flavor" with Paulared, Akane, Jonamac, Gala, Spartan, McIntosh, Melrose, Jonagold, Gravensteins. Over 30 varieties. Also Spanish Roja/red garlic. We sell only what we grow. We feature "Lisa" Low Input Sustainable Agriculture. Aug 20-Oct 20 Wed-Fri 10am-6pm; Sat-Sun 10am-5pm. *23305 39th Av SE, Bothell 98021. Call for directions.*

KING COUNTY NORTH

18   Woodinville Fmrs' Mkt   425-788-3697
Open air market in downtown Woodinville, next to city hall. Nearby are wineries, the Burke Gilman Trail and Molbaks. Fresh seasonal fruits and vegetables from local WA farmers. Beautiful flowers and perennials, baked goods and handmade crafts. *Open every Sat, May3-Oct, 9am-4pm.*

19   Lydon's Blueberry Farm 425-788-1395
U-pick blueberries. Mid-Jul-frost. Wed-Sun 9am-dusk. Closed Mon-Tue. Call first. *14510 Kelly Rd NE, Duvall 98019: 6 miles east of Duvall.*

20 Game Haven Greenery   425-333-4313
Vegetable plants in spring. Field grown nursery stock. We pick or U-pick pumpkins. Salad greens. Natural grass fed beef. Call for availability. *7110 310th Av NE, Carnation 98014: 1 mile north of Carnation on Carnation Farm Rd.*

21 Harvold Berry Farm   425-333-4185
U-pick strawberries mid-Jun thru mid-Jul. U-pick raspberries Jul 1-mid-Aug. Daily: 8am-8pm. Free containers. *32325 NE 55th, Carnation 98014: north city limits on the Carnation Duvall Rd, Hwy 203.*

22 Pfeiffer Farm   425-333-4934
Largest sheep farm in King County. Naturally grown lamb and mutton available year round. We now have meat rabbits, chickens, ducks, geese and goats. Call for availability. Custom farm slaughter facility now approved. Special farm days by appointment. Featuring shearing, hands-on petting baby animals and a straw maze (minimum of 20 children). In business over 30 years. Please call first! *31439 W. Commercial, Carnation 98014.*

23 Remlinger Farms   425-451-8740
Direct Farm Market seasonal fruit & vegetables. Old fashioned fun on the farm & U-pick. Seasonal Festivals & Entertainment. Farm animals: viewing & petting. Nursery, garden shop & consignment handcrafts. Bakery (featuring fresh frozen "U-bake" pies). Restaurant, catering & location for company picnics. Rent the party barn for the theater for your birthday parties complete with a puppet show. Apr-Dec. call for Ripe n Ready Report. *NE 32nd St, Carnation 98014: 1 mile S of town, off Hwy 203.*

24 Fall City Farms   425-222-7930
Open in July with U-pick garlic, organically grown rice and herbs. Specialty garlics, shallots, elephant garlic, corn, pumpkins, apples, cider, honey, dried tomatoes, gourds and more. Thur-Mon, 10am-6pm Jul-Nov 1st. Open Sun 11am-6pm. Hours and days may vary. Self-service from Nov until sold out. We use only recycled bags. Bring your own please. Tours for school & general public, garlic braiding lessons. Look for our Garlic Weekend in Aug; Apple Day in Sept and Winter Weekend in Dec. *3636 Neal Rd: take 1st left off of Hwy 203 heading N from Fall City.*

25 Bybee-Nims Farms   425-888-0821
Blueberries: U-pick. Open mid-Jul to mid-Sept, daily 9am-dusk. Picnic tables available, bring your lunch and your camera. *42930 SE 92nd St, North Bend 98045: take I-90 exit 31, turn left, continue through next 2 signal lights, go to signal light at North Bend Way, turn right, go 2 blocks to Ballarat Ave N, turn left, continue north and east on arterial to 428th "T". Continue left. After crossing river, turn right, watch for signs. Farm is about 1 3/4 miles from town.*

26 Redmond Sat Market   425-882-5151
The Eastsides original open air Farmers' Market features organically grown vegetables, fruits and berries. Flowers and plants for sale direct from grower. Craft items made & sold by the vendors, some made on site. Meet local artists & buy direct. Open Sat 8am-2pm. May 3 thru Oct 11th. Promotional days throughout season with special activities for children. *Located at 7730 Leary Way, in downtown Redmond.*

27 Serres Farm   425-868-3017
Strawberries: U-pick Jun-mid-Jul daily 9am-7:30pm. Containers furnished. Pumpkin patch October 11-31, 10am-5pm weekends; weekdays 2-5pm. Christmas trees, cut & u-cut, Nov 29 thru Dec, weekends 9am-5pm, weekdays 2-5pm. **20306 NE 50th St, Redmond 98053: 3 miles east of Redmond on Redmond-Fall City Hwy (SR 202) to Gray Barn, then south (right) 1 block (.15 mile) on Sahalee Way, then west (right) .25 mile on NE 50th to farm.**

**28 University District Farmers' Market
      206-633-1024**
Come visit Seattle's "growers-only" Farmers' Market. Buy direct from over 50 WA state farmers; seasonal fresh fruit and vegetables from both sides of the state. Fresh organic produce, herbs and flowers, mushrooms, cheese, eggs, nuts, preserves, honey, plants and nursery items, fresh baked goods. Weekly entertainment and free gardening, composting advice. Sat May 31-Nov 1, 9am-2pm. *On the "Ave" at the corner of NE 50th St and University Way NE. From I-5 take 50th St exit. Head east on NE 50th for 1/2 mile to corner of 50th & Univ. Way. Located outdoors at Univ. Heights Community Center. Parking tokens available for one hour free parking at U-District lots.*

29 Pike Place market   206-682-7453
The Market features 120 farms from WA, OR and Canada, selling by the day, the week, the season. Over 230 different crops-over 100 varieties of vegetables. Complete line of seafood, bakeries, hand-crafted items, over 200 merchants, and 60 places to eat! Spend a day at the oldest continuously operating Farmers' Market in the country. Open year-round, Mon-Sat 9am-6pm. Open Sun 11am-5pm. *Pike Place Market, First Ave & Pike Place in downtown Seattle, 98101.*

Vashon Island

30 Vashon Green Market   206-463-6557
Vashon Islands small farmers come together to bring you the best in locally grown vegetables, fruits, berries, cut flowers, and nursery plants. *Easy to find on Vashon Hwy in the middle of Vashon town: 5 miles south of the north end ferry dock, 10 miles north of the south end ferry dock. Open Sat, Mar 29-Oct 11, 10am-3pm.*

**31 Family Trees Gardens/
     Peter's Pumpkin Patch   206-463-3256**
U-pick or we pick fruit, nuts, veggies and flowers. Self service farm stand is always open. Full service weekends and holidays. Mar 1-Oct 31. Pumpkin sales start after our free "Great Pumpkin" raffle Oct 4th. It's a fun trip to Vashon Island and to our wonderful farm! This is a diversified family farm with many great products. At times, we may not have large quantities of some items. *7316 SW 240th, Vashon 98070: From the Vashon Hwy, follow the signs toward Dockton on Maury Island. 23724 Dockton Rd SW, Vashon Island.*

KING COUNTY SOUTH

32 Overlake Blueberry Farm 425-453-8613
Open Mon-Fri 10am-6pm: Sat 9am-6pm; Sun 11am-5pm. Season starts mid-July thru Sat before Labor Day. Cleaned and sorted picked blueberries available in pints, 5# and 10# flats and 5# freezer-ready containers. Also U-pick. Raspberries will be available during the season. Call ahead in case of inclement weather. *2380 Bellevue Way SE, Bellevue 98004.*

33 Issaquah Farmers' Mkt   425-392-2229
Located at the Community Center, every Sat from Apr19 thru Oct 9am-3pm (except the Sat of Salmon Days weekend). Produce, nursery items, crafts, espresso and much more. Special Saturdays; youth specials and community activities. Lots of parking. *301 Rainier Blvd S.*

**34 Kennydale Blueberry Farm
                              425-228-9623**
Blueberries: U-pick mid-July until picked out in Sept. Please call before coming. Call between 8am-7pm to hear U-pick and order information. Closed Sun. Picked berries by advance orders only, in 5 & 10# flats. No sprays used on our berries. *1733 NE 20th St, Renton 98056: take exit 6 off 405. We are on the east side of the freeway. Follow fence around school, turning R on NE 28th then L on Jones Av. Go 8 blocks to NE 20th, turn L. We are the 3rd house from the corner, on the R.*

35 Grandpa's Farm   425-432-4269
Strawberries: U-pick or we pick. Boxes and carriers provided. Open daily, Jun-Jul 8am-6pm. *26825 SE 208th St. Maple Valley, WA 98038.*

36 Cruz-Johnson Farms   253-872-8017
A little country left in the Kent Valley. 3 varieties of raspberries beginning in Jul. 11 varieties of sweet corn including yellow, bicolor and white. Picked fresh daily beginning Aug. Open Mon-Sat, closed Sun. Jun-Aug 8am-6pm; Sept & Oct 10am-6pm. Call for recorded info on product availability. *22243 Frager Rd, Ken 98032: from I-5, take exit 152, go east on Orillia Rd 2 miles. Turn rt onto Frager Rd. One mile south on rt. From Kent, 3 miles north of golf course.*

**37 Carpinito Bros. Farm Stand
                              253-854-5692**
Strawberries, raspberries, blueberries, corn, beans, beets, carrots, cabbage, lettuces, cauliflower, broccoli, peppers, potatoes, tomatoes, cucumbers, and pickling accessories. Cherries, pears, apricots, prunes, grapes, apples. Garden store/nursery-bedding plants, screened valley topsoil & bark. Oct-pumpkins; Dec-Christmas trees, green & flocked. Open all year, daily 9am-6pm. *1148 N. Central Av, Kent 98032.*

38   Kent market   253-813-6976
The Market opens for the 23rd year providing an outlet for farmers, gardeners, artists, and hand crafters to sell their products. Vendors are welcome by reservation or as walk-ins. The Market opens on Sat, Apr 12 9am-4pm; Sun 10am-3pm through Oct 25th. *Located in the Municipal Parking Lot at the corner of 4th & Smith Sts in downtown Kent.*

39   T&M Berry Farm   253-941-1435
U-pick raspberries. Centennial & Tulameen raspberries begin early July. Open daily 8am depending on availability of ripe berries. Please call ahead. Free containers. No sprays on berries. Children welcome with parents, but please no school or care groups. We do not have the facilities to accommodate them. *South of Kent on 3rd about 1.5 miles, or go north of 277th on 78th about 1/2 mile. Watch for signs.*

40   The Fat Hen Farm   253-631-9553
Let the kids visit with the farm animals, while you browse thru our display gardens. Over 300 varieties of herbs, perennials and everlastings. Fresh herbs in season. Classes offered on herb growing, crafting and cooking. Open Mar-Dec Wed-Sun 10am-6pm. *28040 152nd Ave SE, Kent 98042: Take SE 272nd (Kent-Kangley Rd) to 152nd Av SE (Kent-Black Diamond Rd) go 1/2 mile south. App. 1 mile from Lake Meredian.*

41   Auburn Farmers' Market 253-735-2957
come visit the Wed market on the *corner of Auburn Way and Cross Street, 1/2 block off Hwy 18.* The Market features fresh off the farm fruits and vegetables. We also have beautiful bedding plants, flowers, arts & crafts as well as food to munch! Season begins Wed June 11 and runs through Oct. Hours 9am-3pm.

42   Mosby Brother's Farm Stand
**   253-863-9733**
Find a full line of produce and seasonal fruits and berries at our roadside stand. We also have a U-pick pumpkin patch in Oct. *East of Auburn on the Green Valley Rd. From Hwy 18, take the Auburn-Black Diamond Rd exit. Stay to the right past the Neeley Mansion. Go app. 1 mile. Located on the corner of Academy Dr & Green Valley Rd. Open Jun-Oct daily 9am-6pm. Open all holidays.*

43   John Hamakami Strawberry Farm
**   253-833-2081 (evenings)**
U-pick strawberries. Nothing like fresh U-pick berries for freezing, preserving and/or fresh eating. Please call for availability and picking times. *14733 SE Green Valley Rd, Auburn 98092: 5 miles east of Auburn on the road to Flaming Geyser Park.*

44   Edeldal Farm   253-939-1350
Purebred Jacob sheep, Angora goats, wool and mohair. We specialize in nantucket Rug Hooking, a uniquely American pioneer craft. We welcome custom orders for handspun yarn, rugs, stuffed animals, etc. Call about classes in rug hooking. Visitors welcome but please call first. *15429 SE Green Valley Rd, Auburn 98092*

45   Bob's Produce   360-825-5994
Complete line of local and Yakima fruits and vegetables. Bedding plants, vegetable starts and flower starts. Hanging baskets and hanging tomato baskets. handmade gifts, wishing wells, windmills, cow-planters and more. Fresh made jams & honey. Open May 15th to Nov 1, 9:30am -7pm daily. *41126 SE 264th Enumclaw 98022: Hwy 169 just 2 miles N of Enumclaw.*

46   The Enumclaw Country Market
**   253-939-1707**
A Saturday Market in *downtown Enumclaw, across from the library at Griffin and Railroad.* Join us at the Gazebo for fresh fruits, vegetables, herbs and arts & crafts, including homemade soaps. Open Sat, April 26-Oct 25, 9am-4pm. See the listing each Wed in the Courier Herald for what will be currently available.

47   Rockridge Nashi Orchards
**   & Bamboo Grove   360-825-1962**
We are a small 10 acre custom Nashi (Asian Pear) orchard located 5 miles NW of Enumclaw. There are 17 different varieties to choose from, each with its own ripening season. We sell single fruit and cases (straight & mixed). Open Sept 1-Oct 15, Wed-Sun 10am-6pm. *41127 212th AV SE, Enumclaw 98022.*

48   Susie's Produce   360-825-7429
Complete line of local and Yakima produce. Some organic produce available. Bedding plants, vegetable starts, herbs and flower baskets. Eggs and honey. See product reference guide for complete listing. Call for availability on U-pick. We give farm tours in Oct by reservation. Open 10am-7pm Jun-Oct 31. *Auburn-Enumclaw Hwy & 196th Av, Enumclaw.*

49 Pete's Farm   253-833-1121
Farm fresh raspberries. Fresh picked and U-pick. Please call ahead to order picked berries. Also please bring your own containers. Open 7 days a week during season, 9am-7pm. *From Seattle, go south on 167. Exit at 8th St (south of City of Pacific). Go east on 8th to Valentine Av. Turn left. Go north app. 1 mi. Farm on right at 519 Valentine Av. From Tacoma go north on 167, rest of directions the same.*

PIERCE COUNTY

**50 Love's Puyallup Raspberry Resort
    & Farm Direct Market   253-845-3125**
We grow acres of yummy raspberries, boysens, marions, and strawberries. Also Blues, Logans and blacks. Love's grown and fresh picked daily white & yellow corn, lettuce, cabbage, zucchini, cukes, potatoes, beans, rhubarb, squash & much more. Local & Eastern WA produce by box or bag. Fall pumpkin festival and holiday trees. *One big location to serve you off Hwy 167 at Puyallup, just north of downtown on meridian at Valley Av. Open May-Dec 8:30am-6:30 pm.*

**51 Adams Valley Av Greenhouse
    and Produce Farm   253-770-2588**
Full line of bedding plants, vegetable starts, gallon tomatoes, perennials and many baskets. Several varieties of unusaul flowers from England, organic vegetables, we-pick, possible u-pick. Salad greens, herbs, beans, onions, garlic, squash and more. Free range chickens. Greenhouse opens late Apr. Produce available Jun-Sept. Call ahead for U-pick & product availability. *11623 Valley Av E, Puyallup 98372. (between N Puyallup and Sumner).*

52 Gwendon Farm   253-848-2108
Raspberries and apples. U-pick or picked raspberries in Jul. Mon-Sat 9am-5pm. Sun 1pm-5pm. No spray used on berries. Call to ensure availability. Apples available late Aug thru Nov. 50 varieties, but principally Jonagold, Spartan, Melrose, Gravenstein, Jonamac, Liberty, Chehalis, Akane, Discovery, Macoun, Mitsu, Summerred. U-pick or picked apples available Thur-Sat 11am-5pm. Make your own apple juice with our apple press by appointment. *6613 114th Ave Ct E, Puyallup 98372: between Puyallup and Sumner on North bank of the Puyallup River.*

53 Spooner Farms   253-841-2876
We pick daily for you. Our own strawberries, raspberries, boysenberries, kotata and Sylvan blackberries and English peas. Jun-Jul, daily 9am-6pm. *Two locations in Puyallup: 1725 E Main (across from Daffodil Bowl) and 9622 SR 162 E, Puyallup 98374 (Old Sumner-Orting Hwy at Alderton). U-pick strawberries available at latter address. Containers furnished.*

54 Foster's Riverbend Farm 253-863-4816
Raspberries, pie cherries, kotata blackberries, rhubarb and eggs. U-pick: pie cherries & raspberries. July & 1st part of Aug. *7619 SR 162 E, Sumner 98390: one mile south of Sumner.*

**55 Scholz Farms & Gardens,
    Pumpkin Palace   253-848-7604**
Open daily 9am-6pm, Mar 1 thru Oct 31. We offer fresh seasonal produce and flowers including Strawberries (fresh & frozen), other berries. Yellow Finn Potatoes, our famous sweet corn varieties, daffodils, lilies, hanging baskets and dahlias. Our new gift shop is open. In Oct we open the entire farm to the public for pumpkins, painted pumpkins and a wide variety of other fall crops. We also give group farm tours in Oct by reservation. *From Puyallup, head East on Pioneer to Hwy 162 (Sumner-Orting Hwy) and turn right. Continue 3 miles. We're on the right, past 128th St. or call for directions.*

56 Sunrise Blueberry Farm 253-845-2856
Certified organic blueberries: hand-picked at their peak of freshness! Fresh picked, ready to freeze, frozen. Quantity discounts for 10 pounds or more. We sell plastic netting for bird control. Season: Jul-Sept. Open Mon-Sat 8am-5pm. *Easy to find in Puyallup off E Pioneer. Turn at Spinning School on 13th St SE and look for the Red Shed at the end of the road. Please call ahead for large orders.*

57 Puyallup Farmers' Mkt 253-845-6755
The freshest fruits and vegetables (some organic), a vast variety of nursery stock, unique handcrafted items, and tasty foods. Our 15th season, open Sat May 3-Sept 6, 9am-2pm in and *around Pioneer Park, 4 blocks N of the fairgrounds.*

58   Terry's Berries   253-922-1604
Certified organic: raspberries (summer & fall), strawberries (Jun & Aug), blackberries, vegetables: green beans, corn, squash, pumpkins, other. Apples: Gravensteins, Jonogold and Liberty. Apple/pumpkin harvest festival: Make your own apple cider! Great family fun Oct weekends! Apple picking/cider making farm tours. Hours vary with crops and weather so call before you come. U-pick by appointment only. *Farm stand just 2 miles from I-5, exit 135 at 4520 River Rd, between Tacoma and Puyallup.*

59   Pioneer Blueberry Farm   253-770-0941
Blueberries: U-pick or fresh picked daily for highest quality and flavor. Roadside stand features a wide variety of seasonal fruits and vegetables, all locally grown. Open Jul-Sept, 10am-6:30pm daily. *5169 Pioneer Way E, Tacoma 98443: between Puyallup and Tacoma at bottom of Canyon Rd.*

**60   The Meat Shop of Tacoma, Inc.
                                  253-537-4490**
Complete line of highest quality organic meats. Beef, pork, fryers, lamb, veal and rabbit. We use original recipes for our cured meats: ham, bacon, sausage, cold cuts, beef jerky, etc. All made without preservatives, coloring, fillers, or additives. Complete cutting, wrapping and processing of beef, pork, lamb, veal and wild game. Custom poultry kill available by appointment. *Open 8am-6pm Mon-Fri; 10am-5pm Sat. 13419 Vickery Rd E, Tacoma 98446.*

61   Tacoma Farmers' Market 253-272-7077
Downtown Tacoma, Antique Row, 9th & Broadway. Thur 10am-3pm, Jun 5-Sept 4. Fresh from local farms: produce, berries and fine fruits, traditional to organically grown. Fresh honey. Fresh baked goods. Cut and potted herbs. Lovely cut and potted flowers and unusual shrubs. Quality crafts by local artisans. Variety of foods for lunch and entertainment.

62   Proctor Farmers' Market 253-756-8901
Our open air farmers' market is located in the heart of Tacoma's historic North end Proctor District. Features: farm fresh produce, organic fruits, berries and vegetables, specialty herbs, bedding plants, cut flowers and delicious fresh herbs, bedding plants, cut flowers and delicious fresh breads/bakery. Enjoy a lunch al fresco while listening to local musicians. Open Sat, Jun-Aug 9am-2pm. *From I-5 City Center exit take Schuster Pkwy to N. 30th St. Turn left onto Proctor St. Market located in the US Bank parking lot (Proctor & N 26th).*

Kitsap County

Kitsap County Farm Trails Map

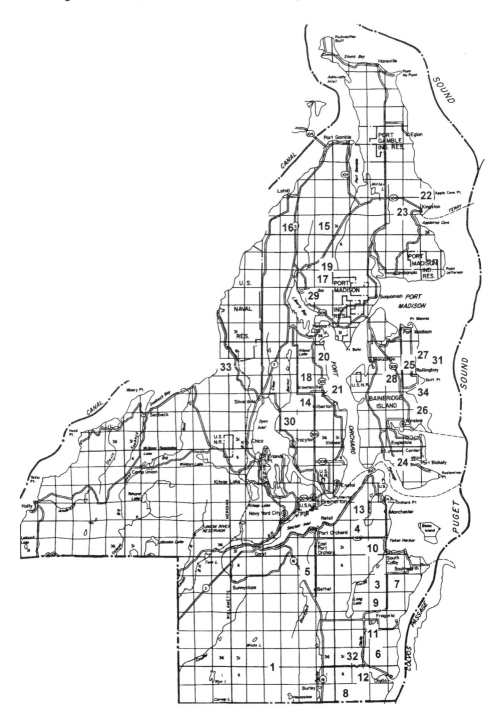

Credit: Sound Farmers Education Foundation

Produce Reference Guide

FRUITS & VEGETABLES

Apples: 12, 28
Basil: 30
Beans: 14
Blackberries/Blueberries: 34
Carrots: 34
Chard: 34
Cider: 28
Corn: 25, 27, 28, 34
Cucumbers: 34
Dill: 30
Fruit: 22
Grapes: 26
Gourds: 25, 27, 28
Grape Cuttings & Plants: 26
Herbs: 4, 24, 30, 34
Herb Seeds: 30
Herb Starts: 30, 34
Leeks: 34
Lettuce: 34
Onions: 34
Peas: 34
Pickles: 14
Pumpkins: 25, 27, 28, 34
Raspberries: 1, 12, 27
Salad Greens: 4, 34
Squash: 25, 27, 34
Strawberries: 17, 25
Vegetables: 22, 34

FLOWERS & ORNAMENTALS

Bedding Plants: 24
Classes: 24, 26, 29
Dried Flowers: 24, 28, 34
Flowers Arrangements: 22, 24, 28, 30, 34
Flowers Edible: 4
Tours: 1, 24, 26, 28, 32
Holly Nursery Stock: 31
Nursery Stock: 26, 27, 31

FOREST PRODUCTS

Boughs: 8, 15, 33
Christmas trees: 8, 15, 27, 33
Christmas tree stands: 15
Garlands: 15, 33
Holly: 13
Wreaths: 15, 24, 26, 31, 33

LIVESTOCK

Cattle & Calves: 0, 3, 5
Chickens: 9
Emus: 16
Goats: 23, 29
Hogs: 1, 9
Horses: 7, 13, 32
Lambs: 9, 12, 18, 19, 20, 21, 22, 23
Llamas: 10, 11
Peacocks: 6, 21
Rabbits: 29
Sheep: 6, 9, 12,. 18, 19, 20, 21, 22, 23
Trout: 2

MEAT/FISH/ANIMAL PRODUCTS

Angora: 29
Beef: 0, 3, 5
Eggs: 6, 9, 22
Feathers: 6
Honey: 23
Lamb: 5, 9, 12, 17, 18, 19, 20, 21, 23
Pork: 1, 5, 9
Sheepskins: 9, 12, 18
Smoked Meats: 5, 14
Wool, Mohair, Fleece: 6, 9, 12, 18, 22, 23, 29

MISCELLANEOUS

Art: 14, 29
Antiques: 14
Beauty Bark & Top Soil: 14
Books, Herbal: 29, 30
Border Collies: 18
Compost: 9, 13, 18, 20, 23
Yarn, Woven & Knit Articles: 6, 12, 22
Herbal Products: 30
Horse Boarding/Training: 7, 13
Stud Service: 7, 13, 20
Manure: 7, 9, 13, 14, 18, 20, 23
Soap: 12
Spinning Wheels, Lessons: 12, 29
Tractor Service: 13
Vines: 26
Welding Repair: 20
Wine: 26
Slaughter/Cut/Wrap: 5

Farm Index

0. CHRISTIPAUL FARM
Chris & Paul Schlicht   360-275-4739
13807 Voctor Rd, Belfair 98528
Available year round are feeder calves and bottle calves. Beef by the side must be ordered in advance. Informational help for new farmers on all types of livestock. Please call for directions.

1. B&H FARM
Bill & Helen Nation   360-876-9687
11520 Abbey Ln SW, Port Orchard 98366
Please call before coming. 1 mile W of Sidney on Wildwood, S on Abbey Ln. Swine: We have pigs of all ages with different genetics; purebred & crossbred Hampshire, Berkshire, Duroc and Landrace breeding stock. Quality weaner, BBQ and butcher pigs. Raspberries in season, we pick. Call to order, no insecticides used. Tours by appt.

2. BELFAIR FISH FARM
Ray Mastel   360-275-8220
NE 170 David Farm Rd, Belfair 98528
Season Mar 1-Oct 31. Hours Mon-Sat 11am-7pm and Sun 12pm-7pm. Located on Davis Farm 3/4 mile N of Belfair on Old Belfair Rd. Featuring Rainbow and Steelhead Trouth, U-fish.

3. DJ LIMOUSIN
Dave Berry   360-871-3542
6845 SE King Rd, Port Orchard 98366
Go S on Banner from SR 160 (Sedgewick Rd). R on King Rd, to farm. Full blood Limousin cattle: bulls, cows, heifer, calves.

4. NATURE'S COMPLIMENT
Julia Ratmeyer Folkerts   360-871-7972
5257 Bulman Rd SE, Port Orchard
Please call before coming and to place orders. Call for directions. Most items available year round. Organically grown, field washed salad greens, fresh cut herbs and edible flowers.

5. FARMER GEORGE'S MEATS
Joe Keehn   876-3186
3870 Bethel Rd, Port Orchard 98366
Open Mon-Sat 9am-5:30pm. Farm slaughtering, custom cutting and wrapping, smoking, freezer beef and pork, sides and quarters, freezer packs, retail meats, homemade sausage, hams and bacon.

6. SWALLOW LANE FARM AND FIBERWORKS
Mark & Cathie Williams   206-857-2669
8323 SE Millihanna Rd, Olalla 98359
Please call before coming. Located off Banner Rd (to the E) between LaLa Cove and Willox. Registered Jacob sheep, Jacob wool and mohair. Handspun yarns and handwoven gifts, brown eggs, peacock feathers.

7. SAWDA ARABIANS AND PINTOS
Herman Aguayo   360-871-2796
5322 Peterson Rd SE, Port Orchard 98366
Please call before coming. Tue-Sun 8am-5pm. 5.5 miles E of Hwy 16, 1/2 mile S on Sedgwick Rd. Arabian stallion service (breeding), Prince Sawda, sweepstakes sire-pinto approved, Beau Kelli-Comar Bey Beau+++ son horses for sale (Arabians & pintos), free manure available year round.

8. FIVE SPRINGS TREE FARM
Doug & John Kingsbury   206-857-5423
15331 Bandix Rd SE, Olalla 98359
Please call before coming out. Open weekends after Thanksgiving 9am-5pm. Other hours by appointment only. From Hwy 16 follow Burley-Olalla Rd E 1/2 mile to Bandix Rd. Turn right on Bandix 1.7 miles to farm. Choose & cut Christmas trees: Douglas fir, Grand fir, Noble fir and Scotch pine.

9. ARBOR MEADOWS FARM
Joy & Sarah Garitone   206-857-6096
8134 Orchard Av SE, Port Orchard 98366
Please call before coming. Hours 8am-6pm. Take Hwy 16 S to Mullenix, go left (E) on Mullenix to Orchard and L on Orchard to 4th. Farm on left. Eggs, laying hens, sheep (purebred Dorset, NCWGA Natural Colored sheep, Moorit colored Fine wooled CVM purebreds. Breeding, show stock, 4-H project lambs), manure and compost (U-haul), meat (lamb and mutton for freezer, all year) wool, sheepskins (white and dark). Custom raised hogs. All meat naturally raised without drugs or hormones.

10. WINTERCREEK FARM
Mike & Dannie Sayers   360-871-3136
1140 Woods Rd E, Port Orchard 98366
Please call before coming and for directions. Wintercreek Llamas was established in 1982. Whether you are looking to buy or for stud service we will help you find your dream llama. We specialize in first-time buyers. Come visit our farm with a preferred herd of llamas born of superior bloodlines and bred for fun and function. We invite you to visit Wintercreek Farm and view our animals.

11. HILLSPRING LLAMA FARM
VanderYacht Family   206-857-7882
6370 SE Mullenix Rd, Port Orchard 98366
Please call before coming. Hwy 16 E on Mullenix Rd, through four way stop (Olalla Valley Rd) first driveway on right. Llamas: Hillspring Farm has been in the llama business since 1985, with over 30 animals on the farm today, making our love for these wonderful animals stronger than ever. If you are interested in learning about or purchasing llamas, we are always happy to share information with you. We have yearlings, geldings, and bred females for sale. Give us a call, there's nothing we love more than talking about, or showing off our llamas.

12. BAA BAA BLACK SHEEP RANCH
Irene & Jim Hudspeth   206-857-3733
13290 Wallace Rd SE, Olalla 98359
Leave message. We'll return call with directions. Open by appt. Wool shop, fleeces, carded roving and commercial fiber. Shacht and Ashford spinning wheels and supplies. Natural colored NCWGA Merino-Romney cross, Merino breeding stock. Organic locker lambs, sheepskins, raspberries, U-pick apples, and hand spun yarn. Handcrafted natural beauty bar soap, spinning lessons.

13. CHEECHAKO ACRES
Ollie & Sharon Call   360-871-2953
2363 Mt. View Rd, E, Port Orchard 98366
Please call before coming out. Hours 10am-10pm, call for directions. Light tractor service, horse boarding and training, composted horse manure.

14. MINDER FARMS
Jim & Cathy Carlson   360-692-9271
1000 NE Gluds Pond Rd, Bremerton 98310
Please call ahead. On Waaga Way and Gluds Pond Rd intersection. Open Wed-Fri 12pm-5:30pm; Sat-Sun 8:30am-5:30pm. Beauty bark, topsoil, fertilizer, antiques, smoked products, jerky, pickled asparagus, dilly beans, pickles and jams. Local talent's art work.

15. JONES TREE FARM
Art Jones   360-779-7840
1795 NE Sawdust Hill Rd, Poulsbo 98370
Hours: Daylight, Nov 15-Dec 24. North of Poulsbo, 1 mile E of Big Valley Rd on Sawdust Hill. Christmas trees, boughs, wreaths, cedar garlands, tree stands, (mainly Noble, Douglas and grand fir). U-cut.

16. HILLTOP EMU RANCH
Ron & Paula Phillips   360-779-5614
22244 Port Gamble Rd, Poulsbo 98370
Open 8am-5pm. Emus: naturally raised, 3 mo. old unrelated pairs, emu yearlings, bonded breeding pairs, micro chipped, DNA tested. Emu products: oils, shampoo and conditioners, emu sun care products.

17. Olson Berry Farm
Olsons   360-779-1737
3255 NE Lincoln Rd, Poulsbo, WA 98370
2 miles E of downtown Poulsbo. Please call for days open. U-pick strawberries, fresh picked flats and half flats also available. Locker lambs: call during Aug to reserve your organically raised lamb.

18. RAINBOW FARM
Tom & Barbara Creed   360-692-9716
201 NW Sigurd Hanson Rd, Poulsbo 98370
Please call ahead. 1 mile N of Hwy 303, 1 block W of Central Valley Rd. By appointment only. Locker lamb, registered black & white Romney sheep, breeding stock, registered Southdown sheep, breeding stock, registered Border Collies, handspinning fleeces, sheep hides, manure.

19. AL STADTLER   360-779-4465
Urdahl Rd, Poulsbo, 98370
Please call before coming out. Registered Horned Dorset Sheep.

20. NEUMANN FARM
Fred & Cathy Neumann   360-779-9231
13003 Old Military Rd NW, Poulsbo 98370
Please call ahead. Hours: 10am-6pm. Central Valley Rd, E on Walker to "T" intersection, then N on Old Military. Suffolk sheep (registered & slaughter), feeder lamgs (control your grass), breeding rams (for lease), freezer packs, manure, metal products (custom made), welding repair.

21. O'HARA SUFFOLKS AND SOUTHDOWNS
Leroy O'Hara   779-4138
12901 S. Keyport Rd NE, Poulsbo 98370
Please call ahead. (Hours 8am-10pm) Between Brownsville and Keyport on S. Keyport Rd. Suffolk and Southdown sheep (registered), breeding stock, 4-H market lambs, project animals, locker lambs, peacocks, naturally raised.

22. FIR HOLLOW FARM
Susan and Teague Parker   360-297-4466
29625 Rash Rd NE, Kingston 98346
Please call before coming out. (Hours Mon-Sun 9am-6pm). 1.5 miles W of Kingston to Parcrel Rd. Go N 1 mile to Rash Rd, turn Left, second drive on left. Shetland sheep and fleeces, handspun yarn and natural fibers, eggs, flowers, fruits and vegetables organically produced.

23. RAIN SHADOW FARM
Marcia Adams   360-297-4485
2510 Chris Ln NE, Kingston 98346
Please call ahead. S on Miller Bay Rd from Rt 104. E on West Kingston Rd for 1/4 mile then S on Chris Ln. Cashmere and angora goats, Coopworth sheep. Wool, mohair, cashmere yarn, honey, manure (year round), hand-spinning fleeces and locker lamb. Organically raised.

24. ROSE OF SHARON'S
Sharon Soames   206-842-6883
10359 NE Seaborn Rd, Bainbridge Island
From ferry, W on Winslow Way, R (N) on Madison Av, W on Wyatt. Travel S about 4.75 miles. Follow signs to Port Blakely along Blakely Av. At 5 way intersection, proceed across to second house on Seaborn Rd. Open year round by appointment only. Rose of Sharon's is a seaside garden and floral design studio where Sharon grows, preserves and designs nature's art. Rose of Sharon's has a wide selection of dried flowers, herbs and some seeds. Ready made wreaths, seaside collage pieces, and arrangements as well as do-it-yourself craft materials available. Classes offered Sept-Apr. Custom design always. "Christmas in the Country" open house/sale early Dec. Occasional offerings of specialty Plants, garden tours.

25. BAINBRIDGE ISLAND FARMS
Karen Selvar   206-842-1429
9229 Day Rd E, Bainbridge Isl. 98110
Strawberries: fresh picked daily, available from the end of May through the first week of July. Call for exact dates. Squash: Acorn, Buttercup, Butternut, Delicata, Sweet Dumpling and more. Ornamental corn and gourds also, located at the Pumpkin Patch.

26. BAINBRIDGE ISLAND VINEYARDS AND WINERY
JoAnn & Gerard Bentryn   206-842-9463
682 Hwy 305, Bainbridge Isl 98110
Open to public Wed-Sun 12pm-5pm. Located 1/4 mile from ferry terminal on Hwy 305 in Winslow. We are growing European grape varieties that are suited for our climate, both for eating and wine making. Vinifera cuttings to start your own vines and prunings for gourmet cooking and wreath and basket makers available late winter. Plants available in summer and fall. Our wine is sold only at the winery. Tasting room, wine museum and gardens. Picnic area. Call about our tours and classes. No insecticides used.

27. SUYEMATSU FARM
Akio Suyematsu 206-842-4388
9229 Day Rd E, Bainbridge Isl. 98110
Raspberries: fresh picked daily available end of Jun-Aug 7th. U-pick, call for dates and hours. Pumpkin patch: U-pick, many different varieties. Squash, ornamental corn and gourds also. Christmas trees: U-cut, Noble fir, Grand fir and Norway spruce. Located at 13610 Manzanita Rd. Fresh cut lot on Hwy 305 in Bainbridge Island. Nursery Trees: unusual and usual deciduous trees field grown. Call 206-842-1429, ask for Karen for hours and appt.

28. WILLOW BROOK FARMS
Mike Ryherd and Dottie Parcheski
206-842-8034
12600 Miller Rd NE, Bainbridge Isl. 98110
W of Hwy 305 at Day Rd. This 24 acre farm is open to the public on Oct weekends only. Pumpkins, specialty apples, fresh pressed cider, ornamental corn, gourds, fresh and dried flowers and other produce in season. Gardens, orchards, barns (miniature horses), hayfields and berry patch open for self-guided tours on sale days. Group guided tours by appt. at other times (fee).

29. VICTORIA'S ATTIC AND COSMOS RABBIT FACTORY
360-779-3666
18846 E. Front St, Poulsbo 98370
(Shop, studio and gallery located in historic downtown Poulsbo). Hours: 10am-5pm Mon-Sat; 12pm-4pm Sun. We raise Angora rabbits and Angora goats. We sell looms, spinning wheels, fibers, commercial knitting and weaving yarns, dyes and books. Classes in spinning, weaving, knitting, and crochet. Our gallery features dolls, Austrian crystal jewelry, handknit designer sweaters, handspun angora, mohair, wool and silk yarns; weavings and wall hangings by local artists.

30. SILVER BAY HERB FARM
May Preus 360-692-1340
9151 Tracyton Blvd, Bremerton 98311
Hours: Tue-Sun 11am-5pm. Closed Mon. Jun-Sept. From Silverdale, go E up Bucklin Hill rd. Turn R on Tracyton Blvd. Sign on right. From Bremerton, take Riddell Rd to Tracyton, cont. to Tracyton Blvd, 1 mile S of Fairgrounds Rd on left. Herb plants, herb seeds, fresh cut herbs, cut flowers, gift shop with books and herbal theme garden. Organically raised.

31. ISLAND HOLLY FARM
Gordon & Chris Wilson 206-842-6116
11060 NE Madison, Bainbridge Isl. 98061
Please call ahead for nursery stock in spring and fall. For Christmas items, drop by. Hours: Retail shop opens first weekend after Thanksgiving Sat-Sun 10am-5pm; Mon-Fri 12pm-5pm. Holly, wreaths, candy canes, Noble fir swags, cut holly sprays, potted holly trees.

32. PETS GALORE HORSEBACK RIDES
Mark & Wendy Buczkowski
206-857-7506
13659 Cedar Glenn Ln SE, Olalla 98359
Ride unguided on our private 2 miles of wooded trails at your own level (walk, trot or canter) or guided trail riding lesson. We have 10 acres of park-like setting with an outside areana area and picnic area. Appt. only/up to groups of 6. If you miss riding or would like to learn, call us and come out!

33. KUNEY'S TREE FARM
Fred Kuney 360-830-5284
11175 NW Pioneer Rd, Seabeck 98380
Hours: 9am-5pm daily. Take Hwy 3 from Silverdale/Bremerton, turn W on Newberry Exit, go 2 miles and turn right on Seabeck Hwy, go 2 miles turn left on Pioneer Rd. Go to end of blacktop Rd. Christmas trees: Douglas, Grand and Noble fir, Pine and Spruce). U-Cut.

34. OCEAN SKY FARM
Art Biggert & Suzy Cook 206-842-7431
5191 Taylor Ave NE, Bainbridge Isl. 98110
A family operated farm using organic and sustainable farming techniques to grow a wide variety of vegetables from a to z. Specialties include ready-to-eat salad mix, fresh and dried herbs, dried tomatoes, sweet corn, everlasting flower bouquets, asparagus, blueberries. Produce is available at the farm's roadside stand Mon, Wed, Fri 12pm to dusk. Bainbridge Island Farmers' Market Apr-Oct. Special orders welcome. Please call ahead.

Snohomish County

Snohomish County Farm Trails Map

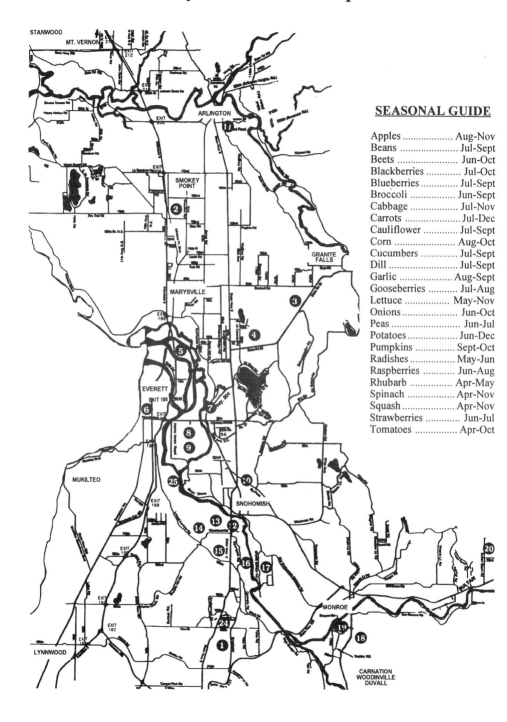

Produce Reference Guide

Apples: 6, 7, 10, 12, 13, 17, 23, 25
Autumn Decorations: 5, 6, 9, 10, 12, 13, 17, 23, 24, 25
Basil: 6, 9, 10, 12, 13, 23, 25
Beans: 3, 6, 7, 9, 10, 11, 12, 13, 16, 23, 25
Bedding Plants: 3, 6, 23, 25
Beef, Live: 12
Beets: 3, 6, 7, 9, 10, 11, 12, 13, 16, 23
Blackberries: 6, 8, 10, 23, 25
Blueberries: 3, 4, 13, 15, 20, 23, 25
Boysenberries: 23
Breed & Stock Sheep: 21
Broccoli: 3, 6, 10, 11, 13, 23, 25
Brussels Sprouts: 6, 10, 23, 25
Cabbage: 3, 6, 10, 11, 12, 13, 23, 25
Carrots: 3, 6, 7, 10, 11, 12, 13, 14, 16, 23, 25
Cauliflower: 3, 6, 10, 11, 13, 23, 25
Cherries: 6, 10, 12, 13, 23, 25
Chicken: 12, 21
Chinese Vegetables: 6, 10, 11, 23
Christmas trees: 5, 23, 25
Cider: 5, 6, 10, 12, 13, 17, 23, 25
Corn: 3, 5, 6, 7, 9, 10, 11, 13, 16, 17, 22, 23, 25
Corn Stalks: 3
Cucumber Pickling: 3, 6, 7, 9, 10, 13, 16, 23, 25
Cucumber, Slicing: 3, 6, 7, 9, 10, 11, 13, 16, 23, 25
Dill: 3, 6, 7, 9, 10, 11, 12, 13, 14, 16, 23, 25
Ducks: 1, 19, 21
East WA Fruit: 3, 23, 25
East WA Vegetable: 3, 23, 25
Egg Plant: 13
Eggs: 6, 10, 12, 19, 23
Feathers & Down: 19
Flowers U-cut: 1, 6, 12, 13, 14, 16
Flowers Cut: 1, 3, 7, 7, 10, 13, 14, 16, 24, 25
Garlic: 3, 6, 7, 10, 11, 12, 13, 14, 16, 23, 25
Geese: 18
Goats/Kids: 12, 19, 21
Gooseberries: 23
Gourds: 3, 5, 6, 7, 9, 10, 12, 13, 14, 16, 17, 23, 25

Grapes: 6, 10, 13
Hay: 25
Herbs: 3, 6, 10, 23, 24, 25
Honey: 3, 5, 6, 10, 12, 13, 17, 23, 25
Kohlrobi: 3, 6, 10, 12, 13
Leeks: 6, 10, 11, 13, 23
Lettuce: 3, 6, 10, 11, 13, 23, 24
Manure: 16, 19
Milk: 12, 23
Nursery Stock: 3, 5, 6, 10, 23, 24, 25
Onions: 3, 6, 7, 10, 11, 12, 13, 23, 25
Parsnips: 6, 10, 23
Peas: 3, 6, 10, 12, 13, 23
Peppers: 3, 6, 7, 10, 11, 13, 25
Picnic Tables: 5, 9, 13, 14, 17, 25
Pigeons: 20, 23
Pigs/Pork: 12, 23
Potatoes: 3, 6, 7, 10, 11, 12, 13, 16, 23, 25
Preserves: 3, 4, 5, 6, 10, 12, 13, 17, 23, 25
Prunes: 6, 10, 23, 25
Pumpkins: 3, 5, 6, 7, 9, 10, 11, 12, 13, 16, 17, 23, 25
Rabbits: 12, 21, 23
Raspberries: 3, 4, 5, 6, 8, 9, 10, 12, 13, 17, 18, 22, 23, 25
Rhubarb: 6, 10, 12, 13, 23, 25
Shallots: 6, 10, 23, 25
Sheep/Lambs: 3, 12, 19, 21, 23
Spinach: 3, 6, 10, 11, 13, 16, 23, 25
Squash: 3, 6, 7, 10, 11, 12, 13, 17, 23, 25
Staw: 5, 25
Strawberries: 2, 3, 6, 10, 12, 13, 17, 22, 23, 25
Tayberries: 5, 17, 23
Tomatoes: 3, 6, 7, 10, 11, 12, 13, 23, 25
Trees: 6, 10, 12, 23, 25
Turnips: 6, 10, 23
Vegetables: 3, 6, 7, 9, 10, 11, 12, 13, 16, 19, 23, 25
Wool: 21, 23
Zucchini: 3, 6, 7, 10, 11, 12, 13, 16, 19, 23, 25

Farm Index

1. **CAPROZ DAHLIAS**
206-481-7917
4510 174th SE, Mill Creek 98012
Go east 2 miles on 180th from Bothell-Everett Hwy or west from Clearview (Hwy 9) to Sunset Rd. On Sunset Rd turn right at 174th (look for blue sign). Over 500 varieties of dahlias of all sizes and colors; tubers available til May 1. Mid-Aug best time to visit gardens or order tubers for next year. Cut dahlias and other flowers available. Gift certificates. Hours: 9am-5pm or call.

2. **DUE'S BERRY FARM**
206-659-3875
14003 Smokey Pt. Blvd, Marysville 98271
Smokey Point Blvd: Take exit 116th St off I-5 N. Strawberries (Shuksan, Rainiers). U-pick, mid-Jun-mid-Jul. Weekdays 8am-8pm; Sat-Sun 8am-5pm. Commercial quality, clean fields. Plants on mounded rows. Senior citizen discount. Bring this map to field and receive a discount on your purchase. Call before coming to insure good picking and possible time changes because of weather conditions.

3. **BAKKO'S FARM MARKET & NURSERY INC.**
206-334-3581
7808 SR 92, Lake Stevens 98258
We are located 5 1/2 miles from Hwy 9 on Hwy 92 (Granite Falls Hwy). The nursery is open 9am-5:30pm seven days a week from Mar to the end of Oct. Our summer hours are 8am-6pm. We stock fruit trees, landscape trees, shrubs, bedding plants, hanging baskets, and related items. The Farm Market opens with the strawberry season. Shuksan and Rainier strawberries, Meeker raspberries, blueberries, (U-pick or We-pick on berries, vegetables, eastern Washington fruit, Bodacious Seneca Daybreak, and Platinum Lady corn (we can supply large gatherings with corn). Pumpkin patch opens Oct 1. Orders taken for fruit and vegetables. Please see Product Guide for complete listing.

4. **THE BLUEBERRY PATCH**
206-334-5524
10410 54th St NE, Everett 98205
Organically grow, well-tended blueberries. U-pick or fresh picked (early, mid and late varieties). Available late Jul to mid-Sept. Call ahead for pre-picked orders. Open 7 days a week, Mon-Sat 8am-7pm; Sun 9am-5pm. A great family outing. Located near Lake Cassidy, Centennial Trail and waterfowl sanctuary. Children welcome to accompany adults. From I-5, Marysville exit 199. East on Hwy 528, 3 1/2 miles to Hwy 9, then south (right) to Lake Cassidy Rd, past lake to 54th Place NE. (about 3/4 mile). Turn east (left) on 54th for 1/2 mile to Blueberry Patch.

5. **BIRINGER FARM**
206-259-0255 (Berry Line)
Marysville, WA 98271
Seasonal: U-pick & Farm Market. Strawberries (mid Jun-Jul); raspberries, tayberries (Jul); Pumpkins (Oct); Christmas trees (Dec). Trolley to field, special events, farm tours, farm kitchen, picnic area. Join us! Country fun! Hours vary with crops. Call Berryline before you come. From I-5, Marysville exit 199, rt to State St light. Rt on Hwy 529 S, rt 50 feet past 2nd bridge to Farm Gate.

6. **EVERETT FARMERS' MARKET**
206-347-2790
12311 4th Place W, Everett 98204
This market is located on the scenic waterfront and showcases the very best in handmade and home-grown goods. We feature farm fresh fruits and vegetables, organics, too. Flowers and plants, herbs, baked goods and crafts by local artists. Jun 9-Oct 6, Sun 11am-4pm. West Marine View Dr next to the Chamber of Commerce (just north of the entrance to Marina Village).

7. **CARLETON FARM**
206-334-2297
830 S. Sunnyside Blvd, Everett 98205
From I-5, exit 194 onto Hwy 2 (Hewitt Av) trestle, turn left at end of trestle onto Hwy 204 then take first left onto Sunnyside Blvd. Watch for stand on left. Mid-Aug to Oct 31, daily 10am-7pm. Corn, beans, carrots, cukes, beets, dill, onions, potatoes, and summer & winter squash. Pumpkins, old-fashioned pumpkin patch, U-pick or we pick. Fall decorations: corn stalks, straw etc. Horse boarding, full care and self-care, covered arena, outside turnouts, outside area year round.

8. EBEY ISLAND BERRY FARM
206-337-1932
1516 51st Av SE, Everett 98205
Raspberries & blackberries, State Certified Organic, mid-Jun-Aug. U-pick or we pick, open daily 8am-6pm; Sun 9am-5pm. Take exit 194 off I-5 (or Hewitt Ave from Everett), take first rt off trestle onto Home Acred Rd, then first left to 51st SE about 1 mile to Berry Farm on left.

9. LAURA & BOB JOHNSON
206-252-3181
5211 52nd St SE, Everett 98205
Located 3 miles from Everett. Take Exit 194 off I-5 (Hewitt Av). Take first rt turn off trestle onto Home Acres Rd for 2 1/2 miles. At bridge, bear left, down lane to stand. Raspberries, beans, beets, basil, dil, pickling cucumbers, corn (yellow & white, bi-colored), squash, cornstalks, pumpkins (at stand, with ride or U-pick in field). Pumpkin wagon tours in October by appointment weekdays. No appointments needed on weekends. Open July-Oct.

10. SNOHOMISH FARMERS' MARKET
206-347-2790
12311 4th Place W, Everett 98204
Open Thur, Jun 6 for 5th season. This lively market will feature fresh fruits and vegetables, organics too. Fresh & dried herbs, plants and flowers, honey, baked goods and arts & crafts direct from local growers and artists. 1st St, 2 blocks west of the bridge, by the river in downtown Snohomish. Thur 5pm-9pm until Sept 26.

11. STEEN'S PRODUCE
360-435-9625
8904 Tveit Rd, Arlington 98223
Hwy 9 to Arlington, E on Highland Dr past Burn Rd. Watch for sign on south side of rd. Hours 9am-6pm. Closed Mon.

12. STOCKER'S "THE CORN KING"
360-568-2338
10622 Airport Way, Snohomish 98290
1/2 mile S of Harvey's Airport, near Hwy 9 & Marshland Rd Crossing. Sweet corn in small or bulk quantities, including special white corn. Beets, basil, dill, broccoli, cabbage, cauliflower, carrots, peas, summer & winter squash, beans, cucumbers, u-pick pumpkins (including some X-large varieties) and flowers. Local milk, eggs, honey, corn stalks, Eastern Washington produce including decorative corn, gourds, other vegetables, apples, cherries, peaches, other fruits and berries as available. Watkins products, apple cider year-round, free petting zoo. Stand open daily. Polled Hereford bull rentals plus feeding and feeder stock year-round. Live rabbits, chickens and ducks. Christmas trees and local jams.

13. HAGEN VEGETABLES FARM & MKT
360-568-4120
8203 Marsh Rd, Snohomish 98290
Between Hwy 9 & Larimer's Corner. Open Mon-Sat 9am-7pm; Sun 11am-6pm; Jun 1-Oct 31. Farm stand, fresh-picked vegetables: beets, blueberries, raspberries, strawberries, eggplant, broccoli, cabbage, carrots, cauliflower, corn, slicing cucumbers, dill, garlic, basil, lettuce, potatoes, winter squash, leeks, green onions, turnips, zucchini, onions, Brussels sprouts, tomatoes, kohlrabi and more. Green beans & pickling cucumbers u-pick/we-pick. U-cut flowers and dried flowers. Peas & pumpkins, u-pick. Eastern Washington fruit. Free hayride to the pumpkin patch in Oct.

14. STANLEY'S STEMS
360-568-4252
Marsh Rd, Snohomish 98290
We only sell what we grow! Open from late July to Oct 6. Hours: Wed-Sun, 10am-4pm on Mon & Tue. Go 1 mile S of Snohomish on Hwy 9. Turn W (rt) at the first stoplight onto Marsh Rd, continue W for 1.8 miles. Look for the scarecrows in the field. Everlastings at their best, offered wholesale and retail at reasonable prices. We import seed to create an English Garden that offers a unique selection of fresh flowers for the U-cut market. Vase rental program, Asiatic & Oriental Lilies. U-pick carrots, fresh herbs including Italian, Purple, Anise & Thai basil. Our own garlic by the pound, braided and/or decorated.

15. MOUNTAIN VIEW BERRY FARM
360-668-3391
7617 E. Lowell-Larimer Rd, (131st SE) Snohomish 98290
Blueberries, U-pick or boxed at farm. Aug; sometimes U-pick extends into Sept. 9am-7pm Mon-Fri; 9am-4pm Sat-Sun. May be closed occasionally due to weather or being picked out. Call before coming. Orders taken.

16. BAILEY VEGETABLES
360-568-6826
12711 Springhetti Rd, Snohomish 98290
3 miles S of Snohomish. Fresh vegetables in season, u-pick. Green beans, new potatoes, pickling cucumbers, beets, flowers, fresh-picked corn, squash, u-pick pumpkins and carrots. Composted manure and perennial flower starts are also available. 7 days a week, 8am-8pm.

17. CRAVEN FARM & PUMPKIN PATCH
360-568-2601
13817 Short School Rd, Snohomish 98290
Strawberries (Jun), raspberries, marionberries, tayberries (Jun/Jul). Call for availability. The farm's jams, jellies, syrups also for sale. "Tailgate" antique sales, Annual Country Antique Sale. Craven Pumpkin Patch Oct 1-31. Story, cookie, farm animals, nursery rhyme pumpkin scenes and a pumpkin. Tour admission $3.75 per child, adults free. Call for a weekday appointment. Weekends open to public 9:30-4:30. No appointment needed. Harvest Market with fall produce, gift shop, antique store, snack bar, espresso and every size pumpkin! Harvest Bazaar in Oct.

18. SNOW'S BERRY FARM
A CENTENNIAL FARM
360-794-6312
18401 Tualco Rd, Monroe 98272
From Monroe, drive on mile S on Duvall Hwy (203), turn rt onto Tualco Rd, watch for sign on left. Raspberries: 3rd or 4th week in June til mid-Aug. U-pick and picked to order or can usually buy directly from field. Open daily 7am-7pm including Sunday.

19. TUALCO VALLEY ANIMAL FARM
360-794-6326
17910 SR 203, Monroe 98272
1/2 mile S of Lewis St Bridge on Monroe-Duvall Hwy 203. Eggs: organic, fertile; hen (blue and brown), duck and goose. Sheep: ewes and lambs for pets or butchered on order year-round. Milk goats and kids. Geese and pigeons. Wool: (black, brown and white). Organic garden manure by truckload or bag. Open daily afternoons year round.

20. GREEN'S ACRES BLUEBERRY FARM
360-793-1714
32326 132nd SE, Sultan 98294
Blueberries (early, mid and late varieties) available Jul-mid-Sept. Young, heavy-bearing bushes with large berries. Easy picking. Call before coming. U-pick, we pick. The best!

21. PFEIFFER FARMS
360-333-4934
31439 W. Commercial, Carnation 98014
Largest sheep farm in King County. Naturally grown lamb and mutton available year round. We now have meat rabbits, chickens, ducks, geese and goats. Call for availability. Custom farm slaughter facility. Special farm days by appointment. Featuring shearing, hands-on petting baby animals and a straw maze (minimum of 20 children). In business over 30 years. Please call first.

22. HARVOLD BERRY FARM
360-333-4186
32325 NE 55th St, Carnation 98014
U-pick strawberries (mid-Jun-mid-Jul) and raspberries (Jul). Containers are provided at no charge. U-pick fields open every day, 8am-8pm. Call ahead in case of varying hours. Convenient parking close to fields. Located N of Carnation on Carnation-Duvall Rd (#203).

23. REMLINGER FARMS
206-451-8740
32610 NE 32nd St, Carnation 98014
1 mile south of town off Hwy 203. Open Apr-Dec. Call for Ripe'n Ready Report. Direct Farm Market seasonal fruits & vegetables. Old fashioned fun on the farm & u-pick. Seasonal festivals & entertainment. Farm animals viewing & petting. Nursery, garden shop and consignment handcraft. Bakery featuring fresh frozen "u-bake" pies. Restaurant, catering and location for company picnics. Private birthday parties complete with puppet shows and more.

24. TONNEMALER FAMILY ORCHARD
360-668-2799
17809 SR 9, Clearview 98290

We specialize in farm fresh fruit from our Eastern WA farm. Picked fresh, tree-ripened fruit. Alfalfa hay and grass mix. Open year-round. Hours 10am-6pm Mon-Sat; 11am-6pm Sun. Expanded hours in the summer. We have dried flower arrangements and wreaths.

25. THE FARM
206-334-4124
7301 Rivershore Rd, Everett 98205

The Farm is a working dairy. We have a pumpkin patch in the fall and feature a wagon ride, hay maze, petting zoo, Peter Rabbit story trail and family fun. We also have nursery stock, perennials, annuals, cut flowers, herbs, sweet corn, and a gift shop. Hours vary seasonally, so call ahead.

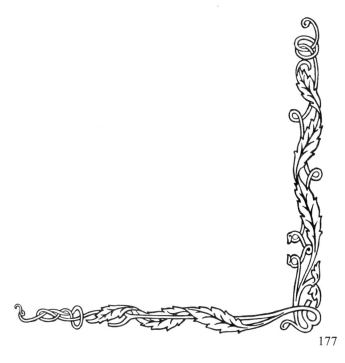

Spokane County

Green Bluff Orchard Location Map

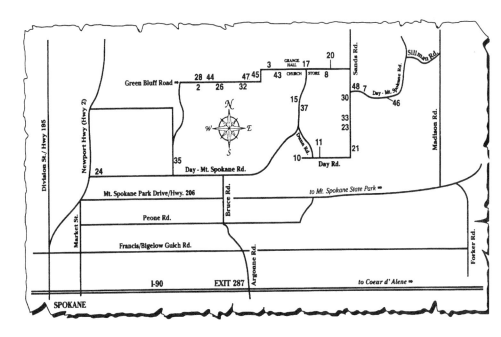

FRUIT & VEGETABLE CALENDAR

Strawberries .... Jun-Jul
Cherries .... Jul-Aug
Raspberries .... Jul-Aug
Apricots .... Jul-Aug
Apples .... Aug-Winter
Cucumbers .... Aug-Sept
Peaches/Nectarines .... Aug-Sept
Corn .... Aug-Sept
Prunes/Plums .... Aug-Oct
Carrots .... Aug-Winter
Pears .... Sept-Winter
Cabbage .... Sept-Winter
Potatoes .... Sept-Winter
Grapes .... Sept-Oct
Pumpkins .... Sept-Winter
Squash .... Sept-Winter
Christmas trees .... Winter

Credit: Green Bluff Growers Association

Farm Index

2. **HUCKABA ORCHARDS**
   238-2967
   E 8022 Greenbluff Rd, Colbert 99005
   20 acres of orchards with mowed grass and driveways, hiking and picnicking. Sweet and pie cherries, 20 varieties of apples, u-pick/picked. Pears, prunes, squash, pumpkins, cabbage, etc. Homemade apple cider since 1966.

3. **SMITH'S HILLTOP ORCHARD U-PICK**
   238-4647
   9423 E. Greenbluff Rd, Colbert 99005
   Cherries (Bing, Lambert, Rainier, & pie), Peaches (Red Haven & Daroga Red. Prunes and Nectarines. Apples (Macs, Jonathan, Red & Golden Delicious, Jonagold, Empire, Granny Smith and more). U-pick/picked. Cider, Jam and Pumpkin Patch.

7. **SEIMER'S PICK & PACK**
   238-6242
   24 Hour Information/Fax 238-4893
   Rides: U-pick strawberries, cherries & peaches. Applefest: Corn patch maze, rides, fun & games, music, food, educational tours, arts & crafts, apples, organic sugar carrots, potatoes, pumpkins, squash, cabbage, cider, honey, jam, straw flowers, corn stalks and gourds. Lots of easy parking!

8. **EDBURG'S ORCHARD**
   238-4271
   1/4 mile east of Green Bluff store.
   U-pick or picked strawberries; Bing, Lambert, Rainier and Royal Ann cherries; apricots, peaches, Red & Golden Delicious apples, summer & fall raspberries.

10. **WALTER'S FRUIT RANCH**
    238-4709
    Ride that "Fruit Loop Express." U-pick strawberries, cherries, peaches, nectarines, apricots and apples. Homemade: apple butter, preserves, take-n-bake pies, cinnamon rolls, cherry & apple cider. Log Cabin Gift Shop with crafts & gifts. Experienced educational tours. Cherry, peach and apple festivals. Pumpkinland.

11. **HIDDEN ACRES**
    238-2830
    U-pick/picked: raspberries, blackberries, cherries, cots, peaches, prunes. Apples: 12 delicious varieties of cooking & eating apples. Jams, apple butter & huckleberries. Gift shop and picnic area. U-pick pumpkins, corn maze, giant talking pumpkin and more during October Apple Festival.

15. **ANDERSON'S ACRES**
    238-6760
    Cherries: u-pick, Bings, Rainiers, Vans & Lamberts. Apples: U-pick/we pick. Transparents, Gravensteins, Gala, Red & Golden Delicious, Jonathan, Spartans & other varieties. Prunes, squash & pumpkins. 1/2 mile south of the Green Bluff Store, 17715 N. Day-Mt. Spokane Rd.

17. **HARVEST HOUSE & ORCHARD**
    238-6970
    Fresh fruit, berries & vegetables available daily May-Dec. Cherry & apple cider, "Apple Shop" country gifts, honey & jams. Homebaked goodies, ice cream & lunch available. Enjoy the beauty of the "Bluff" from our large covered deck. Tours, lots of parking, buses welcome. Cherry, peach & apple celebrations with country BBQ, live music & family fun!

20. **YARYAN'S ORCHARD**
    238-6261
    1/2 mile east of the Green Bluff Store. U-pick/picked to order. Cherries, apricots, peaches (early and late Red Havens, Daroga Red), apples (Red & Golden Delicious, Jonathan, McIntosh, etc), honey.

21. **WELLENS' LUSCIOUS FRUIT & ANTIQUES**
    238-6978
    Bing, Rainier & pie cherries, four varieties of Apricots, Freestone peaches, nectarines, plums, prunes and 14 varieties of apples. Family fun at our cherry, peach & apple festivals featuring Luscious Pie, country cooking, live music, craft booths, pony rides, face painting, antique shop and lots of easy parking.

23. THORSON'S COUNTRY FARM
238-6438
N. 17007 Sands Rd. U-pick/picked cherries, apricots, freestone peaches (HerbHale, Golden Monarch), Bartlett and d'Anjou pears, apples (Spartan, Paulared, Wagener, Rome, Winesap, Red & Golden Delicious), seedless & juice grapes, vegetables, pickle cukes, pumpkin patch. Lots of easy parking, carts provided.

24. McGLADE'S TREEMENDOUS FRUIT
467-8340
100 yards off Newport Hwy at Green Bluff turnoff. Fresh cut flowers, fruit trees, berry plants, garden produce and pumpkins, strawberries, raspberries, blackberries, blueberries, cherries, huckleberries, apricots, peaches, pears, apples, cider, gift apples, honey, apple butter, creamy fresh fruit milkshakes. Specialty food gifts, homemade pies. Closed Sun.

26. GREEN BLUFF HIGH COUNTRY ORCHARDS
238-4963
8518 E. Greenbluff Rd. U-pick or picked: sweet cherries (Bing, Rainier), pie cherries, strawberries, apricots and raspberries. Bring your own containers. Open summer fruit season only. Always call for hours and availability. Orders encouraged.

28. GREEN BLUFF CHRISTMAS TREE FARM
238-4067 / 238-6742
Grand fir, Concolor fir, Fraser fir, Balsam fir, Blue spruce, Norway spruce, choose & cut plantation. Visit our growing trees to look at an enjoy. Tree cutting from Thanksgiving until Christmas. U-cut trees stay fresh longer!

30. GRANNY'S ORCHARD
238-4991
U-pick Rainier & Bing cherries, apricots & peaches.

32. GREENBLUFF COUNTRY INN & ORCHARD
238-6971
Greenbluff's premier bed & breakfast. U-pick/picked cherries, peaches, apples, pears, walnuts. Jams (unique varieties). Fabulous fruit pies & pastries, honey, vegetables, dried flowers, gift baskets, country crafts. Giant pumpkin seasonal activities. Our own special cider. Warm pioneer hospitality!

33. WICKLUND'S APPLE LANE
238-4294
N. 17425 Sands Rd. At the Big Red Barn: cherries (Bing, Lambert, Rainier, pie), apricots, peaches (freestone varieties: Late Red Haven, Fair Haven), prunes, apples (many varieties). Asian pears, squash, cider, pumpkin patch, honey. Fall produce. Good parking. Easy picking & carts provided.

35. TOWNSHEND FARMS
238-4346
N. 16112 Greenbluff Rd. Choose & cut your own Christmas trees: Scotch pines & fir. All sizes. Saws provided. Open the day after Thanksgiving.

37. DIETZ U-CUT CHRISTMAS TREES
238-6975
17713 N. Day-Mt. Spokane Rd. Choose & cut a fresh fragrant Grand fir, Concolor fir, Scotch pine or spruce. All sizes, table tops and up. Fresh wreaths, tree stands. Saws furnished. Open for cutting starting the day after Thanksgiving.

43. CARMICHAEL'S GREENBLUFF GARDEN
238-4128
Strawberries, cherries, pickling cukes. October Apple Festival, gigantic pumpkin patch. The Great Round Corn Maze. Petting zoo, pony rides, potatoes, cabbage, corn bundles, gourds, picked apples. School tours.

44. HANSEN'S ORCHARD
238-4902
E. 8215 Greenbluff Rd (1.4 mile west of the store). 37 varieties of apples including Gala, Golden, Empire and Early Criterion. Chilled fresh barrel-pressed cider. Strawberries, cherries, apricots, peaches, prunes, tomatoes, carrots. Homemade jams and apple butter. Hand-loomed rag rugs, country kitchen items. Country store.

45. COLE'S ORCHARD
   238-4962
N. 18423 Greenbluff Rd (1/2 mile W of Store) Apricots, prunes, apples (Gravenstein, Spartan, MacIntosh, Golden Delicious, Jonathan, Rome, Winter Banana, Ida Red & Granny Smith), potatoes, squash, pumpkins, cabbage, honey & cider.

46. ALPACAS ON GREEN BLUFF
   238-4116
E. 11726 Day-Mt. Spokane Rd. Alpacas, originally form the Andes of S. America, produce luxurious fiber. Come see why alpacas are the world's finest livestock investment. Alpacas and alpaca products for sale including fiber, roving, yarn gloves, sweaters and Alpaca Blend coffee. Educaton tours. Open 10am-5pm Fall weekends and by appointment. Visits welcome.

47. "OLE" CIDER PRESS FARM
   238-2670
8903 E. Greenbluff Rd. (one mile west of store). Come join the harvest fun. Juicy and delicious fruit in season fresh off the tree. Cherries (Bing, Lambert, Rainier, pie), apples (Paulared, Gravenstein, MacIntosh, Spartan, Winesap, Red/ Golden Delicious). Fresh apple cider.

48. ELEVEN ACRES
   238-9473
7/10 mile east of Greenbluff Store on Day-Mt. Spokane Rd. Strawberries, raspberries, peaches, rhubarb, tomatoes, peppers, cukes, sweet corn, herbs, fresh flowers, apples, squash, pumpkins, ornamentals and more!

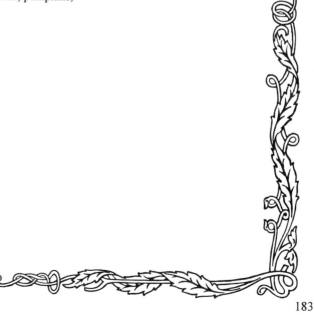

Thurston County

Thurston County Farm Map

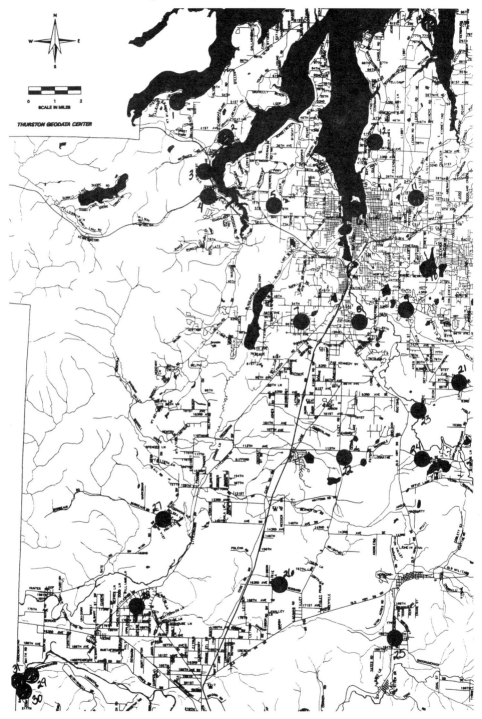

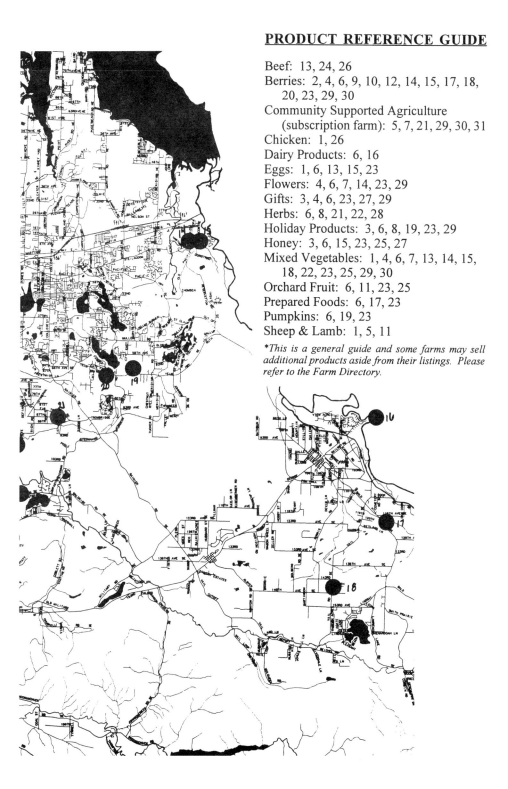

PRODUCT REFERENCE GUIDE

Beef: 13, 24, 26
Berries: 2, 4, 6, 9, 10, 12, 14, 15, 17, 18, 20, 23, 29, 30
Community Supported Agriculture (subscription farm): 5, 7, 21, 29, 30, 31
Chicken: 1, 26
Dairy Products: 6, 16
Eggs: 1, 6, 13, 15, 23
Flowers: 4, 6, 7, 14, 23, 29
Gifts: 3, 4, 6, 23, 27, 29
Herbs: 6, 8, 21, 22, 28
Holiday Products: 3, 6, 8, 19, 23, 29
Honey: 3, 6, 15, 23, 25, 27
Mixed Vegetables: 1, 4, 6, 7, 13, 14, 15, 18, 22, 23, 25, 29, 30
Orchard Fruit: 6, 11, 23, 25
Prepared Foods: 6, 17, 23
Pumpkins: 6, 19, 23
Sheep & Lamb: 1, 5, 11

This is a general guide and some farms may sell additional products aside from their listings. Please refer to the Farm Directory.

SEASONAL AVAILABILITY GUIDE

Animal Meats .... Year round
Apples .... Aug-Nov
Apple Cider .... Year round
Asparagus .... Apr-May
Basil .... Jun-Sept
Beans .... Jul-Oct
Beets .... Jun-Dec
Blueberries .... Jul-Sept
Broccoli .... May-Sept
Brussels Sprouts .... Aug-Nov
Cabbage .... Jul-Nov
Carrots .... Apr/Jul-Dec
Cauliflower .... Jul-Nov
Celery .... Sept-Nov
Cherries .... Jun-Aug
Corn .... Aug-Oct
Cucumbers .... Jul-Sept
Dill .... Jul-Sept
Eggs .... Year round
Fish .... Year round
Garlic .... Aug-Dec
Herbs .... Mar-Nov
Honey .... Year round
Kohlrabi .... Apr-May/Aug-Nov
Lettuce .... May-Nov
Loganberries .... Jul-Aug
Marionberries .... Jul-Aug
Onions .... Jun-Nov
Oysters .... Year round
Peas .... Jun-Jul
Peppers .... Aug-Oct
Potatoes .... Apr-Dec
Pumpkins .... Sept-Nov
Radishes .... Sept-Dec
Raspberries .... Jul-Aug
Rhubarb .... Apr-Jun
Spinach .... Apr-Nov
Squash .... Jul-Dec
Strawberries .... Jun-Jul
Tomatoes .... Jul-Oct
Zucchini .... Jul-Oct

Farm Directory

1. **Oyster Bay Farm**   866-9424
   4931 Oyster Bay Rd, Olympia
   Self-serve egg pick-up year-round. Prearranged sales of lamb & chicken. Small seasonal vegetable farm stand: Saturdays, mid-July to mid-Sept. No chemical sprays or fertilizers used. *Two miles off Hwy 101, on Burns Cove.*

2. **Steamboat Island Farm**   866-1753
   5735 Young Rd, Olympia
   Raspberries, marionberries and apples available seasonally. Market pigs for sale year-round. Fruit stand: late June-Oct, Mon-Sat 8am-7pm, Sun 1pm-7pm. *Hwy 101 to Steamboat Isl Rd exit. Turn right onto Steamboat Isl Rd then right onto Gravelly Beach Rd and left onto Young Rd.*

3. **Four B's Farm**   866-7708
   2448 Madrona Beach Rd, Olympia
   Raw honey & beeswax candles availalbe year-round. Old English and variegated holly Dec 1-25. Open daily, please call first. *Follow Mud Bay Rd to Madrona Beach Rd. 1.9 miles on the right.*

4. **Perry Creek Farm**   866-2588
   6149 Old Olympic Hwy, Olympia
   Sheep & lambs, early rhubarb, vegetables, fruits, berries, flowers, handmade soaps and other crafts. All produce and lambs grown without commercial pesticides or herbicides. Small quantities, excellent prices. Jun-Sept, Fri-Sun 10am-3pm; other times by appt., please call. *Hwy 101 to 2nd Av exit, south to Old 410. Turn right onto Old Olympic Hwy, farm sign will be on left.*

5. **Common Ground CSA**   866-9527
   4004 11th Ave NW, Olympia
   Community Supported Agriculture. Members receive a weekly box of fresh, organic vegetables, herbs and flowers. Please call for information about membership. Also available: goats, sheep, lambs, wool and mohair fleece.

6. **Olympia Farmers' Market**   352-9096
   700 N. Capitol Way, Olympia
   Brand new market on Olympia's scenic waterfront offering a wide selection of fresh, organic produce, fruit, plants, herbs, honey, baked goods, meats, seafood, crafts, art, hot lunches and entertainment. Apr, Nov & Dec: Sat-Sun 10am-3pm; May-Sept: Thur-Sun 10am-3pm; Oct: Fri-Sun 10am-3pm. *Located at the extreme north end of Capitol Way.*

7. **Kirsop Farm** 352-3590
6136 Kirsop Rd, Olympia
A wide variety of certified organic vegetables and flowers, including a crop of very hot peppers! Some CSA shares available, please call for information. Farm stand: mid-May to Nov, Sat-Sun. Also look for our farm stand on weekends at the Blue Heron Bakery. *Take I-5 to Trosper Rd W, continue 1/2 mile to Krisop Rd.*

8. **Fairie Herbes** 754-9249
6236 Elm SE, Tumwater
Nursery & demonstration gardens. We sell fresh and potted herbs and perennials plus a large selection of handmade, herbal bath, skin and sleep aids. Mar-Oct, 7 dyas a week, 10am-6pm. *Follow Capitol Blvd just under a mile south of Trosper Rd to X St. Turn left and continue three blocks to the corner of X & Elm Sts.*

9. **Spooner Farm** 456-4554
3327 Yelm Hwy, Olympia
U-pick & ready-picked strawberries, raspberries and marionberries. Early Jun-mid-Aug. *On Yelm Hwy between Rich and Wiggins Rd.*

10. **Johnson Farms** 493-2350
2908 Wiggins Rd, Olympia
Certified Organic red, black, yellow and purple raspberries and eight varieties of blackberries. We also offer Fall raspberries! Frozen berries available. Mid-Jun-mid-Sept, please call for hours. *Take I-5 to College St; turn right onto 37th, then right onto Wiggins Rd.*

11. **Hedgerow Farm** 352-9352
3238 Lindell Rd NE, Olympia
Lamb meat, Suffolk rams, sheep skins, filberts, black walnuts and apples. Open year-round, product availability dependent on season. Call anytime! *Follow South Bay Rd north past Skateland; turn right onto Lindell. The farm is on the right.*

12. **Carr's Organic Blueberry Farm**
943-2277
3844 1/2 Gull Harbor Rd, Olympia
Certified Organic Blueberries. U-pick and custom orders filled. large size and older varieties available. Bring a picnic and enjoy the tranquil surroundings! Please phone ahead for special orders. Jul-Sept, 10am-dusk. *Travel north on East Bay Dr past Priest Point Park and turn right onto 36th Av. At the first stop sign, turn left onto Gull Harbor Rd and travel 1/3 mile to the address on the right. Follow signs to off-road parking.*

13. **Esterly's The Farm** 943-7129
7816 Libby Rd NE, Olympia
Organic eggs year-round. Organic beef and free-roaming stewing hens when available. Self-serve and u-pick produce seasonally. Please phone ahead for large orders. *Travel north on East Bay Dr/Boston Harbor Rd. Turn right onto Woodard Bay Rd, which magically turns into Libby Rd. Continue north and the farm will be on the right.*

14. **Nisqually Produce Farm** 456-8195
Olympia
Wide variety of Certified Organic vegetables, berries and flowers. Farm stand: Jun-Sept, 7 days a week, 10am-6pm. *Take I-5 exit #114; follow Nisqually Cut-Off Rd 1 1/2 miles to the corner of Steilacoom Rd & 7th Av. The farm is on the right.*

15. **Pigman's Organic Produce Patch**
491-FARM
10633 Steilacoom Rd, Olympia
Certified Organic vegetables and berries. We have strawberries (Jun-Sept). Come right in, even if the stand isn't set up. May-Oct: Mon-Sat 10am-dark. *Take I-5 to exit #114; follow Nisqually Cut-Off Rd 1/2 miles to the corner of Steilacoom Rd & 7th Av. The farm is on the left.*

16. **Wilcox Farms** 458-7774
40400 Harts Lake Valley Rd, Roy
Dairy products (milk, whipped cream, half & half, etc.), juices and egg products. Farm store: year-round, Mon-Fri 10am-5pm. *Follow Hwy 507 to McKenna; turn right onto Hwy 702, then right onto Harts Lake Valley Rd. The farm store is on the first road on the left.*

17. **Blueberry Hill Farm** 458-4726
18811 119th Av SE, Yelm
Fresh, Certified Organic strawberries, raspberries, blueberries and blackberries. Also offering homemade jams and overnight lodging. Jun-Sept (jams available year-round). Please call ahead to order berries and jam and/or make reservations. *Go one mile past Four Corners off of Bald Hill Rd, then follow signs.*

18. **Gorley's Gardens** 894-2548
15641 Vail Rd SE, Yelm
Assorted vegetables and blueberries. Come and see our demonstration gardens and dome greenhouse! Jul-Oct, Mon-Sat 10am-6pm. *From Yelm, turn right at 5 corners onto Bald Hill Rd; turn right onto Vail Rd and continue 5 miles. The garden is on the right.*

19. Hunter's Christmas Farm   456-0466
7401 Yelm Hwy, Olympia
Pumpkins, winter squash, Christmas trees, wreaths and garlands. Enjoy the holiday fun of our petting farm, hay maze and live reindeer! Oct 5-31, seven days a week 9am-5:30pm; Nov 22-Dec 22, seven days a week 10am-5pm. *Located 1/3 mile east of the Amtrak Station on the Yelm Hwy.*

20. Ward Farms   456-1345
7725 Yelm Hwy, Olympia
Berry Barn selling strawberries. Late May-Jun, 7 days a week. *Located 1/2 mile east of the Amtrak Station on the Yelm Hwy.*

21. 9th Heaven Herbs and Vegetables   493-1107
Olympia
Membership program and subscription sales. No on-site sales. Call for delivery or pick-up at the Olympia Farmers' Market. Specialty salad mix, basil, garlic (including garlic braids), cut flowers, limited amounts of assorted greens and fresh herbs. May-Oct.

22. Shady Grove Organic Farm   705-0189
Olympia
Certified Organic produce and herbs, specializing in fresh basil, winter squash, and sweet and hot peppers. Bulk orders must be placed one day in advance. Please call ahead for directions and to place orders; no drop ins!

23. Lattin's Country Cider Mill   491-7328
9402 Rich Rd SE, Olympia
In addition to our famous home-made cider, we sell honey, eggs, vegetables, fruit, pumpkins, pies, jams, dried fruit and gifts! Come and see our farm animals and enjoy our horse-drawn wagon rides every Sat in Oct. Our annual Applefest will be held September 28&29, 10am-4pm. Open year-round, Mon-Sat 9am-6pm, Sun 12pm-5pm (closed Sun, Jan-Jun). *Travel south on Capitol Blvd; 3 1/2 miles past Airdustrial Way turn left onto Rich Rd. The farm is 1/2 mile down, on the right.*

24. Nelson Bros.   352-1761
3624 Waldrick Rd SE, Olympia
Natural, grass-fed beef for sale throughout the fall. We use no feed additives, hormones or chemicals. WSU research has shown our breed of longhorn beef-cattle to produce meat lower in cholesterol than other steer. Please call to place orders.

25. Richard McNair   264-2995
2820 180th Av SE, Tenino
On-farm sales of honey (year-round), apples (some until Apr), pears, grapes, produce and garden plants. Open year-round, 9am-dark. *Two miles south of Tenino on the east side of the railroad tracks. The farm is on the corner of 180th Av and Crowder Rd.*

26. Natural Prairie Farm   273-9965
3312 163rd SW, Tenino
Organic beef and eggs from organically-raised chickens. We are open year-round, but please call ahead!

27. Robertson's Honey   352-9512
Mima Rd SW, Olympia
Local, raw and unprocessed honey from fireweed, blackberries and wildflowers. Raw beeswax and beeswax candles. Open year-round. *Two miles SW of Littlerock at the corner of Mima and Bordeaux Rds.*

28. Scatter Creek Nursery   273-6730
8550 173rd St, Rochester
Bedding plants, perennials, hanging plants and fresh herbs seasonally. Open mid-Apr -mid-Jul. Tue-Sun 10am-50m. *Take I-5 to exit 88 and turn towards Rochester onto 12 West. Turn right at the first light, then bear a hard left onto Sargeant Rd. Turn left onto 173rd and the nursery will be 1/2 mile on the right.*

29. Helsing Junction Farm   273-8557
12013 Independence Rd, Rochester
Community Supported Agriculture program Jun-Nov. Certified Organic vegetables, apples, Asian pears, pears, raspberries and flowers. Fruit gift baskets and everlasting herb and flower wreaths. We ship UPS!

30. Independence Valley Farm   273-5882
13136 201st St, Rochester

Community Supported Agriculture shares. U-pick, special orders and bulk sales. Certified Organic strawberries, pickling cukes and other produce. Open June to November. *Take I-5 south to exit 88. Travel west on Hwy 12 to Rochester. At light, turn left onto Albany Rd, then right onto 185th, which curves left to Marble Rd, and becomes Independence Rd. Bear right after bridge over river. Continue 2.2 miles, and turn right onto 201st St. Go to the first house past the first barn.*

31. Rising River Farm   273-5368
13136B 201st St, Rochester

Community Supported Agriculture program offering fresh, Certified Organic vegetables and herbs. Some trades are available and we accept food stamps. Please call ahead for more information. Open May-Oct. *See #29 for directions to 201st St. Third driveway on the right.*

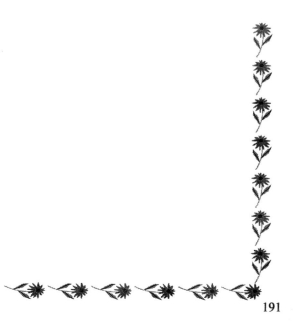

Yakima County

Yakima Area Farm Trails

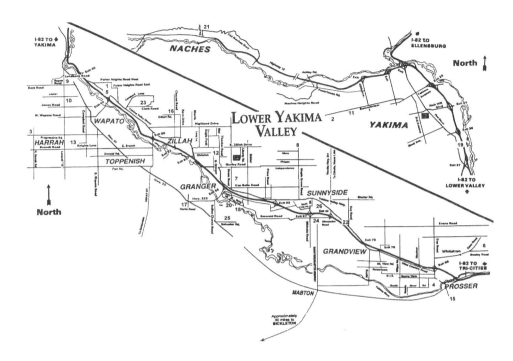

QUICK REFERENCE GUIDE:

1. Belzer Orchards
2. Residential Fruit Stands
3. Caribou Ranches, Inc.
4. Chukar Cherries
5. Donald Fruit & Mercantile
6. Durfey Farms
7. Granger Berry Patch
8. Guerra's Produce
9. Husch & Sons
10. Imperial's Garden
11. Johnson Orchards
12. Jones Farm
13. Krueger Family Peppers & Produce, Inc.
14. Mtn. View Produce & Hauling
15. Prosser Farmers' Market
16. RML Orchards, Inc.
17. Schell Farms Bean & Produce
18. Sky^e Ranch
19. Spring Creek Ranch
20. Stewart Vineyards
21. Thompson's Farm
22. Tucker Cellars, Farmers' Market
23. Turcott Orchard, Benson Ranches
24. Darigold Dairy Fair
25. Guerra's Produce
26. Sunnyside Dowtown Farmers' Market

Credit: Yakima Farm Trail Group, Lino Guerra 509-837-8897

Farm Products Guide

1. Belzer Orchards 509-877-4359
620 E. Parker Heights Rd, Wapato 98951
Location: From I-82 take exit 44. At end of exit turn north to Donald (not toward Wapato) & go to end of road (about 1/3 mile). Turn left toward Yakima, then take 1st paved road to right. (This puts you on E. Parker Heights Rd). Cross over bridge and keep to the right. We are 3/4 mile from bridge on right. Watch for big rock painted with BELZER ORCHARDS.
CHERRIES: U-pick Bings, Vans, Rainiers, Jun 25-Jul 10. Best to call before coming.
PEARS: Bartlett & D'Anjou, Aug 10-Sept 15; Bosc, Oct.
APPLES: Red & Golden Delicious, late Sept; Rome, Oct.
Fruits boxed at farm. Open daily 11am-7pm when fruit is available. Other times by appointment. Please call before coming. To hear recording of what's available or to leave a message let phone ring at least 5 times.

2. Residential Fruit Stands 509-575-5358
1103 S. 3rd Av, Yakima 98902
Stands: S. 2nd & 3rd Av, & Nob Hill / also S. 58th & Summitview Av (next to Smooty's)
Location: Take Exit 34 off of I-82. Turn West. Go 2 miles to SE corner of S. 3rd Av & Nob Hill.
We've been serving the Yakima Valley since 1960 with fresh local fruit, vegetables and berries. Produce stands open 9am-dusk every day from early Jul-Nov. Gift/Kitchen shop open year round. Fresh bread baked daily. Christmas Trees in December.

3. Caribou Ranches, Inc. 509-848-2277
7281 Progressive Rd, Wapapto 98951
Location: From Yakima, take exit 37 off I-82 onto Hwy 97. Then take the Lateral A exit. Follow lateral A south 5 miles to the 4-way stop at Kiles Korner. Continue south another 2 miles to Progressive Rd. Turn right and follow spuds signs 3 1/4 miles.
ASPARAGUS: Mid-Apr-mid-Jun, by order only.
POTATOES: Norkotah - white, Norland - red, Yukon Gold - yellow. We have been raising potatoes in the same location for 37 years. We are your personal potato grower.
One box or a truck load. We never close. TRUCKERS WELCOME.

4. Chukar Cherries 509-786-2055
320 Wine Country Rd, Prosser 99350
Location: From I-82 take exit 80 (Gap Rd) south toward Prosser. Find Chukar Cherries between the airport and the Yakima River bridge, app. one mile from the exit. Open daily from 10:30am-5pm.
Tasting Room! "The Year-Round Cherry & Berry Company" offers tasting samples of award winning products for your enjoyment. Find a variety of choice dried cherries and berries, chocolate coated cherries and berries and other regional special foods. Fresh cherries in season.

5. Donald Fruit & Mercantile 509-877-3115
2560 Donald-Wapato Rd, Wapato 98951
Location: 15 miles south of Yakima on I-82, take exit 44, on the north side of the interchange, in Donald, next to mini-mart; or Donald Rd. turnoff from Yakima Valley Hwy.
We have a fun, old fashioned general store-farm market where we sell our fruit from our Centnennial family farm. We also have a good selection of Yakima Valley gift foods, fresh apple cider, unique gifts and cards, and great fresh peach sundaes that can be eaten in our picnic area. Easy access for RV's. We also have a collection of antique apple varieties growing next to the store.
APRICOTS: July 1-30, Tiltons, Perfections, Goldrich, Goldbar
ASPARAGUS: June
CHERRIES: June 12-July
PEACHES: July 15-Sept, Red Haven, Flavorcrest, Rosa, Suncrest, Golden Elberta, Flamecrest, Angeles, and Gold Medal
NECTARINES: July 25-Aug
PEARS: Bartletts, Aug 15-Sept; Winter & Asian pears, Sept-Oct
APPLES: Summer apples, Aug. Many fall varieties, Sept-Oct, including Criterions and Jonigolds.
PLUMS, PRUNES, GRAPES, SWEET CORN, MELONS, TOMATOES, POTATOES, ONIONS and **VEGETABLES** in season.
U-PICK PUMPKIN PATCH: Oct
APPLE GIFT PACKS: Shipping Oct-Dec 15
CHRISTMAS TREES
Open daily, 9am-6pm Memorial Day through Christmas.

6. **Durfey Farms**   509-973-2202
Rt. 2, Box 2538, Swaley Rd, Prosser 99350
Location: Take Gap exit off I-82. North on Gap to Johnson Rd. Turn right on Johnson Rd to Old Inland Empire Hwy (OIE). Follow OIE east through Whitstran. Turn left off OIE onto Case Rd going north. turn right on Swaley Rd. First driveway to the left.
PEACHES: July 20-Sept 15, Red have, Rosa, Suncrest, Cresthaven, J.H. Hale, Golden Elbertas.
APPLES: Aug 15-Dec 1, Golden, Red Delicious, Romes.
MONUKKA GRAPES: Sept 1-Oct 31
ENGLISH WALNUTS: Oct
VEGETABLES OF ALL KINDS: June-Oct
Open anytime. Truckers welcome. We specialize in tree ripe fruit.

7. **Granger Berry Patch**   509-854-1413
1731 Beam Rd, Granger 98932
Location: Take exit 58 off of I-82, turn East. Go 1/2 mile, turn left onto Beam Rd. Go 1 1/2 miles. Farm on East side of Beam Rd.
RHUBARB
CURRANTS: red & black
GOOSEBERRIES: pink, green, English
RASPBERRIES: red, yellow, purple, black
MARION-, LOGAN-, BOYSEN-, STRAW-, BLACKCAPS, BLUE-, BLACK-, and HUCKLEBERRIES.
CONCORD GRAPES
BERRY FESTIVAL: July - games, contests, petting zoo, family fun. Tours.
HUCKLEBERRY HAPPENING: End of Aug-Labor Day. Petting zoo, huckleberry desserts, tours, games.
PUMPKIN FESTIVAL: Oct: weekends, displays, hay rides, pony rides, giant straw maze, tours, petting zoo, entertainment, family fun. U-pick pumpkins, gourds, Indian corn.
CHRISTMAS TREE FESTIVAL: U-cut by appt.
BERRY JAM AND SYRUP: samples, gift packs, wholesale, retail sales, year round.
FROZEN BERRIES: year round.
Berries, grapes and pumpkins are u-pick or ready-picked at the farm. Open 8am-5pm daily, June-Oct. Call for dates and times of festivals. Truckers welcome. Please call ahead for availability and large orders.

8. **Guerra's Produce**   509-837-8897
4800 Maple Grove Rd, Sunnyside 98944
Guerras's Produce Annual Chile Festival: Aug
Location: Take exit 63 off of I-82. Go North to Yakima Valley Hwy & turn East. Turn left (North) onto Maple Grove Rd. Go app. 5 miles. Watch for signs.
GUERRA'S GOURMET NATURAL SEASONINGS: Hot red salsa, pickled Jalapenos, spicy pickled cukes, sample gift packs, wholesale-retail, year round.
HOT PEPPERS: Jalapenos, Serrano, Hot Portugal, Ancho, Pasilla, New Mexico Chile, Cayenne Pepper, Habanero.
SWEET PEPPERS: Bell, Anaheim, Banana, Red Bell
APPLES
CILANTRO
TOMATOES: Mid-Jul-frost
MELONS: watermelons, cantaloupes, mid-Jul through frost.
GARLIC, ONIONS: Aug & Oct
PINTO BEANS
CUCUMBERS: Slicers & pickling, mid-Jul through frost.
DRY PEPPERS: Sun-dried whole red chiles, ristras, and wreaths years round.
Open Mon-Sat 9am-6pm, Sun 10am-6pm. Truckers welcome. Please call ahead for large orders. Easy access for trucks & RVs.

9. **Husch & Sons**   509-877-4485
400 Lundberg Rd, Wapato 98951
Location: From Yakima take Exit 37 off of I-82 onto Hwy 97. Take Lateral "A" exit. Ranch located corner of Lateral A & Lundberg Rd.
PEACHES: Roza, Early August - Golden Elberta, late Aug until early Sept.
PEARS: Bartlett, mid-Aug to early Sept.
ITALIAN PRUNES: mid-Aug
APPLES: Criterion, Ryan Red, late Sept-Oct products at roadside stand are boxed at farm or U-box from bins. Truckers welcome. Call ahead for large orders. Bring containers or there are boxes for sale.

10. Imperial's Garden   509-877-2766
2701 Corner Lateral A & Lateral I
Wapato 98951
Location: Driving south from Yakima, take exit 37 off I-82 to Hwy 97, then take the Lateral A exit. Go South to Lateral I & turn left. First roadside stand on the right.
PEAS: mid-Jun
TOMATOES, BEETS, PEPPERS, BEANS, SUMMER SQUASH, CUCUMBERS, EGGPLANT, SWEET CORN: Jul-Oct
MELONS: Jul-Sept
ONIONS: Aug-Oct
WINTER SQUASH: Sept-Oct
Open daily 7am-7pm, Jun-Oct. Roadside stand and U-pick. Truckers welcome.

11. Johnson Orchards   509-966-7479
4906 Summitview Av, Yakima 98908
Location: Orchard, warehouse, and roadside stand located close in on Yakima's westside. 9 blocks west of 40th Av on Summitview Av.
Family owned & operated in the same location since 1904.
CHERRIES: Tree ripened, picked fresh daily. mid-Jun to mid-July. Bing, Rainier, Van & Lambert. Also available, 12#, 1/2 Bing, 1/2 Rainier boxes packed for shipping.
APRICOTS: July, 3 varieties
NECTARINES: Aug-Sept, 2 varieties
PEACHES: Aug-Sept, 4 varieties, including Golden Elberta
BARTLETT PEARS: Aug-Oct, red & green
WINTER PEARS: Aug-Dec
PRUNES, PLUMS: Aug-Sept
APPLES: Aug-Dec, summer apples include Lodi & Tydeman; fall apples include Red, Golden, Starking, and Standard Delicious, Gala, Jonagold, Jonathan, Spartan, Criterion, Fuji, Granny Smith, Rome, Winesap & Braeburn.
Apple and pear gift packs available Sept-Dec. 1, 2, and 4 layer boxes, any combination. All fruit sold by pound, box or bin. Open daily 9am-6pm.

12. Jones Farms   509-829-6024
2020 Thacker Rd, Granger 98932
Location: Off I-82 at exit 54, 1 1/2 miles North on Yakima Valley Hwy, turn right and go 2 1/2 miles East on East Zillah Dr, turn right. Stand is 1 block South on Thacker Rd on the right.
CHERRIES: Bing, Rainier, Van, Lapin, Attika; Jun-Jul
PEACHES, NECTARINES, TOMATOES, SWEET COEN, WATERMELONS, PEPPERS: Aug-Sept.
CANTALOUPE, CUCUMBERS: Aug
APPLES: Red Delicious, Golden Delicious, Criterions, Romes, Winesaps, Molly Gold, Ginger Gold, Fuji, Braeburn; Aug-Oct
Open Sun 7am-5pm Aug-Sept. All fruit and produce listed is grown on our farm. Truckers welcome.

13. Krueger Family Peppers & Produce, Inc.
509-877-3677
462 Knights Ln, Wapato 98951
Location: From Yakima take Exit 37 onto Hwy 97. At the stop light at the Fort Restaurant at Wapato, turn west. Go 1/2 mile to Campbell Rd & turn left. Go 2 1/2 miles to Knights Ln and follow signs.
PEPPERS: Hot & sweet, 70 varieties including Bell, Pimentos, Jalapeno, Green Chilies, Serrano, Habenero and a number of exotics from Europe and Mexico. Aug 1-frost.
PICKLING CUKES, SUMMER & WINTER SQUASH, EGGPLANT, PUMPKIN, WINTER SQUASH: 18 varieties, Sept-frost.
TOMATOES: 4 varieties.
WATERMELONS: 6 varieties
CANTALOUPES: 4 varieties after Jul 15
HONEYDEW, CASABA, CRENSHAW AND OTHER EXCLUSIVE MELONS
GRAPES: Concord & Campbell
CHERRIES
APRICOTS: 4 varieties
APPLES: 4 varieties
PRUNES
ONIONS: Winter Yellow, Red, White & Walla Walla Sweet.
Your containers, recipe books. Open Sun-Thur, daylight hours. Fri until 3pm. Closed Sat. Truckers call ahead. U-pick, roadside stand. Boxed at farm.

14. **Mtn. View Produce & Hauling**
    509-829-3899
    823 N. Liberty Rd, Granger 98932
Location: Take exit 54 off I-82. From Yakima Valley Hwy, turn towards Zillah. Turn right on Zillah Dr and go 5 miles. Turn right on N. Liberty Rd, 2nd place on left at the dairy.
We specialize in many different vegetables & fruit from apples to zucchini. We have a large truck and will deliver farm fresh fruit & vegetables to your store or fruit stand. Please call a few days ahead from date you actually want your order delivered. To assure a stop on our routes call early in the season before routes are full.

15. **Prosser Farmers' Market 509-786-3600**
    Prosser Economic Development Assn.
    1230 Bennett Ave, Prosser 99350
Location: Take Gap Rd exit off I-82 at Prosser. drive into town on Wine Country Rd. Turn right on 7th St at the Jackpot Minimart, stay on 7th until you reach the Public Library. Take a left on Sommers, we're located next to the City Park.
ALL THE VALLEY FRUITS AND VEGETABLES AVAILABLE IN SEASON, CRAFT ITEMS AND BAKED GOODS.
Open Sat 8am-1pm, Jun-Oct.

16. **RML Orchards, Inc.   509-829-6313**
    2970 Gilbert Rd, Zillah 98953
Location: From I-82, exit 52, North on Cheyne 3 miles, NW corner of Cheyne and Gilbert Rds.
    Naches Farmer (RML)   509-653-2434
    12160 Hwy 12, Naches 98937
Location: The stand is located on the left side of Hwy 12 on the north edge of town. Just pass the lumber mill and before the "Y" in the hwy.
CHERRIES: Bing, Jun-Jul
APRICOTS: Rival, Perfections, Patterson - Jul
PEACHES: Golden Elberta, J.H. Hales, Angelus - Aug-Sept
NECTARINES: Red Gold - Aug
PEARS: Bartletts, Aug
APPLES: Red, Golden, Criterions, Winesaps, Grannys - Sept-Oct.
Plus ice cream, pop, Washington honey, jams, many goods. Gift shop. Call ahead. Bin, box or truckload. Truckers welcome.

17. **SCHELL FARMS BEAN & PRODUCE**
    509-865-4511
    10 Harris Rd, Toppenish, 98948
Location: Take exit 58 off I-82 and go south on Hwy 223, 3 miles to Hwy 22. Turn right onto Hwy 22. Go 1/4 mile to Harris Rd. Stand is on left. Or 4 miles east of Toppenish on Hwy 22 and Harris Rd.
APPLES: Sept-Oct
APRICOTS: Jul 1-Aug
BEANS: Green & Yellow, Jun-Jul
BEETS: Jun-Jul
CABBAGE: Jun-Jul
CANTALOUPE: Aug-Sept, 3 varieties honeydew, (pink & green) Casaba, Sharylene, & other exotic melons.
CHERRIES: mid-June-Jul
CORN, INDIAN: Sept-Oct
CORN, SWEET: Jul-Sept (Chief O'Ray)
CUCUMBERS: Jul-Sept
DRY BEANS: Pinto, Reds, Whites, Black & Mixed year round.
NECTARINES: Jul & Aug
ONIONS & GARLIC: Aug-Oct
PEACHES & PEARS: Aug-Sept
PEPPERS: Bell, Jalapenos, Jul 15-Oct 1
POTATOES: Aug-Oct
PUMPKINS: Sept-Oct 30, mini & large
SQUASH: Aug-frost, summer & winter varieties
TOMATOES: Aug-Oct
WATERMELONS: Aug-Sept
ZUCCHINI: June-Sept
Open Mon-Sat, 9am-6pm; Sun 9am-4pm; mid-Jun through Oct 30.
Wholesale & Retail. All truckers welcome. Call ahead for large orders. Easy access for trucks and RVs.

18. **Sky^e Ranch   509-854-1866**
    800 Nass Rd on Cherry Hill, Granger 98932
Location: From I-82 take exit 58. Turn S on Hwy 223 for 1 1/2 miles to Emerald Rd exit & go E for app. 2 miles then turn left on Cherry Hill Rd. to Nass Rd. Watch for signs to Sky^e Ranch.
CHERRIES: mid-Jun-Jul 1. Large, sweet, fully ripened Bing and Van cherries. Fresh picked daily. Packed and hydro-cooled in the orchard. Sales by the pound or by the ton. Telephone orders accepted. Truckers welcome. Please call ahead for large orders.

19. Spring Creek Ranch   509-248-6621
3213 Tacoma St, Union Gap, 98903
Location: 6 minutes from downtown Yakima. Take exit #36 off I-82. Turn W onto Valley Mall Blvd. Go 1/4 mile and turn S on Main St. Go 3/4 mile and turn E on Columbus St (at Jean's Cottage Inn). Drive straight and you are at Spring Creek Ranch. Follow signs. Easy access for RV's and buses. Restrooms.
22 ACRE PRODUCE AND FLOWER FARM WITH A LARGE MARKET ON THE FARM. FARM TOURS, PETTING ZOO, FRESH PRODUCE.
Watch our farm crews care for and harvest the crops. Cross the beautiful spring-fed creek and stop to feed the 50 wild Mallard ducks, who will eat out of your hand. Watch the quiet parts of the creek for the schools of native fish. The beautiful old farm was first settled by the Goodwin Family who led the first wagon train in to the Yakima Valley in 1864. We have strived to retain their heritage. Choose farm fresh grown fruits, vegetables and colorful bouquets of fresh and dried flowers from our Farm Market located in the old barn built in 1897. Learn about farming as we practice it today, while enjoying the visible presence of the past.
PRODUCE: Apples; apricots; asparagus; beans-green; beans-dry; beets; broccoli; blueberries; cabbage; carrots; cauliflower; celery; cherries; corn-sweet; cucumbers; dill; eggplant; garlic; gourds; grapes; leeks; lettuce; melons-cantaloupe, watermelon & honeydew; nectarines; nuts-Hazelnuts,peanuts, walnuts & almonds; onions-yellow, red, Walla Walla sweet & white; peaches; pears; peas-snow, snap & pod; peppers-green, red, yellow, orange, lavender bell peppers; peppers-hot 25 varieties; plums; prunes; pickling cukes; potatoes; radishes; raspberries; rhubarb; spinach; squash-butternut, spaghetti & buttercup; strawberries; tomatillos; tomatoes-slicing & Roma; turnips; Indian corn; mini-pumpkins; gourds; carving pumpkins. Wide selection of dried fruit.
FLOWERS: Fresh cut flowers, over 30 varieties. Also dried flowers.
Open 9am-6pm daily, May 15-Oct 31.

20. Stewart Vineyards   509-854-1882
1711 Cherry Hill Rd, Granger
Location: From I-82, take Exit 58, S on Hwy 223 App. 1/2 mile. Take first left, then left again immediately. Follow rd 1 1/2 miles to top of Cherry Hill.
Premium varietal wines including: **CHARDONNAY, CABERNET SAUVIGNON, CHERRY HILL BLUSH, GEWURZTRAMINER, RIESLINGS, and MUSCAT CANELLI.**
We welcome visitors to the winery and the second floor tasting room for fine wine, cordial hospitality, and a beautiful view of the Lower Yakima Valley. Picnic facilities in the surrounding cherry orchards are available. Winery hours: Mon-Sat 10am-5pm; Sun 12-5pm. Please phone ahead for large groups and tours.

21. Thompson's Farm   509-653-2589
9535 Old Naches Hwy, Naches 98937
Location: Our farm borders the NE corner of the town of Naches. Traveling on Hwy 12, turn N onto Shaffer Av between Country Basket Fruit and the old blue gas station. About half a mile N our driveway is located at the intersection of Shaffer and the Old Naches Hwy.
Since 1898 Thompson's Farm has been a family owned orchard. We grow over 35 varieties of fruit and sell both commercially and directly to the public. Bring your family and visit our farm. Tour the orchard, see old and new equipment, you are welcome to sample tree ripened fruit right off the tree, or select from fruit harvested daily.
BLOOM DATES: Call during Mar & Apr for specifics.
CHERRIES: Bings, Rainiers and Lamberts. End of Jun-Jul.
PEACHES: old and new varieties: Red Haven, Red Daroga, Hale, Veteran Slappy, Suncrest, Red Globe, Early and Late Elberta, and more. Available most of Aug & Sept.
PEARS: Red & green Bartlett, D'Anjou, Comice, Bosc. End of Aug-Sept.
NECTARINES: Jul-Aug
PRUNES: Early & Late Italian, Sept.
PLUMS: Aug
APPLES: new and old varieties of Red Delicious, Goldens, Winsaps, Romes. End of Sept-Oct.
CIDER, VINEGAR, HONEY, JAMS & JELLIES: Available all year.
Call ahead or take a chance. Truckers welcome.

22. **Tucker Cellars, Farmers' Market**
   509-837-8701
   70 Ray Rd, Sunnyside 98944
Location: Located on Yakima Valley Hwy between exit 69 & 73 off I-82.
WINE TASTING ROOM: Tucker's offers you a selection of fine wines to sample along with gourmet foods such as popcorn, pickled vegetables and more in the gift shop.
FARMERS MARKET: Our Farmers' Market, which is adjacent to our wine tasting room, has a wide selection of home grown fruit & produce. Available by the pound, box or truck load. Open daily 8am-6pm (summer) 9am-4:30 pm (winter).

23. **Turcott Orchard, Benson Ranches**
   509-877-2688
   801 Clark Rd, Wapato 98951
Location: From I-82 take exit 44 N through Donald to Yakima Valley Hwy, right on Yakima Valley Hwy to Sawyer. North on Lombard Loop to Clark Rd, 4th house on left.
PEACHES: Roza (Aug 10), J.H. Hale & Golden & Giant Elberta (Aug 28), Gold Medal (Labor Day).
NECTARINES: Red Gold (Aug 20)
PEARS: Bartlett, Bosc (Aug 20)
APPLES: Prime Gold (Aug 25) good keeper.
All fruits are u-pick or boxed at ranch. Open daily (except Tue) 8am-6pm. Boxes for sale or bring own containers. Truckers call one day ahead.

24. **Darigold Dairy Fair**   **509-837-4321**
   400 Alexander Rd, Sunnyside 98944
Location: from I-82 take exit 67 (Sunnyside Central exit). Darigold Dairy Fair is located on the south side of the freeway.
The Darigold Dairy Fair offers hand-dipped ice cream (with seating available either inside or outside on the veranda), cheese, gift items, cow memorabilia and a tour of the cheese factory. Open daily.

25. **Guerra's Produce**   **509-854-1745**
   501 Schuster Rd, Granger 98932
Location: Take Exit 58 off of I-82. Go S 1 1/2 miles on Hwy 223, take left on Indian Church Rd for 1 1/2 miles. Turn left on Schuster Rd for 1/2 mile. We are the first house on the left.
SWEET CORN: Jul-Oct
MELONS: Watermelons, Cantaloupes, Honey Dew, Casaba and Rocky Sweet Melons Jul-Oct.
TOMATOES: Aug-Oct
CUCUMBERS: Pickling & slicing Jun 15-Oct
PEPPERS: Bell, Jalapeno, Thai, hot
DRY BEANS: Pinto, red, white, & black beans
DRY PEPPERS: New Mexico Chile.
Call ahead for large orders.

26. **Sunnyside Downtown Farmers' Market**
   509-839-8275
   Uptown Sunnyside Assn.
   PO Box 329, Sunnyside 98944
Location: 534 S 6th St, Downtown Sunnyside in Pocket park. Take exit 67 off I-82, follow green and yellow signs to Downtown Sunnyside. Market is on 6th St (nearest cross street is Franklin).
Fresh picked and quality fruits and vegetables from the Yakima Valley area can be found at our market. Wonderful crafts and homemade foods available. Family activities going on every Sat. Open 9am-2pm Jun-Oct.

Guerra's
3rd Annual
Pacific Northwest

Chile Pepper Festival

Saturday & Sunday • August 2 and 3

Admission Includes:
- *Family Fun & Games*
- *Food & Refreshments*
- *Enjoy our Famous Grilled Peppers & Barbecued Shish-kabob*
- *Live Entertainment*
- *Door Prizes*
- *And Much More!*

509-837-8897

Location: *Take exit 63 off of I-82. Turn right onto Yakima Valley Highway and then left onto Maple Grove Road. Go North approximately 5 miles.*

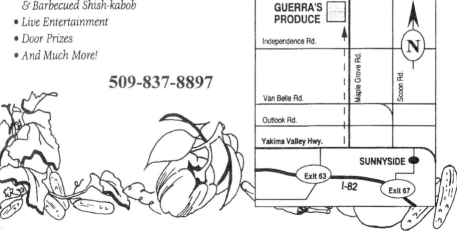

Areas for Washington Farmers' Markets

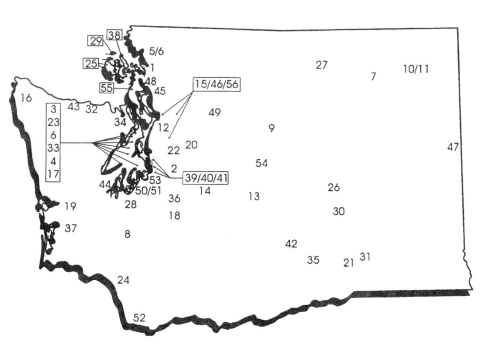

Washington Farmers' Markets

1. Depot Farmers' Market
Location: 7th St & "R" Av, Anacortes
May 17-Oct 11, 10am-2pm Sat
Contact: Kathy Janke 360-293-4803
PO Box 224, Anacortes 98221

2. Auburn Farmers' Market
Location: 118 Cross St SE, Auburn
Jun-Oct, 9am-3pm Wed
Contact: Donel Brinkman 206-735-2957 or
206-804-9567; 3215 "M" St, Auburn 98002

3. Bainbridge Island Farmers' Market
Location: Municipal pkg lot,
410 Madison Ave N, Winslow
Easter to Oct, 9am-1pm Sat
Contact Suzy Cook 206-842-7431
PO Box 10225, Bainbridge Isl 98110

4. Belfair Farmers' Market
Location: Hwy 3, across from Theler Ctr
May-Oct, 9am-3pm Sat
Contact: Glenda Jillson 360-895-2401
PO Box 1649, Belfair 98528

5. Bellingham Farmers' Market Assn.
Location: Railroad Av & Chestnut St
Jun-Sept, 3pm-8pm Wed
Contact: Karen Durham, 360-647-2060
304 - 36th St #146, Bellingham 98225

6. Fairhaven Wednesday Farmers' Market
Location: 11th & McKenzie
Jun-Sept, 3pm-8pm Wed
Contact: Leone Moene 360-738-1574
PO Box 4083, Bellingham 98227

7. Bridgeport Farmers' Market
Location: Hwy 17, parking lot next to
Quickie Mart. Jun-Sept, 10am-2pm Sat
Contact: Rick Lynn 509-686-3971
1804 Raymond Av, Bridgeport 98813

8. Lewis County Farmers' Markets
Locations:
Centralia - Pine St between Tower & Depot
Chehalis - City parking lot at National &
Market Sts. Last week Apr-last wknd Oct
Centralia 9:30am-1pm Fri
Chehalis 9:30am-1pm Sat
Contact: Mary Lewis 360-785-3101
PO Box 272, Chehalis 98532

9. Chelan Valley Farmers' Market
Location: Johnson St next to Chamber of
Commerce. Jun 14-Oct 18 9am-Noon, Sat
Contact: Karen Koch 503-687-3171 or Jody
Powers 509-687-9487
Rt 1 Box A-100, Chelan 98816

10. Colville Farmers' Market
Location: Corner of Hawthorne & Elm
Apr 26-Oct 2pm-7pm, Wed; 8am-1pm
twice/month, Special Event Saturdays
Contact: Pam Harrison 509-669-6438
Dick Dell 509-684-5912
1133-A Aladdin Rd, Colville 99114

11. Northeast Washington Farmers' Market
Location: 3rd & Main
May-Oct, 8:30am-1pm Sat
Contact: Todd Kowitz 503-738-6219
PO Box 647, Colville 99114

12. Edmonds Museum Summer Market
Location: Bell St between 5th & 6th
July 5-Sept 27, 9am-3pm Sat
Contact: Bette G. Bell 206-775-5650
PO Box 952, Edmonds 98020

13. Kittitas County Farmers' Market
Location: Washington School, 6th &
Anderson; May-Oct, 9am-1pm, Sat
Contact: Jackie Charlton 509-925-1776
110 W 6th, Box 242, Ellensburg 98926

14. Enumclaw Country Market
Location: Railroad St & Griffin Av
Apr 26-Oct 25, 9am-4pm Sat
Contact: Suzanne Cohen 206-939-1707
PO Box 871, Enumclaw 98022

15. Everett Farmers' Market
Location: Everett Marina, W. Marine View Dr., North of the Navy Homeport & Marine Village. Jun 1-Sept 28, 11am-4pm Sun
Contact: Marie Brayman 206-347-2790
12311 4th Pl W, Everett 98204

16. Forks Farmers' Market
Location: Thriftway Parking lot
May-Oct, 10am-3pm Fri-Sat
Contact: Joanne McReynolds
360-374-6623, 21 Bunker Rd, Forks 98331

17. Gig Harbor Farmers' Market
Location: Pierce Transit Park & Ride, Kimball St.
May-Oct, 9am-3pm Sat & 1 Sun in mid-Jul
Contact: Janice Piercy 206-884-2496
PO box 1014, Wauna 98395

18. Graham Farmers' Market
Location: Town Center, Meridian & 224th
May-Aug, Noon-6pm Sun
Contact: Trudy A. Liebe 360-893-3303
Diane Tucker, 20015 Orting Kapowsin Hwy E, Graham 98338

19. Grays Harbor Farmers' Mkt & Craft Fair
Location: 1956 Riverside Dr.
Year round, 9am-6pm Tue, Fri, Sat
Contact: Phyllis N. Shrauger 360-538-9747
PO Box 228, Aberdeen 98520

20. Issaquah Farmers' Market
Location: Community Center, 301 Rainier
Apr 19-Oct, 9am-3pm Sat
Contact: Dorothy Knitter 206-392-2229
PO Box 1307, Issaquah 98027

21. Kennewick Farmers' Market
Location: Kennewick Av & Benton St.
Jun-Nov, 8am-Noon Wed & Sat
Contact: Ken Silliman 509-586-3101
Po Box 6552, Kennewick 99336

22. Kent Market
Location: Municipal lot, 4th & Smith
Apr-Oct, 9am-4pm Sat; 10am-3pm Sun
Contact: Candy Howard 206-813-6976
PO Box 557, Kent 98035

23. Kingston Farmers' Market
Location: Kingston Marina Park
May-early Oct, 4pm-6pm Wed; 9am-2pm Sat
Contact: Naomi Maasberg 360-297-2876
26059 Barber Cut-off, Kingston 98346

24. Cowlitz Community Farmers' Market
Location: Cowlitz County Fairgroiunds
Apr (Sat only) -Oct, 8am-1pm Tue & Sat
Contact: Terrence Miracle 360-425-1297
3296 Nebraska, Longview 98632

25. Lopez Island Farmers' Market
Location: Village House, Lopez Village
Memorial Day to Labor Day
10am-2pm Wed & Sat
Contact: Christine Langley 360-468-2857
Rt 1 Box 2221, Lopez 98261

26. Columbia Basin Farmers' Market
Location: Lyon Field behind Frontier Junior High School. Jun 15-Oct 15 8am-1pm Sat
Contact: Alice Parker 509-346-9383
PO Box 691, Moses Lake 98837

27. Okanogan Valley Farmers' Market
Location: American Legion Park
May-Oct, 4pm-6pm Tue; 9am-Noon Sat
Contact: Mary Rabchuk 509-422-4128
1107 N. 3rd, Okanogan 98840

28. Olympia Farmers' Market
Location: 700 N. Capitol Way
10am-3pm Sat & Sun (Apr, Nov & Dec); Thur-Sun (May-Sept); Fri-Sun (Oct)
Contact: Rick Castellano 360-352-9096
PO Box 7094, Olympia 98507

29. Orcas Island Farmers' Market
Location: Village Green, Eastsound
Apr-Oct, 10am-3pm Sat
Contact: Sandra Green 360-376-6159
PO Box 1202, Eastsound, 98245

30. Othello Farmers' Market
Location: 4th & Main
May-Oct, 8am-Noon Sat
Contact: Betty Lanning 509-488-5385
755 N. 7th, Othello 99344

31. Pasco Farmers' Market
Location: Corner of 4th Av & Columbia
1st Sat in May to 3rd Sat in Nov;
1st Sun in Jun to 1st Sun in Sept;
8am-Noon Wed & Sat; 11am-3pm Sun
Contact: Rosemary Doupe 509-545-0738
PO Box 842, Pasco 99301

32. Port Angeles Farmers' Market
Location: 8th & Chase St
Year round, 8:30am-4pm Sat
Contact: Nash Huber 360-683-7089
230 Simpson Rd, Sequim 98382

33. Kitsap Regional Farmers' Market Assn.
Location: Parking lot on Bay St, behind
Peninsula Feed Store
Apr-Oct, 9am-3pm Sat
Contact: Bill Olson 206-857-2636
PO Box 8247, Port Orchard 98366

34. Jefferson County Farmers Market
Location: Water St. btwn Elevated Ice
Cream & Police Station
Apr 19-Oct 12, 9am-1pm Sat
Contact: Greg Mitchell 360-385-9747
PO Box 1384, Port Townsend 98368

35. Prosser Farmers' Market
Location: Prosser City Park, 7th & Sommers
Jun-Oct, 8am-1pm Sat
Contact: Linda Hall 509-786-3600
1230 Bennett Av, Prosser 99350

36. Puyallup Farmers' Market
Location: Pioneer Park
1st week in May to 1st week in Sept
9am-2pm, Sat
Contact: Sonie Waltier 206-845-6755
PO Box 1298, Puyallup 98371

37. Willapa Farmers' Market
Location: Riverfront Park, 3rd & Alder
July-Oct, 10am-3pm Sat
Contact: Nancy Foley 360-942-3489
Rt 3, Box 455, Raymond 98577

38. San Juan Island Farmers' Market
Location: County Courthouse parking lot,
Friday Harbor
Mid-Apr-late Oct, 10am-1pm Sat
Contact: R. Bruce Gregory 360-378-2309
6451 Mitchell Bay Rd, Friday Harbor 98250

39. Fremont Farmers' Market
Location: N. 34th St & Evanston Av
May-Oct 10am-4pm Sun
Contact: Michaele Blakely 206-333-6386
PO Box 301, Carnation, WA 98014

40. Pike Place Market
Location: 1st Av & Pike St.
Year round, 9am-6pm Mon-Sat;
11am-6pm Sun
Contact: Merlyn Goeschl 206-682-7453
85 Pike St, Rm 500, Seattle 98101

41. University District Farmers' Market
Location: Corner of NE 50th & University
Way NE
May 31-Nov 1, 9am-2pm Sat
Contact: Chris Curtis 206-633-1024
4512 University Way NE, #102
Seattle 98105

42. Selah Farmers' Market
Location: Old Fire Stn bldg & pkg lot
110 W. Naches Av
May 17-Oct 25, 9am-2pm Sat
Contact: Jill Wise 509-697-5545
Carolyn Miller 509-697-7220
PO box 415, Selah 98942

43. Sequim Open Aire Market
Location: 2nd & Bell St
Jun-Oct, 9am-2pm Sat
Contact: Su Howat 360-683-9446
PO Box 1817, Sequim 98382

44. Shelton Farmers' Market
Location: 414 W. Franklin St
Jun-Oct, 9am-3pm Sat
Contact: Karin Olsen 360-427-7461
PO Box 1986, Shelton 98584

45. Silvana Farmers' Market
Location: Ding Dong Park, Downtown
Apr 26-Sept 27, 2pm-4pm, mid-summer Wed; 10am-4pm Sat
Contact: Joy Song Morgan-Nelson 360-652-5708, PO Box 237, Silvana 98287

46. Snohomish Farmers' Market Assn.
Location: First St 2 blocks West of Bridge
May 8-Sept 25, 5pm-9pm Thur
Contact: Marie Brayman 206-347-2790
PO Box 1994, Snohomish, 98291

47. Spokane Market Place
Location: 1202 W. First Av
10am-4pm Wed & Fri-Sun (May-Sept); Wed & Sat (Oct-Dec)
Contact: Jackie Rappe 509-482-2627
525 E. Mission Av, Spokane 99202

48. Stanwood Farmers' Market
Location: American Legion parking lot
May-Sept, 9am-2pm Sat
Contact: Gayle Ricci 360-653-9356 or Joy Martin 360-629-4357
4217 128th St NE, Marysville 98271

49. Sultan Saturday Market
Location: Riverpark on Main St.
May-Oct, 9am-2pm Sat
Contact: Debbie Coppel 360-793-2565
PO Box 46, Sultan 98294

50. Proctor Farmers' Market
Location: Bank Parking lot, 3916 N. 26th
Jun-Aug, 9am-2pm Sat
Contact: Leah Walker 206-756-8901
3722 N 31st St, Tacoma 98407

51. Tacoma Farmers' Market
Location: Broadway between S. 7th & 9th
Jun 5-Sept 4, 10am-3pm Thur
Contact: Randy Chiarovano 206-272-7077
PO Box 707, Tacoma 98401

52. Vancouver Farmers' Market
Location : Broadway & 5th St.
Mar 29-Oct 25
9am-3pm Sat
Contact: Madeleine Dulemba 360-737-8298
PO Box 61638, Vancouver 98666

53. Vashon Farmers' Market
Location : 1/2 block S of Bank Rd on W side of Vashon Hwy. across from Bobs Bakery, Vashon
Late Mar-early Oct, 10am-3pm Sat
Contact: Richard O'Dell 206-463-6557
PO Box 1448, Vashon 98070

54. Wenatchee Valley Farmers' Markets
Locations:
Leavenworth: next to City Pool
Wenatchee: Riverfront Park, base of 5th
Jun-Oct
Leavenworth: 9am-1pm Tue
Wenatchee: 8am-Noon, Wed & Sat
Contact: Valerie Fulleton 509-884-6412
PO Box 2824, Wenatchee 98807

55. Coupeville Farmers' Market
Location: 8th & Main, Coupeville
Apr-Oct, 10am-2pm Sat
Contact: Irene Thomas 360-678-6757
2445 S. Rocky Way, Coupeville 98239

56. Woodinville Farmers' Market
Location: 175th St. next to City Hall
Mar 29-Oct 17-18, 9am-4pm Sat
Contact: Grant Davidson 206-485-1042
PO Box 1927, Woodinville 98072

Travel Notes
WASHINGTON

Date　　　　**Place**　　　　**Comments**

We hope you enjoy your roadside travels.

ORDER FORM

ROADSIDE STANDS and FARMERS' MARKETS
A Travel Guide to Westcoast Produce

Name: _____

Address: _____

_____

Phone: _____

Copy this order form or detach and send to:

First Edition 1997-1999
ISBN 0-9658650-0-2

Creekside Publishing
PO Box 250
Scotts Mills, Oregon 97375

Please allow 2-4 weeks for delivery.

If you own a fruit and produce roadside stand, or are not included in this edition and would like to be included in our future editions, or have an organization with a farm trail map not included, please drop us a note or call 503-873-2021. We welcome wholesale inquiries.

Index

California State Roadside Stands
Counties:
Calaveras County
Contra Costa County
El Dorado County
Fresno County
Lake County
Napa County
Nevada County
Placer County
San Mateo County
Santa Clara County
Santa Cruz County
Sonoma County

Oregon State Roadside Stands
Counties
Clackamas County
Hood River County
Linn County
Marion County
Multnomah County
Polk County
Washington County
Yamhill County

Washington State Roadside Stands
Counties
Bainbridge Island
King County North
King County South
Kitsap County
Pierce County
Skagit County
Snohomish County
Spokane County
Thurston County
Vashon Island
Whatcom County
Whitby Island
Yakima County

California Farmers' Markets
Counties:
Alameda, Amador, Butte, Calaveras, Contra Costa,
El Dorado, Fresno, Glenn, Humbolt, Imperial, Kern,
Kings, Lake, Los Angeles, Marin, Mariposa,
Mendocino, Merced, Monterey, Napa, Nevada,
Orange, Placer, Riverside, Sacramento, San Benito,
San Bernardino, San Diego, San Francisco,
San Joaquin, San Luis Obispo, San Mateo
Santa Barbara, Santa Clara, Santa Cruz, Shasta,
Siskiyou, Solano, Sonoma, Stanislaus, Sutter,
Tehama, Trinity, Tulare, Tuolumne, Ventura, Yolo

Oregon Farmers' Markets
Areas:
Albany-Corvallis, Ashland-Medford, Astoria,
Beaverton, Bend, Canby, Eugene, Grants Pass,
Gresham, Harrisburg, Hillsboro, Hood River,
Independence, Klamath Falls, La Grande,
McMinnville, Medford, Newport, Portland, Sandy,
Roseburg, Tigard, Tillamook, Tualatin,
(over the border) Vancouver, WA

Washington Farmers' Markets
Areas:
Anacortes, Auburn, Bainbridge Island, Belfair,
Bellingham, Bridgeport, Centralia/Chehalis,
Chelan, Coville, Edmonds, Ellensburg, Enumclaw,
Everett, Forks, Gig Harbor, Graham, Hoquiam,
Issaquah, Kennewick, Kent, Kingston, Longview,
Lopez Island, Moses Lake, Okanogan, Olympia,
Orcas Island, Othello, Pasco, Port Angeles,
Port Orchard, Port Townsend, Prosseir, Puyallup,
San Juan Island, Seattle, Selah, Sequim, Shelton,
Silvana, Snohomish, Spokane, Stanwood, Sultan,
Tacoma, Vancouver, Vashon Island,
Wenatchee/Leavenworth, Whidbey Island,
Woodinville

References

(A note from the authors: Please support your local county home extension departments. They are excellent resources for information regarding educaational programs, and answers related to agriculture, home economics, 4-H, and many other related questions and issues. Also, with government dollars being reduced and programs being eliminated for many state and federal agencies, our home extensions and farm funding all need a good word from you to your local, state and nationally elected officials in the form of letters, phone calls, and most importantly your voice at the voting booth. Thank you.)

County Extension Offices	Phone #
● **California**
Calaveras County	209-754-6477
Contra Costa County	510-646-6540
El Dorado County	916-621-5502
Fresno County	209-456-7285
Lake County	707-263-6838
Napa County	707-253-4221
Nevada County	916-273-4563
Placer County	916-889-7397
San Mateo County	415-726-9059
Santa Clara County	408-299-2635
Santa Cruz County	408-763-8040
Sonoma County	707-527-2621
● **Oregon**
Clackamas County	503-655-8631
Hood River County	541-386-3343
Linn County	541-967-3871
Marion County	503-588-5301
Multnomah County	503-731-4104
Polk County	503-623-8395
Washington County	503-725-2300
Yamhill County	503-434-7517
● **Washington**
Bainbridge Island	206-679-7327
King County North	206-296-3900
King County South	206-296-3900
Kitsap County	366-876-7157
Pierce County	206-591-7180
Skagit County	206-336-9322
Snohomish County	206-338-2400
Spokane County	509-533-2048
Thurston County	206-786-5445
Vashon Island	206-679-7327
Whatcom County	360-676-2600
Whitby Island	206-679-7327
Yakima County	509-575-4218

Credits

California
Calaveras Farm Trails, Calaveras County Master Gardeners
California Federation of Certified Farmers' Markets, Davis, CA
Coastside Harvest Trails, produced and provided by San Mateo County Farm Bureau
Country Crossroads, Farm Country Crossroads Map, Santa Clara/Santa Cruz County, Watsonville, CA 95076, 408-724-1356
El Dorado County Ranches & Farms, El Dorado County Farm Trail
Fresno County Farm Bureau, Blossom Trail Committee, Fresno Chamber of Commerce, 209-495-4800
Harvest Time in Brentwood, Harvest Time in Brentwood, Inc.
Lake County California Farm Trails, Lake County Marketing Program
Napa County Farming Trails, Napa County Farming Trails, Inc.
Placer Grown Farm Trails, Sonoma County Farm Trails, PO Box 6032, Santa Rosa, CA 95406

Oregon
Hood River County's Fruit Loop, Hood River Grower-Shipper Association
Mid-Valley Growers Guide, (copyright) Courtesy of *Albany Democrat-Herald Growers Guide*
Oregon Trail Farms, Oregon Trail Farms Direct Market Association, 1417 Orchard heights Rd NW, Salem, Oregon 97304
The Oregonian, "Farmers' Markets 1997", May 13, Oregonian Publishing Co, Portland, OR
Tri-County Farm Fresh Produce, Tri-County Farm Fresh Produce

Washington
Farm and Garden Kitsap County, Sound Farmers Education Foundation
Farm Fresh Guide, Puget Sound Farm Direct Marketing Association
Fields of Plenty, Skagit Valley Herald
Green Bluff Growers Farm Fresh Produce, Green Bluff Growers Association
Snohomish County Local Farm Guide, Courtesy of Sno-Isle Direct Marketing Association, Mary Bakko & Ed Stocker
Thurston County Direct Sales Farm Map, Washington State University Cooperative Extension (Thurston & Lewis County) Courtesy of Carol Miles, 360-740-1295
Washington State Farmers' Market Association
Yakima Valley Farm Products Guide, Yakima Farm Trail Group, Lino Guerra, 509-837-8897 & Angie Bosna, 509-829-3899